Theatre and Globalization: Irish Drama in
the Celtic Tiger Era

Also by Patrick Lonergan

THE METHUEN DRAMA ANTHOLOGY OF IRISH PLAYS (*editor*)

'INTERACTIONS': The Dublin Theatre Festival, 1957–2007
(*co-editor with Nicholas Grene*)

'ECHOES DOWN THE CORRIDOR': Irish Theatre – Past, Present and Future
(*co-editor with Riana O'Dwyer*)

Theatre and Globalization: Irish Drama in the Celtic Tiger Era

Patrick Lonergan

palgrave
macmillan

First published 2009 by
PALGRAVE MACMILLAN

Palgrave Macmillan in the UK is an imprint of Macmillan Publishers Limited,
registered in England, company number 785998, of Houndmills, Basingstoke,
Hampshire RG21 6XS.

Palgrave Macmillan in the US is a division of St Martin's Press LLC,
175 Fifth Avenue, New York, NY 10010.

Palgrave Macmillan is the global academic imprint of the above companies
and has companies and representatives throughout the world.

Palgrave® and Macmillan® are registered trademarks in the United States,
the United Kingdom, Europe and other countries.

ISBN-13: 978-0-230-21428-6   hardback
ISBN-10: 0-230-21428-2   hardback

This book is printed on paper suitable for recycling and made from fully
managed and sustained forest sources. Logging, pulping and manufacturing
processes are expected to conform to the environmental regulations of the
country of origin.

A catalogue record for this book is available from the British Library.

Library of Congress Cataloging-in-Publication Data

Lonergan, Patrick.
    Theatre and globalization : Irish drama in the Celtic Tiger era /
    Patrick Lonergan.
       p. cm.
    Includes index.
    ISBN-13: 978-0-230-21428-6 (alk. paper)
    ISBN-10: 0-230-21428-2
    1. English drama—Irish authors—History and criticism.   2. English drama—
    20th century—History and criticism.   3. Theater—Ireland—History—
    20th century.   4. Theater and globalization—Ireland—History—20th century.
    5. Literature and globalization—Ireland—History—20th century.   6. Culture
    and globalization—Ireland—History—20th century.   7. National characteristics
    in literature.   8. Multiculturalism in literature. 9. National characteristics in
    the theatre.   I. Title.   II. Title: Theatre and globalization : Irish drama in the
    Celtic Tiger era.

    PR8789.L66   2009
    792.09415'09049—dc22   2008029941

10 9 8 7 6 5 4 3 2 1
18 17 16 15 14 13 12 11 10 09

For Thérèse, with love and thanks

Contents

Acknowledgements

I am grateful to my students and colleagues at the English Department, NUI Galway, and owe particular thanks to Kevin Barry, Ros Dixon, Adrian Frazier, Frances McCormack, Hubert McDermott, Riana O'Dwyer, and Lionel Pilkington. I gratefully acknowledge funding support from the NUI Galway Millennium Fund, and also wish to thank the staff of the university's James Hardiman Library.

Parts of this book were originally written for a PhD dissertation on the Internationalization of Irish Literature, for which I received funding from the Irish Research Council for the Humanities and Social Sciences. I gratefully acknowledge the Council's support. I wish to thank Lionel Pilkington, who supervised that research, and Brian Singleton, who examined it.

All efforts have been made to secure rights for material used in this book. I gratefully acknowledge Gallery Press for permission to reproduce extracts from plays by Marina Carr and Brian Friel; Methuen for permission to reproduce extracts from the works of Martin McDonagh and Brendan Behan; Nick Hern Books (www.nickhernbooks.co.uk) for permission to use material by Conor McPherson, Elizabeth Kuti, Marie Jones, Tony Kushner, and Enda Walsh. Thanks also to Faber for permission to reproduce material from Friel's *Dancing at Lughnasa* and texts by Seamus Heaney and Harold Pinter. Full publication details for all quoted texts appear in the list of texts cited in this book. If any material used here is not credited appropriately, please contact me through my publishers.

Parts of Chapter 2 appear in John Harrington (ed.), *Irish Theatre in America* (Syracuse University Press, 2008). Chapter 3 was first published in Karen Fricker and Ronit Lentin's *Performing Global Networks* (Cambridge Scholars Press, 2005). Parts of Chapter 4 first appeared in Richard R. Russell's *Martin McDonagh: A Casebook* (Routledge, 2007). I am grateful to the editors of those books for permission to revise and re-use that material.

Many members of the Irish theatre community answered questions, provided unpublished material, or otherwise offered help. I wish to thank the staff at the Abbey Theatre, Druid Theatre, the Dublin Theatre Festival, Fabulous Beast, Focus Theatre, Guna Nua, Rough Magic, and the Royal National Theatre (UK). I must pay particular tribute to the Abbey Theatre archivist Mairead Delaney. I also wish to thank Druid Theatre and Simon Annand for allowing me to reproduce the image from *Long Day's Journey Into Night* on the cover of this book. Particular thanks to Sinead McPhillips of Druid.

Many colleagues gave invaluable advice and help as this book progressed. I have benefited greatly from discussing the ideas presented in this book at events organized by the International Association for the Study of Irish Literatures and the Irish Theatrical Diaspora group. Between 2002 and 2004, I attended the Keough Notre Dame Irish Seminars, where I had an opportunity to discuss many of the ideas developed herein. Thanks to the Seminar's Directors, Seamus Deane, Luke Gibbons, and Kevin Whelan. I want particularly to thank Joan Dean, Karen Fricker, Nicholas Grene, Helen Meany, and Shaun Richards, all of whom have been immensely generous with advice and support. I also want to thank Shannon Steen, whose 2003 Seminar on Critical Race theory at UC Berkeley was extremely helpful in my early drafting of chapter 8. Any errors or oversights are entirely my own.

Finally, I must thank my parents, brothers, and sister for their support, and I dedicate this book to my wife Thérèse, who has been a source of constant encouragement throughout this process.

Abbreviations and Terminology

The following abbreviations are used throughout the text:

ATA: Abbey Theatre Archive, Dublin
FDI: Foreign Direct Investment
IDA: Industrial Development Agency Ireland
IRA: Irish Republican Army
NLI: National Library of Ireland
NTS: National Theatre of Scotland
RNT: Royal National Theatre, London
RSC: Royal Shakespeare Company
RTE: Radio Telefís Éireann, the Irish national television and radio network

I also make regular use of the following Irish terms:

Dáil Eireann: the Irish parliament
Gaeltacht: regions of Ireland in which Irish is spoken as the first language
Taoiseach: the Irish Prime Minister
TD (Teachta Dála): an Irish member of parliament

Conversions from the Irish pound to the euro are calculated on the basis that £IR1.00 = €1.27.

Introduction

It's a Sunday afternoon in October 2005, and Harold Pinter has just entered the auditorium. He seems a little unsteady on his feet as he walks down the Gate Theatre's aisle towards his seat, flanked by his wife Antonia Fraser and followed by Michael Colgan, the producer of this weekend-long celebration of his 75th birthday. The Dublin audience is still applauding warmly as the houselights dim; actors are filing quickly onto the stage where, for the next two hours, they will read selections from Pinter's prose, poetry, and drama.

As each actor sits, the audience's excitement grows. There's Jeremy Irons, and beside him is Stephen Rea. Derek Jacobi emerges, then Janie Dee. And there's Michael Gambon, who, like Irons, has apparently 'flown in specially from a foreign movie location' for the event (Billington, 2007: 421). We have barely had time to count the number of performers present – there are 14 in all – when the readings begin.

The auditorium is suffused with the kind of goodwill that we would naturally expect for what is, after all, a birthday party. In performance, scenes from plays like *The Homecoming* would make an audience feel uneasy, but in this setting they are greeted with affectionate recognition. And that recognition works both ways: the Irish audience shows its respect for Pinter's writing, but the actors also emphasize the importance of Ireland to the development of Pinter's career. This dynamic of mutual appreciation is most clearly revealed when Jeremy Irons gives a brilliantly charismatic reading of 'Mac', Pinter's memoir about Anew McMaster, the man who gave him his 'first job proper on the stage', in a company that toured Ireland during the 1950s (Pinter, 2005: 28). It is a lively piece of writing, and the audience is enjoying it – particularly the references to their home country. Irons, who seems fully aware of that enjoyment, pauses, then smiles, before

1

beginning to recount Pinter's story about McMaster's company's tour to Limerick:

> Joe Nolan, the business manager, came in one day and said: Mac, all the cinemas in Limerick are on strike. What shall I do. Book Limerick! Mac said. At once! . . . We opened on the Monday in a two thousand seater cinema, with *Othello*. There was no stage and no wingspace. It was St Patrick's night. The curtain was supposed to rise at nine o'clock. But the house wasn't full until eleven thirty, so the play didn't begin until then. It was well past two in the morning before the curtain came down. Every one of the two thousand people present was drunk. Apart from that, they weren't accustomed to Shakespeare.
>
> (29)

In another setting, the Gate audience might have objected to what is a rather negative description of a group of Irish theatregoers: there's the impoverished quality of the cinema's facilities, the lateness of the show's commencement, the drunkenness and ignorance of the audience. Yet their laughter grows louder with every line that Irons delivers: this, we must remember, is a middle-class urban audience in 2005, laughing at a provincial working-class audience in the early 1950s – the contemporary Irish audience seems to identify much more with Pinter than the Irish people he describes. 'Ireland', Iron concludes, 'wasn't golden always but it was golden sometimes and in 1950 it was, all in all, a golden age for me and others'. And with that he receives the second-loudest cheer of the evening – surpassed only by the reception given to Pinter himself when he takes the stage at the end of the event to read a poem of tribute to his wife.

If you had run quickly enough, it would have been possible to go straight from the Gate to the nearby O'Reilly Theatre, where another performance was starting just as Pinter's reading was finishing. Fabulous Beast's *The Bull* was the only new Irish work in that year's Dublin Theatre Festival, and it had already attracted an enormous amount of attention. Based on the ancient Irish legend *The Táin*, the play features many traits associated with Irish drama: gallows humour, irrational acts of tribal violence, the idealization of women, the celebration of heroic failure – it seems, in other words, like a typical Irish play, featuring typically Irish characteristics. Yet *The Bull* is utterly unlike anything ever seen on an Irish stage before.

It is, firstly, a fusion of literary drama and dance theatre, written and choreographed by Michael Keegan-Dolan, in which text gradually gives way to movement and percussion. The show is delightfully, appallingly, bad-mannered: the most obscene forms of Irish idiom are repeatedly delivered, golf-balls are pelted into the audience, and the most successful piece of Irish theatre ever – *Riverdance* – is ruthlessly parodied, re-imagined as a show called *Celtic Bitch*. The play's final moments involve the entire cast dancing on a stage filled with mud, as rain hurtles down on top of them. They beat found objects with a furious rhythm, howling as they do so: one performer pounds on a barrel, another on a cement mixer, and another beats his tap-shoes on the stage. And in these final moments it feels as if the trait most associated with Irish theatre – eloquence of speech – has been rendered utterly redundant, perhaps killed off for good.

As the play concludes, it seems impossible to ignore the show's treatment of the links between the new and old Irelands. The characters in *The Bull* are, like the Gate audience laughing along with Jeremy Irons, affluent and cosmopolitan – but by connecting their lives with ancient Irish legend, *The Bull* asks them to consider how much things have really changed in Celtic Tiger Ireland. For some audiences, *The Bull* feels like the most important Irish production in years. For others, it feels like an infantile mess. And people are talking about it everywhere: relentlessly, furiously, delightedly.

There are many obvious differences between the Pinter Celebration and Fabulous Beast's *The Bull*. But the performance of both in the same part of Dublin at the same time reveals much about how globalization is changing the way that theatre is being made and received throughout the world. Both productions depend for their impact on the power of global brands: in the case of the Pinter Celebration, from the presence of internationally recognizable celebrities like Jeremy Irons; and in *The Bull* from the transgressive power of satirizing *Riverdance*. Both reveal how globally distributed cultural forms must mix the international with the local: the Pinter readings include a small number of references to Ireland which make the local audience feel recognized, while *The Bull* draws on international dancing styles, blending them with traditional Irish steps to produce something that is simultaneously exotic and familiar. We also see how the category of 'the national' seems less influential in theatrical production than it has been in the past. The Gate is an Irish theatre company celebrating the birthday of one of England's greatest playwrights, and *The Bull* manages to be 'Irish' despite the inclusion in its cast of actors and dancers from Slovakia, France, Italy, the United States, and the UK. Both productions were featured in the Dublin Theatre Festival – which that year had rebranded itself as the Dublin *International* Theatre Festival, thereby emphasizing its history of mixing the best of Irish and non-Irish plays, a strategy that aimed to mark Dublin as an important hub on the international theatre network. Hence, we see that mobility is a significant element of both productions: *The Bull* was a co-production of the Dublin Theatre Festival and London's Barbican Theatre (it opened in London in February 2007 where it was again well received); while a version of the Gate's Pinter Celebration was re-staged for London audiences some weeks after its Dublin premiere. Finally, both productions reveal how a culture of entrepreneurship has had an impact on the development of theatre. *The Bull* was performed in the theatre of Belvedere College, a private school in Dublin's inner city that includes among its former pupils the writers James Joyce, Austin Clarke, and Colin Teevan – though its theatre is named instead in honour of the family of another alumnus, the businessman Sir Anthony O'Reilly, who sponsored its construction. The Gate's Michael Colgan, like O'Reilly, is a shrewd businessman who has used an Irish base to achieve international success. 'If I stage Pinter', he explains to Michael Billington, 'it is because I believe he has totally redefined the nature of drama and because, like Beckett, he appeals to my taste' (quoted by Billington, 2007: 420).

In short, both productions reveal how globalization – as a cultural phenomenon, an economic process, a mode of rhetoric – can help us to understand very different kinds of theatre. Hence, my argument in this book is that theatre worldwide is changing because of globalization – in (at least) four ways.

First, globalization has created new opportunities for writers (like Pinter and Michael Keegan-Dolan) and theatre companies (such as the Gate and Fabulous Beast) to travel internationally. The availability of those opportunities has altered the way in which theatre is made, received, produced, and studied.

Second, playwrights and audiences are now attempting to come to terms with the social changes wrought by globalization. Issues such as asylum seeking, tourism, multiculturalism and interculturalism, universal human rights, and the growth of foreign direct investment (FDI) have become more prominent on the world stage since the early 1990s. Even if these themes are not always considered explicitly by dramatists, they have influenced the reception of many plays.

Third, many recent formal developments in drama may be explained in relation to globalization. Such changes include a reduction of the importance of spoken language in favour of visual spectacle, the compression of action into shorter scenes, the homogenization of setting and dialogue, and the increasing use of monologue.

Finally, globalization complicates – and in some cases renders obsolete – many of the categories used to study dramatic literature and performance. What does 'nation' or 'region' mean in a globalizing world? And has the academy itself come to terms with how globalization has altered the old vocabularies of analysis?

This argument begins in the first chapter, which uses Marie Jones's *Stones In His Pockets* (1999) to set out some working definitions of globalization and its relationship to theatre, which will be clarified and refined as the book progresses. I also explain why I am focusing on Irish theatre during the so-called 'Celtic Tiger' period of c. 1990 to 2005. I move then to a discussion of Brian Friel's *Dancing at Lughnasa* (1990), arguing that this play is an example of how globalization has affected the reception of drama and theatre since the early 1990s. The third and fourth chapters develop that argument by evaluating the impact of globalization upon the category of nation, discussing the Abbey Theatre's 2004 production of Dion Boucicault's *The Shaughraun*, and versions of Sean O'Casey's *The Plough and the Stars* from 1991 and 2002. Globalization has changed the remit and responsibilities of national theatres, I argue; and I discuss the impact of branding on the construction of national dramas.

I move then to considering how place functions as a cultural and critical category, focusing firstly on the career of Martin McDonagh, and then on a 1995 Dublin production of Tony Kushner's *Angels in America*. At the heart of both discussions is a question that dominates considerations of globalization: does that process lead to greater levels of understanding between societies, or does it instead result in cultural homogenization? That question leads on to a consideration of the impact of globalization on theatrical form: if globalization changes the way that we think about space, how does that alter our perception of the space of the theatrical stage? I consider that question by exploring the presentation of the body and monologue within Irish theatre, showing how gender functions within global culture.

The final chapter considers how all of these processes have affected the construction of identity within drama. I offer a genealogy of the nationalized 'brand', which I relate to colonial and nationalist representations of identity. This book concludes with an exploration of how theories of globalization may allow for a deeper understanding of theatre, while pointing out ways forward for dramatic practice and criticism.

Part I   Globalization and Theatre: Definitions and Contexts

1
Globalization and Irish Theatre

'The Irish Know One Thing . . . ' Marie Jones's *Stones In His Pockets*

In 1999, Marie Jones showed that one way to become globally successful is to tap into audiences' fears about globalization. She did so with *Stones In His Pockets*, an internationally successful play in which a Hollywood production company travels to Ireland to make what they hope will be an internationally successful film, about the 19th-century Irish Land War.[1] Jones's drama draws parallels between the imperial past and the global present, suggesting that the 19th-century struggle in Ireland between landlord, agent, and tenant is comparable to the relationship between Hollywood producers, Irish mediators, and a small community of extras in County Kerry in the late 1990s.

Stones is a very funny play – but to see it only as a comedy is to overlook the way that Jones analyses the mass media's presentation of national identities for global consumption. Throughout the action, she illustrates the discrepancy between appearance and reality in the representation of Irishness, often to humorous effect. The filmmakers complain that aspects of the locality, such as the cows and some of the villagers, don't look 'Irish enough' (Jones, 2000: 17). When the locals object to those views, the producers ignore them, arguing that since 'Ireland is only one per cent of the market' it scarcely matters if Irish people know that the film is inauthentic (13). Besides, as the film's leading lady Caroline Giovanni suggests, the Irish need not be taken seriously anyway: 'you people are so simple, uncomplicated [and] contented', she states (15).

Jones shows how many of the local residents are complicit in, and beneficiaries of, their own exploitation. Jake – one of the play's two leading characters – states that the presence of Caroline in the local pub will be used to attract customers there for years to come. Its owner will 'get his wife to make her a sandwich and when the restaurant opens he will have a big plaque saying . . . Caroline Giovanni dined here' (21). The other of the two main characters is Charlie, a mild-mannered local whose association with Caroline raises his profile among his fellow extras. In the play's opening scene, he is refused extra servings of food during his lunch break, but when Jake tells the caterers that 'me and him and Caroline is sort of friends now', he is treated much better: 'yes, fresh cream on both would be lovely . . . no thanks, two helpings is enough' (31).

An audience at *Stones In His Pockets* is most likely to enjoy the play because it gives actors an opportunity to display their versatility and virtuosity. *Stones* is performed by two actors, who between them play 14 roles, signalling character changes with minor alterations in costume, movement, or lighting. The set is also simple, comprising a wooden chest, 14 pairs of shoes, and a backdrop showing the Blasket Islands (an internationally recognized marker of Irishness that has appeared repeatedly in Irish literature since Dion Boucicault's 1874 play *The Shaughraun*). Much of the humour in the production thus arises from old-fashioned theatricality: from the actors' quick changes from one character to another, from their crossing of boundaries associated with gender, nationality, and age.

This emphasis on live performance suits the play's themes very well: the skill of the actors creates a contrast between the excitement of live performance and the homogenized and superficial quality of the Hollywood film. And by showing how one body can be used to perform multiple identities, the actors in *Stones* counteract the tendency within mass culture to present homogenized versions of identity as if they are authentic. The play may thus be seen as a reassertion of the value of theatre in a mass-mediatized world. Because everything to do with Hollywood in the play is presented as obviously inauthentic (from the leading lady's accent to the national identity of the cows), the audience must infer that anything that is marked as being 'not Hollywood' must therefore be authentic.

Jones also has much to say about the ownership of Irish identity in the global marketplace. One of the play's more amusing passages involves the attempt by Caroline to seduce Charlie, in the hope that he will help her to speak Hiberno-English more authentically – a practice which her colleagues refer to as her tendency to 'go ethnic' on film sets around the world (30). Like countless characters in previous Irish plays, Charlie finds himself being feminized and objectified by a sexually assertive woman.[2]

To impress Caroline, he pretends that he writes poetry, and quotes as an example of his own work a poem originally written by Seamus Heaney. He is then embarrassed by the realization that Caroline is much more familiar with Heaney's work than he is himself: his performance 'always works on Irish girls', he complains (26), but does not fool the American star.

Charlie is quoting from 'Exposure', a work from Heaney's 1975 volume *North* – a poem that he also recited as part of his acceptance speech for the 1995 Nobel Prize for Literature. Jones's use of this poem probably arises because it is one of Heaney's most famous – but it can also be seen as an attempt to focus her audiences' attention on the issue of artistic responsibility. 'Exposure' was written in response to the Northern Irish Troubles, which Heaney presents in *North* as being rooted in the clash of essentialized notions of Irish identity: he rejects what he calls the 'diamond absolutes' that mark people out as different from each other. 'I am neither internee nor informer', he writes, but an 'inner émigré', who is 'taking protective colouring / From bole and bark' (Heaney, 1990: 91). Like the actors playing Jake and Charlie, Heaney is like a performer putting on different costumes, refusing to be fixed perpetually by one adjective or one identity.

It makes sense that an actress like Caroline would be attracted to those sentiments. But Jones's use of a poem on this theme is important too, because it allows the audience to consider how the globalization of Irish culture can be seen as another attempt to define and limit national identity, involving the transmission of new 'diamond absolutes' that have little relevance to life within Ireland itself.

Jones is therefore placing together the 19th-century land question, the Northern Irish Troubles, and the globalization of Irish identity. In doing so, she disrupts her audiences' awareness of the gap between present and past, showing that we are still engaged in a struggle over contested territory in Ireland: the difference is that in the 19th century that struggle was about land, but now it is about *meaning*. The Hollywood film shows how the Irish responded to being 'dispossessed' of their land in the past; the irony that Jones reinforces is that the company making this movie is dispossessing the Irish of their entitlement to define their own identity in the present.

This case is made primarily through her presentation of Sean, the young man whose suicide both frames and names the play. He wanted to go to America, we're told, because he 'wanted to be someone' (37); his rejection by the Hollywood crew convinces him that he must therefore be a nobody, and he ends his life on that basis, walking into the sea with 'stones in his pockets'. His death is obviously intended to have a symbolical value. Like a contemporary (if clumsy) version of Michael in Yeats's *Cathleen ni Houlihan* (1902), Sean dies from his belief in an idealized nation – but his death is intended to inspire others to acts of creativity and renewal, which is precisely what happens at the play's conclusion when Jake and Charlie decide to make a film about him. His death is also intended to pose a question to the audience: if Irish identity is created for global consumption, how does that affect the identities of real Irish people?

The play responds to this question not by attacking mass culture, but by proposing that localities should be enabled to contribute to and mediate mass culture. As Zygmunt Bauman states, because of globalization, 'Localities are losing their meaning-generating and meaning-negotiating capacity and are increasingly dependent on sense-giving and interpreting actions which they do not control' (1998: 2–3). Yet as Arjun Appadurai notes, there is 'growing evidence that the consumption of the mass media throughout the world often provokes resistance, irony, selectivity, and, in general, *agency* . . . The images of the media are quickly moved into local repertoires of irony, anger, humor, and resistance' (1996: 7). As a result, 'the residents of a local area will increasingly want to make conscious decisions about which values and amenities they want to stress in their communities', suggests Appadurai (5).

Jones's work, like Bauman's, shows that localities are losing control of 'meaning-generation' but, like Appadurai, she suggests that countries such as Ireland need not simply be passive recipients of a global culture that they do not control. Her play therefore concludes with an act of resistance: Jake and Charlie take control of the narrative by making their own film. The reactions of the villagers in *Stones In His Pockets* to Hollywood are therefore shown not to be passive, but selective: their locality has been transformed by globalization, but they have been inspired to assert the value of their own perspective on Irish life by that transformation.

This action could be seen as inspirational, but the play loses credibility as it moves towards its conclusion. Jones makes clear that new modes of representing the Irish are required, yet her play rarely attempts to present the 'real' Ireland that she calls for: that will be captured in Jake and Charlie's film instead. In that respect, Jones's play again seems reminiscent of *Cathleen ni Houlihan*, a play that famously ends with a revitalized personification of Ireland who is described but never actually shown on stage: the 'young woman with the walk of a queen' must exist in the audience's imaginations, but cannot be represented theatrically.

So too in Jones's play must we imagine the 'big slabbery dribblin' cows [with] udders, tails, arses, in your face' that represent the authentic Ireland that will appear in Jake and Charlie's movie (58). Rather ironically, the play's conclusion thus suggests that cinema rather than theatre will present the 'real Ireland'.

A further problem is that *Stones* taps into the frustration that local communities feel with mass culture – but it does so with such success that the play has itself become an example of mass culture, appearing in countless venues throughout the world. Jones explains the development of her play over time. 'We went on a journey and as the journey progressed, the word of mouth had built and built' she stated in a 2003 interview. 'We had toured and toured, back to Dublin, back to the Tricycle [in London], to Edinburgh, to the Grand Opera House in Belfast, so that the play was a year going around and word of mouth building' (quoted by Foley, 2003: 33–4). Her description of how that success has turned the production of *Stones In His Pockets* into a 'huge industry' is instructive:

> There are a lot of people involved now . . . there are investors and producers and all sorts of PR, press agents, and they are all in there as part of this huge industry. *Stones* is still running in London, it's just finished in Ireland, there's a world tour, it's in Vienna now, it's just come from Perth and there's an American tour. It's on in Winnipeg, about to go to San Francisco, and that's all one producer. The play has also been 'franchised', so there are other productions going on across the world.
>
> (34)

The use of such terms as 'franchised' to describe the international mobility of her play is interesting: although *Stones* is a critique of how mass-mediated entertainment is organized, the production could itself be accused of being a mass-mediated form of entertainment. One might ask, for instance, what it has to offer, other than its liveness, that a Hollywood film cannot deliver. Its plot is largely unoriginal, playing on the standard clash between small-town values and cosmopolitan pretension that is at the heart of Anglophone comedy and much Hollywood cinema. Its characterization therefore tends to be superficial, particularly in its presentation of Sean, which uses the serious issues of drug abuse and suicide to add pathos and depth to a script that is otherwise light-hearted. Indeed, it is probably worth recalling in this context that Jones's treatment of what happens when a Hollywood film-crew arrives in a small town was being considered by many other writers during the same period, as shown in David Mamet's film *State and Main* (2001), not to mention (at least) three different episodes of *The Simpsons*.[3]

This gives rise to an interesting question. When reading the play, it seems indisputable that Jones is genuinely criticizing the use of Irish stereotypes in mass culture, yet when we consider the production, it seems to use audiences' familiarity with those stereotypes to achieve success. The play presents us with Mickey, for example, the oldest surviving extra of John Ford's *The Quiet Man* (1952). 'I don't think that man's liver could survive another movie' (17), says Jake, implying that the stereotype of Irish drunkenness is as likely to be found on a film-set as a film-screen – a point that slightly undermines Jones's suggestion that Hollywood's perspective on Irishness might diverge from reality. Likewise, one of the play's central moments is a second act dance scene that plays with audiences' awareness of mass-mediated presentations of Irish culture. Although Jones's stage directions state only that 'Charlie and Jake dance as if with other people' (41), this scene was among the most memorable in the 1999 production, involving a lengthy and exuberant bout of traditional Irish dancing that would almost certainly have reminded audiences of *Riverdance*. 'The Irish know one thing, it's how to dance', says the Assistant Director Simon upon the conclusion of this scene (41) and, although this line is supposed to present that character as a mediator who exploits the Irish villagers for his Hollywood paymasters, his words probably echo the response of many audiences to the play.

There are many ways of understanding the clash between script and production, and it is possible to analyse Jones's attempt to represent authenticity by using a variety of theoretical approaches.[4] For the purposes of the present argument, I would point out that, just as theatre has recently taken on the language and ethos of multinational business, it is also true that many businesses are starting to organize themselves like theatres.

Stones In His Pockets appeared in the same year as Joseph Pine and Richard Gilmore's influential study *The Experience Economy* (1999). The success of many businesses, they argued, will be determined not by the quality of their services, but by the quality of the experience that they stage for customers. The service has become commodified, they argued: 'we are no longer purchasing a product, but a memory of having experienced an event'. Hence, the value of a trip to Starbucks is not determined by the quality of the beverage we consume. It instead involves participation in a staged experience that allows consumers to perform a sense of connoisseurship, and to be persuaded, while choosing from the many different varieties and recipes for their coffee, that they are exercising something like freedom of choice. Such experiences are offered by other successful multinational companies, from Disney to AOL to IBM. Indeed, one of the most successful Irish multinationals is Ryanair, which markets itself as the only airline that does *not* provide an experience, but instead simply gives customers the service that they actually wish to purchase. The use of theatrical terms in business contexts has become surprisingly common: services are 'the stage' and goods are 'props' used to engage customers, state Gilmore and Pine, who tell us that work is now a form of theatre in which we are all obliged to perform.

The problem with these staged experiences is their ubiquity in the globalized economy: it is difficult to retain the sense that you are participating in an authentic experience when that service is reproduced in thousands of coffee shops around the world. The answer, according to Gilmore and Pine (2007), is that businesses must invest more money in persuading their customers of the authenticity of their experience. They suggest that business leaders can follow five 'influential authenticity principles' in developing their products or services. The new 'authentic' business experiences should appeal to personal aspirations, and then to communal aspirations. They then should 'embrace art', 'promote a cause', and 'give meaning' (76–7).

These five principles are certainly applicable to business, but they can also explain the success of *Stones In His Pockets*. With its references to Heaney and its prioritization of live performance over the mediatized, the play is certainly 'embracing art'. It appeals to personal aspirations, since it performs the possibility that individuals can assert their own vision of the world in the face of globalization; it also asserts the communal value that we can resist the homogenizing tendencies of mass culture. In doing so, it promotes a cause – of the individual against big business, of the small-town country lad who tackles the sophisticated city-bred cynics. Through presenting these issues within the frame of a theatrical experience, Jones suggests that the dilemmas we encounter can be thought of within the linear structure of beginning, middle, and end; she is therefore imposing the illusion of meaning upon our lives. What Jones has to sell, therefore, is *authenticity*. In doing so, she shows herself to be a skilled playwright; and she shows too that she is a skilled businessperson.

The case of *Stones* shows how practices in business and theatre are becoming convergent. This isn't an isolated example: we've recently seen the works of Samuel Beckett being used to inspire business people – who were urged to 'fail better!' in a 2006 article by Stephen Brown (the exclamation point appears in the original article). He identifies seven principles from the pages of *Waiting for Godot* (1955) that can be applied to contemporary business: tenacity, brevity, contingency, ambiguity, narrativity, memory, and something called 'Celticity' which apparently refers to all of the other principles. These seven principles are then applied (convincingly, it must be said) to an analysis of the development of the Apple brand.

One might argue that, just as *Stones* is a comedy that proved to have a successful business philosophy, Brown's article is a business philosophy that has proved to be a successful comedy. Nevertheless, it is noteworthy that an international business journal willingly published an article that featured detailed, credible analysis of Beckett. And that was not the first time that Beckett has been linked to international business. In 2003, the Irish government went on a trade mission to China, the purpose of which was to highlight the quality of Irish products and to persuade Chinese investors of the unique qualities of Ireland's society and, by extension, its workforce. They took with them 127 individuals from 77 companies and education institutions, according to the official press release. And they also brought two theatre productions. One was *Riverdance*. The other was the Gate Theatre's production of *Waiting for Godot*.

For all of these reasons, *Stones In His Pockets* is an excellent example of how globalization affects theatre. The play itself shows Jones's awareness of the interrelationships of cultural and economic globalization, and she neatly satirizes the resultant development of celebrity culture. Its international success is also an example of globalization, not simply because its themes are relevant to audiences internationally, but also because its commercial success was achieved by the use of the business strategies that were first developed by multinational corporations. It is a play that raises questions about how national identity can be exploited as a commodity on international markets, but Jones herself shows an awareness that such values as authenticity and liveness are particularly appreciated by theatregoers throughout the West.

We'll return to all of those themes throughout this book, but I want in this chapter to respond to some of the challenges posed by *Stones In His Pockets*: to consider how globalization affects theatre, to define what globalization might mean for theatre scholars, and to consider how critics, practitioners, and audiences can evaluate and respond to these developments.

Defining globalization

This book focuses on dramatic literature and theatrical production, but it also proposes that the transformation of theatre worldwide is just one example of a paradigmatic shift from geographical to conceptual spaces – as Jones's play suggests, the contested territory nowadays is not land but meaning. In the following chapters, I discuss how that shift has altered the way that culture is produced and received, but I also place that discussion in the context of how globalization has had a much broader impact – on society, politics, and many other features of human activity.

Globalization is evident in the rise of multinational corporations, in the mobility of capital through global currency markets, and in the development of economic bodies such as the International Monetary Fund and the World Bank. It is manifested in the development of supranational federations such as the European Union and in the regionalization of countries like the United Kingdom. It has been realized in the development of internationalized forms of communication, such as the internet and satellite television, which allow for greater levels of intercultural dialogue, while also facilitating the spread of mass-mediated forms of entertainment that have been accused of causing cultural homogenization. And globalization, finally, is apparent in the increasing mobility of people across borders: the wealthy tourists taking package holidays, the business people with investments in several countries, and the refugees, asylum seekers, and economic migrants whose movements are so carefully monitored, and so intensely debated, by governments throughout the West.

The word 'globalization' has been used as an explanation (and sometimes as an excuse) for all of these developments. This gives rise to a problem: there is very little agreement about what the term actually means. As Roland Robertson observes, 'globalization' is 'often used very loosely and, indeed, in contradictory ways' (1992: 8). For Marshall McLuhan (1970), globalization had turned the world into a 'global village', but for Hardt and Negri (2001) it has forced us to live in an 'Empire'. Some scholars claim that our world can be seen as a 'new international information order'; others argue that we live in a 'McWorld', dominated by 'coca-colonization'.[5] We are told that globalization represents something new, yet, as Immanuel Wallerstein argued years ago, the globe has been undergoing social compression since the middle of the 16th century (1974). From shortly after their inception, world religions such as Christianity and Islam showed globalizing tendencies. So did

16th century conquest and 19th century imperialism. And, as Tom Standage shows in *The Victorian Internet* (1999), a process of technology-driven global compression has been underway since the middle of the 19th century – initiated by the invention of the telegraph, accelerated by the development of aviation, radio, and television, and firmly established with the growth of the internet.

A further problem is that your 'globalization' may be different to mine. Goran Therborn points out that there are at least five different discourses on globalization. The first focuses on global capitalism, on the spread of money across national borders, the impact of branding on consumption, and so on. The second involves social criticism, generally dominated by considerations of the ethical dimensions of globalization, with a strong emphasis on exploring the inequalities between the West and the developing world. The third is dominated by discussions about the nation state and its future. The fourth – the one I am most concerned with in this book – is the spread of an international and/or global culture. And the final form of discourse relates to ecology, to such issues as global warming, pandemics, and so on. Rather provocatively (but probably accurately), Therborn suggests that there is little overlap in these fields: 'seldom do these discourses express an awareness of each other and rarely, if ever, an awareness of all the others', he claims (2000: 153). Perhaps Therborn's argument exaggerates the unwillingness of academics to cross disciplinary boundaries in their exploration of globalization. It probably is fair to say, however, that scholars of globalization tend to be concerned primarily with one of the five categories described above (and indeed, this book is no exception in that regard, focusing as it does on culture).

So, in short, does the word 'globalization' refer to anything new – and if so, what on earth does it mean?

This is not a flippant question. If it is unclear what globalization means, it will be even more difficult to establish whether it is a good or bad thing. Globalization is intimately associated with the economic policies of the Reagan and Thatcher governments of the 1980s, which, as Joseph Stiglitz points out, emphasized 'fiscal austerity, privatisation, and market liberalisation' at the expense of other values (2002: 53). The causal relationship between free market economics and other forms of globalization is difficult to define thoroughly. Yes, globalization has been accelerated by the deregulation of national economies, the removal of trade barriers, and the growth of multinational companies. But the economic philosophies that drove these developments could not have become so influential without cultural globalization and the globalization of communications.

As Martin Wolf puts it, 'technology makes globalisation feasible', but 'liberalisation makes it happen' (2004: 9). We need to see globalization not as one process, but as many interlinking processes.

There is also a risk that by condemning globalization we will fail to take advantage of many of its benefits. Globalization, after all, may actually facilitate greater levels of resistance to global capitalism. Books and documentary films that chart the impact of the globalization of capital, especially on countries in the developing world, are widely distributed. In Britain, for example, Naomi Klein's *No Logo* sold over a quarter of a million copies in 2001 alone, outselling new work by such popular writers as Jamie Oliver, Dean Koontz, PD James, Ian Rankin, Cathy Kelly, and Wilbur Smith.[6] Its popularity throughout the world means that *No Logo* is – simultaneously – both a critique of globalization and an example of it. Klein's book (and indeed Klein herself) obviously benefited from globalization, but that does not undermine the arguments that she puts forward against multinational capitalism. Similarly, the spread of so-called 'anti-globalization movements' would be impossible without the globalization of communications and transportation.

The proliferation of such movements, and the appearance of books like *No Logo*, can be seen as evidence of the development of a *global consciousness*. People in the West are becoming aware that their purchase of a particular brand of clothing has an impact upon salaries in South-East Asia; activists are using communications technology to form networks across national boundaries; business people in Ireland look for investment opportunities in China, while Chinese people look for trade opportunities in Ireland. Globalization can also provide the intellectual, political, and cultural infrastructure that might facilitate solutions to problems that transcend national boundaries: global warming, debt in the developing world, the spread of sub-Saharan AIDS, crises in places like Darfur, and so on.

One of the most straightforward definitions of globalization has been offered by Malcolm Waters, who sees it as a social process in which 'the constraints of geography on economic, political, social and cultural arrangements recede, in which people become increasingly aware that they are receding and in which people act accordingly' (2001: 5). That description shows how the influence of globalization is dependent on people's belief that the world is actually becoming more globalized. Some scholars see globalization as an economic process; others suggest that it is a sociological one. I don't disagree with those perspectives, but contend that the most useful way of thinking about globalization – at least insofar as culture is concerned – is as a *meme*. Richard Dawkins's coinage describes the transmission, replication, and evolution of an idea through culture, which, he suggests, occurs in a process similar to that involved in Darwinian biology.[7] Globalization is an excellent example of a meme that is competing well in the cultural pool. As we become aware of the *idea* of globalization, we start making decisions on the basis that the world is globalized. This provides evidence – to ourselves and others – that globalization is real, which further convinces us that the world is globalized, thus inspiring more decisions that are grounded in a global consciousness. 'Globalization' is a belief that replicates itself: when we act globally, we create globalization.

To see globalization as a meme – as a self-replicating cultural motif that survives because individuals choose to believe in it – allows us to become more aware that globalization does not simply involve changes to the social or economic order: it is also a process for which people are responsible, and to which they can and must react. This shows that while globalization may involve many different processes and definitions, all have in common the issue of agency. To illustrate how that approach can be used to understand the different effects of globalization, I want to explore briefly the recent development of three apparently unrelated institutions: Nike, the Irish state, and the National Theatre of Scotland (NTS).

The American footwear manufacturer Nike is one of the iconic examples of globalization. Between 1980 and 1991, the company famously increased its profits tenfold by moving manufacturing to the periphery of its organization, to subcontracted companies in the developing world. This redeployment of its resources allowed it to concentrate instead on advertising and marketing (see Korzeniewicz, 1993; Klein, 2001). This shift means that Nike's power is no longer symbolized by factories or employees occupying physical space, but by the dominance of a concept – a brand – in the imagination of its customers.

Nike's 'downsizing' was completed just as the Irish Peace Process was beginning. That process resulted in the Nineteenth Amendment of the Irish constitution (*Bunreacht na hEireann*) in 1998, which constructed Irish nationality not on the basis of territory, but in terms of individual consent. Before 1998, Articles Two and Three of the Irish constitution had laid claim to the territory of Northern Ireland, defining nationality in relation to the physical space occupied by the island of Ireland. The amendment revoked this territorial claim and redefined nationality as based on personal entitlement. 'It is the entitlement and birthright of every person born in the island of Ireland, which includes its islands and seas, to be part of the Irish nation', the amendment states, its syntax establishing 'the island of Ireland' and 'the Irish nation' as related but separate entities. Before 1998, Irish nationality was defined in terms of an individual's identification with the physical spaces of geographic territory: to be Irish was to be born upon the island of Ireland. Nationality is now defined conceptually: to be Irish is to identify oneself as part of an 'Irish nation' that is related to but separate from physical territory. This entitlement may arise from being born on the island, but it is realized by the exercise of intellectual consent.

This move from the physical to the conceptual is also evident in the establishment in 2003 of the National Theatre of Scotland (NTS). The NTS is not defined in terms of the physical space occupied by a building, as is the case with the national theatres of Ireland and Great Britain. Rather, it is a coordinating organization that may create or support 'Scottish theatre' anywhere. Mark Fisher explains how this system operates: 'The national theatre could team a playwright from Inverness with the production department of the Tron Theatre in Glasgow, and a director from Lithuania. It could take note when the tiny island Mull Theatre did a brilliant show and invest in it, so it could be seen on bigger stages in other places. One week Dundee Rep would be the Scottish national theatre, the next it might be Edinburgh's Royal Lyceum' (2001: 12). Hence, the NTS is not defined spatially by a building in Edinburgh or Glasgow, but by an agreed belief in the concept of Scottish theatre that is closely related to, but not absolutely dependent upon, an association with one physical space.

Each of these cases involves a relocation of power from a physical to a conceptual space, or a *deterritorialization of power*. The example of Nike involves a deterritorialization of economic authority: power is not expressed through the occupation of space by factories, but by the dominance of a brand. The redefinition of Irish nationality is a deterritorialization of political sovereignty: Irishness is defined by the expression of an entitlement, and not by the existence of a physical entity. And the NTS represents a deterritorialization of cultural agency: a play is part of the Scottish canon not because it is produced in one building, but because it is branded as being produced by an organization that can be anywhere and go anywhere. So I am suggesting that the philosophy underpinning globalization is evident in many different contexts: in sweatshops in the developing world, in the Irish Peace Process, in the National Theatre of Scotland.

Globalization, then, is not a coherent process imposed on the individual, but a set of processes to which people and institutions react, with sometimes very different consequences. While a precise and agreed definition of 'globalization' remains elusive, it is nevertheless clear that a social process is underway that is radically altering our perception of space, and therefore of many other things: time, speed, employment, power, nationality – and theatre.

Why Irish theatre?

It might seem odd that I have decided to consider globalization from the perspective of one nation. This is because, as Saskia Sassen points out, 'the theoretical and methodological challenge presented by . . . globalization is that [it] entails a transcending of exclusive national territoriality and of the inter-state system, yet it is implanted in national territories and institutions' (2000: 384). This means that globalization may transcend national boundaries, but it frequently arises from the actions of state-sponsored agencies, and is often regulated by national bodies and laws. As I discuss throughout this book, globalization is experienced from a variety of perspectives – individually, locally, regionally, and nationally. A key concern for this study will be the extent to which the term 'nation' has meaning in a globalizing world – both for makers of theatre and for the scholars and audiences who analyse theatrical works.

It is generally agreed within the literature that the current period of economic globalization began with the collapse of communism in Europe in the early 1990s. In the immediate aftermath of the fall of the Berlin Wall in 1989, both the Irish theatre and the Irish economy experienced a resurgence which, in both cases, was heavily determined by a desire to exploit opportunities that were available internationally, rather than regionally or locally. The so-called 'Celtic Tiger' period of Irish economic growth was matched by what some scholars called a 'third renaissance' in Irish dramatic literature (see O'Toole, 2000). This book is underpinned by the thesis that these two processes were interrelated. I am making the probably obvious suggestion that the resurgence of Irish theatre was aided by economic growth. But I also aim to show something that is probably less obvious: that the performance of the Irish economy was influenced by the international profile of Irish drama.

As I discuss in more detail below, there were many moments before 1990 when Irish theatre was internationalized; and there were moments too, in the country's history, of increased economic globalization. However, my purpose in this book is to illustrate how culture and economics have become far more closely intertwined in the post-Cold War world than ever before, and for that reason I am restricting my analysis of this subject to the 'Celtic Tiger' period of 1990–2005.[8]

At present, it may suffice to state that this book considers the globalization of theatre in relation to Ireland for three reasons: the transformation of Ireland by globalization; the fact that Irish theatre has historically tended to function internationally as well as nationally; and because Irish theatre entered a new period of vibrancy and creativity while the country itself was becoming more globalized.

Ireland has been completely transformed by globalization. A constituent part of the United Kingdom in 1900 and partially independent in 1922, by 2000 it had become the 'most globalized country in the world', according to *Foreign Policy* magazine (2002). That is, it had greater levels of openness to international investment, higher rates of mobility, and more access to global communications than any other country in the world, including (it should be noted) the United Kingdom. It has also become one of the world's wealthiest countries. Gross domestic product (GDP) per capita jumped from €9,846 in 1990, to €23,909 in 1999, and to €33,875 in 2003.[9] Most of that increase was a result of the massive growth of foreign direct investment (FDI) in Ireland during the 1990s, much of it coming from US multinational companies in the software and pharmaceutical industries, such as Microsoft, Intel, and Pfizer. Economic prosperity has had numerous effects on Irish life, some of them very positive. Therefore, because the country is seen widely as an excellent example of the impact of globalization, it may be used to explore in detail the relationship between globalization and theatre.

Irish literature has always tended towards internationalism. Many of the great Irish texts of the 18th century consider the impact of what we would now call the globalization of trade. Swift's *A Modest Proposal* (1729) brilliantly exposes how the production of goods for export and the strategic use of tariffs can have devastating consequences for a vulnerable population. Goldsmith's *The Deserted Village* (1770) imagines the destruction of a rural idyll by the relentless pursuit of wealth through global trade:

> Proud swells the tide with loads of freighted ore,
> And shouting Folly hails them from her shore;
> Hoards, e'en beyond the miser's wish, abound,
> And rich men flock from all the world around.
> Yet count our gains. This wealth is but a name
> That leaves our useful products still the same.

Sheridan's *School for Scandal* (1777) argues that the dissipation of the Surface brothers is a direct consequence of British imperialism: one is a hypocrite and the other financially irresponsible because both know that they can depend on the wealth of their uncle, Sir Oliver, who is due to return to London from the East Indies with their inheritance. And in *Pizarro* (1799), Sheridan draws clear parallels between the Irish rebellion of 1798, the colonization of India, and the conquest of South America by the Spanish Empire.

In the 19th century, Dion Boucicault toured the world with his plays, devising strategies that would allow him to cross cultural boundaries more easily (an issue I return to later in this book). By the end of the century, Oscar Wilde in 'The Decay of Lying' (1891) would deny altogether the possibility of a national literature: when confronted with any nation's art, we must, Wilde believes, remind ourselves that 'there is no such country, there are no such people' (2000: 237).

Even during the Irish Literary Revival (c. 1890–1916), the production of a national literature was always framed in a global context. Yeats aimed to overcome the religious divisions of the country by creating 'a national literature that made Ireland beautiful in the memory' but which had been 'freed from a provincialism by an exacting criticism, a European pose' (1998: 101–2). And all of the great works of the Revival display the influences of international literature on Irish writers: of Ibsen on the plays of Synge and O'Casey, of Turgenev on the fictions of George Moore, of Dante on the works of Joyce and (later) on Beckett too.

The current period of globalization in Ireland has its roots in the 1950s, when the government's decision to embrace economic globalization unleashed a process of cultural globalization. Lionel Pilkington points out that the establishment in 1957 of the Dublin Theatre Festival – which aimed to bring international work to Irish audiences and to promote Irish drama to the world – was closely related to Ireland's integration into the global economy and to its move from a traditional to a modern society. 'The debacle of the 1958 Dublin Theatre Festival may have ended in a triumph for the public authority of the city's Roman Catholic hierarchy', writes Pilkington, referring to the *de facto* clerical banning of Sean O'Casey's *The Drums of Father Ned*. 'The victory was short-lived', he points out, 'The year 1958 also coincided with the publication of T.K. Whitaker's government report, the "Programme for Economic Expansion"'. This gave accelerated momentum to Ireland's economic and social modernization processes (2001: 158). The Whitaker report was a blueprint for the attraction to Ireland of multinational investment, showing how the internationalization of Irish theatre was closely related to state-sponsored movements intended to promote tourism and attract FDI.

The development of Irish theatre during the 1990s hence involves an acceleration of processes that had been evident for centuries. Conor McPherson has spoken repeatedly of his interest in international culture; indeed he admitted frankly in 2007 that 'you could say I've embraced globalisation' (quoted by Khokhar, 2007) – yet he is also doing many of the things that Dion Boucicault did 150 years before him. The plays of Martin McDonagh, similarly, went from Ireland to London and on to Broadway, and include a variety of references to contemporary global culture – and, as such, follow a path and a technique that brought Brian Friel international success with *Philadelphia, Here I Come!* in the mid-1960s. So the second reason for my focus on Irish theatre is that it allows me to explore the links between past and present, placing the globalization of contemporary theatre worldwide in the context of such historical phenomena as colonialism, imperialism, and transatlantic exchange.

Finally, the globalization of Irish society coincides with a revival in its theatre, which achieved unprecedented levels of national and international success during the 'Celtic Tiger' period of economic development. Many recent Irish plays present Ireland as a cosmopolitan society, with writers displaying an awareness of, and comfort with, emerging globalized cultural forms. One of the earliest examples of this tendency was Declan Hughes's groundbreaking *Digging for Fire* (1991). That play articulated the concerns of an emerging generation of Irish people, using international culture and themes to assert a vision of Irish identity that was independent of traditional Irish iconography, and which showed frustration with the idea that Irish drama should be exclusively national in outlook. The characters in Hughes's play move freely from Ireland to elsewhere, and use cultural references that are international without any sense of national displacement. *Digging for Fire* is identifiably Irish, but takes its title from a song by the Boston alternative rock group Pixies, and features music by Tom Waits, New Order, and other internationally recognized artists. It also locates Irish culture within an internationalized literary sphere, while making a series of strong statements about Ireland's national status and its relationship with other countries. This relationship between the national and the international was particularly well illustrated in the original production of the play, which featured a lengthy discussion of Bret Easton Ellis's controversial novel *American Psycho* (1991), which was then receiving much attention throughout the world. Two of the play's characters, Clare and Breda, are discussing the novel. Clare praises it for its modernity, while Breda suggests that stories about serial killers have no relevance to Ireland. This prompts Clare to ask whether the ongoing political violence in Northern

Ireland should not be considered an example of serial killing. 'Oh please', replies Breda, 'spare me the North'.[10]

This exchange highlights the competing views of Ireland that existed in the early 1990s – one emerging, the other passing away. For Clare, Ireland can and should be compared to the United States, but for Breda, the Republic of Ireland still has a village-like atmosphere, in which it is possible to ignore Northern Ireland, to ignore serial killers, and to remain focused only on oneself. The laying bare of these tensions, and the inclusion of such cultural references within an Irish context, place Irish culture within a globalized discourse.

That transformation would become a more explicit feature of Irish writing throughout the 1990s. From that time onwards, Irish theatre acquired a much stronger presence on the international stage than it had hitherto enjoyed, as a result of which many of Ireland's leading writers are now more likely to have their work premiered outside of the country than in it. In 2001, for example, new work by Martin McDonagh was produced in England, a revised version of Tom Murphy's *Too Late For Logic* was premiered in Scotland, and Mark O'Rowe's *Made in China* received its world premiere in Germany.[11] In 2003, Owen McCafferty's *Scenes from the Big Picture* was a success at the National in London, as was McDonagh's *The Pillowman*. And in subsequent years, Irish playwrights such as Marina Carr, Tom Murphy, Marie Jones, Frank McGuinness, Conor McPherson, Sebastian Barry, Christian O'Reilly, Enda Walsh, and many others have premiered their plays not in Ireland, but in London, Edinburgh, or New York.[12] Indeed, many of the best 'Irish' plays that have been produced since 1990 have never been seen in Ireland itself.

This is not a new problem. As Nicholas Grene reminds us, since at least the time of Boucicault, Irish drama has been 'created as much to be viewed from outside as inside Ireland' (1999: 3), and this remains the case at present. However, this situation is no longer exclusively because of characteristics that are unique to Ireland: the relationships between writers, theatres, and nations are changing throughout the world. One example of this is Conor McPherson's statement in 2001 that he would produce his new work only in London because 'he's not going to put up with the level of criticism' in Ireland (quoted by Colgan in Chambers *et al.,* 2001: 87). In making this statement, McPherson identifies problems that in some ways are unique to Ireland: notably its lack of media outlets for serious theatre criticism, and its proximity both to the West End and Edinburgh. However, McPherson's relationship with the London stage may also be considered in the context of a growing flexibility in the relationships of writers with theatres everywhere. In recent years, Neil LaBute and David Mamet have produced new work in London, Patrick Marber has premiered work in New York, and Edward Bond's *The Crime of the Twenty-First Century* (2001), Sheelagh Stevenson's *Enlightenment* (2005), Neil LaBute's *Wrecks* (2005), and Sam Shepard's *Kicking A Dead Horse* (2007) have all premiered in Ireland. The historical mobility of writers and companies in Ireland is now comparable to that pertaining in many other countries – if Ireland sends (or drives) many of its best writers abroad, it is also willing to bring playwrights from other countries to its own theatres. This mobility cannot be explained exclusively by Ireland's status as a small or postcolonial country, since it is a feature of theatre not only in countries like Denmark and India, but also in Britain, the United States, France, and elsewhere.[13]

But as other countries are becoming more like Ireland, Ireland is becoming more like other countries. Breda's injunction in *Digging for Fire* to 'spare me the North' anticipates the development of Irish drama since the 1990s. As I suggest throughout this book (especially in my consideration of Sean O'Casey's *The Plough and the Stars*), a notable tendency in recent Irish drama is to move away from considerations of the impact of the Troubles on Irish life – to reject, ignore, or transcend the postcolonial paradigm established by Field Day and others during the 1980s, and to present the Troubles within an historical context only. As Jones's *Stones In His Pockets* suggests, theatre has considered the conflict of identities in Ireland in the past, but it must now tackle (or exploit) the commodification and essentialization of identity within global culture in the present – a theme that makes Irish drama resonate internationally. This does not mean that plays about the Troubles no longer appear in Ireland: one of the most successful Irish plays on the global stage in recent years was Martin McDonagh's *The Lieutenant of Inishmore* (2001). However, I will argue that globalization – rather than the 'national question' – is now the dominant paradigm in Irish theatre.

To make this argument, I must also clarify my own uses of the terms 'Ireland' and 'Irish'. As I have stated, globalization is frequently (and perhaps paradoxically) facilitated by the policies of the nation state. For example, the decision by the government of the Republic of Ireland to lower the rate of corporation tax led to an influx of FDI, which in turn has made the country more globalized. Because they are governed differently, Northern Ireland and the Republic of Ireland have experienced globalization differently – politically, culturally, and economically. I refer repeatedly to the impact of globalization on what I term 'Irish' theatre in this book, usually drawing on statistics that pertain only to the Republic of Ireland. I do not intend to suggest that these statistics are equally applicable to Northern Ireland. Rather, I aim to show how writers respond to political and social events within one or both of the Irish states in order to create drama that is seen not as 'Northern Irish' or as coming from the Republic of Ireland, but which is seen simply as Irish.

Hence, I argue in the next chapter that Brian Friel's *Dancing at Lughnasa* can be seen in the context of the politics of the Republic of Ireland in the late 1980s and early 1990s – but I also show that when it went abroad its 'Irishness' was received differently. As the example of Jones's *Stones In His Pockets* has already shown, when many plays travel abroad, they are seen simply as *Irish*, whether they originate in Belfast (as Jones's play did), in Dublin (as *Lughnasa* did), or indeed in London (as did many of the most successful Irish plays of the period covered by this book). As I've already suggested, this is because the word 'Irish' has become deterritorialized: it may be used to refer to the physical territory of Ireland, but it also acts as a brand – a commodified abstraction that gives meaning to its purchaser instead of signifying the physical territory of a nation. So when I write about 'Irish plays', I am not necessarily referring to works that were produced in either of the two Irish states, but instead to plays that are marketed or received internationally as corresponding to the Irish 'brand'. I do not wish to elide the differences between the societies and theatrical cultures of Northern Ireland and the Republic of Ireland by using the word 'Irish' to refer to plays from both states. Rather, I wish to draw attention to the tendency within global culture to *ignore* those differences.

I should also state that this book is not a history of Irish drama since 1990. Such an undertaking would have required me to consider many writers, events, and works that do not appear in this book. I have, for instance, referred only in passing to the work of Tom Murphy, mainly because I believe that the major plays he has premiered since 1990 – *The Wake* (1998), *The House* (2000), and *Alice Trilogy* (2005) – are not as relevant to my argument as works by other writers. He is the most important of the dramatists that should feature in any history of this period. Sebastian Barry, Anne Devlin, Thomas Kilroy, Christina Reid, Billy Roche, and others would also merit inclusion in such a work. But none of them is considered here in any depth.

Likewise, a history of the period would probably have dedicated attention to plays in the Irish language, and might have explored in different ways the complex issues of region, race, sexuality, and (particularly) gender. One of the features of globalization, I will show, is that it tends to homogenize, to ignore those elements of a society that are marginalized and hence not easily understood internationally. This has particularly affected the status of Irish women playwrights internationally.

For reasons that are discussed in more detail below, women dramatists do not occupy a central position on the Irish stage, and have therefore tended to have a lower global profile than many male dramatists.

The Irish Playography (a database of all Irish plays produced since 1904) shows that approximately one in four Irish plays produced between 1990 and 2005 was written by a woman – hardly an example of equality, but perhaps a higher number than one might expect. Further examination shows, however, that women are considerably more likely than men to be commissioned to write community drama, plays for children, or collaborative works – all forms that are considered of lesser value than traditional plays, at least insofar as the generation of revenue is concerned. Women writers' work is far more likely to be self-produced than men's in Ireland. Relatively more plays by male authors are published. Relatively more new plays by male authors are produced at the Abbey Theatre, Druid, the Gate, and the other prominent Irish theatres. Only the Dublin company Rough Magic has a record of producing as much new work by women as by men. It is also one of the few companies that consistently encourage women writers to tackle themes other than domestic disharmony, as shown in such recent works as *The Bonefire* by Rosemary Jenkinson (2006) and Elizabeth Kuti's *The Sugar Wife* (discussed in detail in Chapter 8). Of all of the Irish plays that have achieved success throughout the world, only a tiny minority were written by women. *Stones In His Pockets* is one, and we might consider some of the plays of Marina Carr. I do discuss Jones, Carr, Kuti, and other women dramatists in this work. And I attempt to highlight the central role that Garry Hynes and Lynne Parker have played in the development of new Irish writing. Nevertheless, there is always a risk that, in considering how globalization excludes whatever marginalized forms of culture it cannot assimilate, one might reproduce that marginalization, by privileging in any analysis what is dominant or central in global culture. To put it simply, because the majority of globalized Irish plays have been written by men, this book focuses mostly on plays that were written by men. I have tried to be aware of the problems attendant on that imbalance throughout the writing of this book, and to discuss its consequences whenever it is appropriate to do so.

Having stated what I am not trying to do – and what I am trying not to do – I should now explain that my aim is to use Irish drama to chart the emergence of what I will describe as a global theatre network, and to account for the place of Irish drama within that field. Theories of globalization, I suggest, offer one of the best ways of understanding the development of recent theatre. Globalization can be a theme explored by writers, but it can also be a phenomenon exploited for economic gain by producers – and quite often these differing responses to the development can conflict, as I've suggested in the consideration above of *Stones In His Pockets*. As Jones's work shows, a play can simultaneously critique and exploit globalization; it's therefore essential to avoid simplistic approaches to the subject. I make this statement not to call for the creation of a new theoretical model that can be applied universally to every recent play. And I am not attempting to rebrand or reboot the postcolonial franchise that has dominated Irish Studies in recent decades. Instead, I propose that we need a new framework for understanding contemporary developments in theatre in their social and cultural contexts. The ultimate goal of this book, therefore, is to analyse and clarify the relationship between social change arising from globalization, and the different modes of theatre production that have emerged as a result of those changes.

2
Globalizing Irish Theatre: Brian Friel's *Dancing at Lughnasa,* 1990/1999

Brian Friel's *Dancing at Lughnasa* (1990) was an attempt to address problems that would become more prominent during the 1990s. His play is not about globalization, but it can help us to understand better the impact of globalization on our societies – and on our theatre. Furthermore, its production history offers a significant example of how globalization affects theatrical production and reception: a comparison of the play with its production history reveals that although *Dancing at Lughnasa* was one of the most popular international plays of the 1990s, its success appears to have been founded upon a misunderstanding – or perhaps even a misrepresentation – of Friel's script.

Lughnasa achieved classical status with astonishing speed. The play premiered at the Abbey Theatre in 1990 in a production directed by Patrick Mason. It was quite well received but, as we'll see below, there weren't many indications that Irish audiences thought that the play was the masterpiece it is now assumed to be. That changed quickly as Mason's production began to tour nationally and internationally, winning awards, partially inspiring *Riverdance*,[1] and being adapted into a 1998 film that starred Meryl Streep. Within less than a decade, *Lughnasa* had been firmly accepted into the dramatic canon, as shown when it was revived at the Abbey as part of an international 'Friel Festival', held to celebrate the author's 70th birthday in 1999.

The revived *Lughnasa* was, as Karen Fricker (1999) notes, presented as a 'vessel of celebratory nostalgia' (43). This, as Fricker states, is 'deeply ironic': Friel's achievement with *Lughnasa*, and throughout his work, is 'to question the instinct for nostalgia, to expose the gap between experience and understanding, words and meaning, what is institutionally categorized as history and what really happened' (43). Throughout *Lughnasa's* production history around the world, audiences seemed uninterested in the challenging aspects of Friel's script, instead focusing on the play's sentimental and nostalgic qualities. And in Ireland itself, audiences seemed disinclined to see the play as a critique of their society, instead viewing its international success – particularly on Broadway – as evidence of the country's newfound self-assurance on the global stage. In fact, both at home and abroad, the Abbey Theatre's productions of *Dancing at Lughnasa* during the 1990s appear to have been received and remembered in ways that are not only unsupported by Friel's script, but which also seem to conflict with the themes of the play. How can play and production give rise to such divergent responses?

To answer that question, we need to consider how globalization affects the production and reception of theatre internationally. Theories about globalization can allow us to understand Friel's techniques in *Lughnasa*: his use of multiple chronological spaces, his blending of cultures, his focus on the necessity of dramatic uncertainty. Yet globalization can also explain the play's international reception, and its subsequent canonization within Ireland itself.

I am not arguing that *Lughnasa* represents a new departure for Irish drama, world theatre, or indeed for Friel himself, but instead I intend to show that his play's success reveals how many pre-existing features of the Irish theatre would take on increased levels of importance from 1990 onwards.

That said, what we now call 'globalization' has always been central to Friel's work. His breakthrough play, *Philadelphia, Here I Come!* (1964), challenged notions of geographical space, showing us how America is present in Irish life, and Ireland present in America. He continued to develop that theme in *The Loves of Cass Maguire* (1966), which shows how the relationship between personal identity and national space was changing in an Ireland that was beginning to enjoy the first benefits of FDI.

Friel moved from thinking about the relationship between Ireland and America to adopting a global perspective in 1969, when his satire *The Mundy Scheme* appeared. That play was a response to an Ireland that seemed close to bankruptcy, both economically and morally. Focusing on F.X. Ryan, a fictitious Taoiseach who in many ways anticipates such real Irish leaders as Charles Haughey, Friel suggests with Swiftian ire that a possible solution to Ireland's economic woes might be to transform the west of the island into an enormous graveyard for the dead of North America and Europe, its 'useless' land sold off for huge sums of money. That proposal is justified in terms of globalization. 'The days of parochial, provincial, parish-pump thinking are over' in Ireland, states Ryan. 'Either you proudly proclaim your membership of the global village – or you die.

No country can live in isolation. We are all dependent and interdependent. Commerce, trade, and business have made us all brothers' (Friel, 1970: 272).

As a statement of the imperatives (and the risks) associated with globalization, this speech anticipates the many similar declarations made by Irish leaders during the Celtic Tiger period: participation in globalization is not simply desirable, Friel's protagonist states, but a matter of life and death. For this reason, *The Mundy Scheme* seems many years ahead of its time: if we placed it side-by-side with *Dancing at Lughnasa*, it is possible that some readers would find it difficult to determine which play appeared in 1969, and which in 1990. Friel's suggestion seems to be that Ireland can only succeed in the emerging global economy if it chooses to become an enormous memorial for the dead of the civilized West. For this and other reasons, *The Mundy Scheme* is a deeply cynical play; it lacks Friel's usual subtlety, but it makes a strong point.

It is a point that Friel wouldn't return to until decades later, however. *The Mundy Scheme* premiered in June 1969; only two months later, in response to the worsening sectarian violence in Northern Ireland, British troops arrived in the province; not long after that, the 'Battle of the Bogside' began in Derry, and what we now call the 'Troubles' had begun. Friel's response to that situation was to move away from writing plays that sought to consider Ireland in its global context. Beginning with *The Gentle Island* (1971), Friel's attention turned inwards, to an exploration of Ireland itself – and we see from that time the emergence of plays that portray Ireland as a country in which the threat of violence is constantly present. That violence is shown to be quite literally just below the surface of Irish life in *Volunteers* (1975), in which a team of republican prisoners takes part in an archaeological dig; it is also present in *Faith Healer* (1979) and *Living Quarters* (1977), both of which conclude with the violent deaths of their principle male characters. For Friel, mapping the Irish landscape seems to have become a way of historicizing the Troubles, helping his audiences to understand how a country that had seemed peaceful – as peaceful, in fact, as a graveyard – could have descended into ferocious violence from 1969 onwards.

That exploration led ultimately to the foundation of Field Day Theatre Company, and to the premiere of Friel's 1980 masterpiece *Translations*. Both events have been explored in detail elsewhere (see Richtarik, 2004), so I do not wish to provide a detailed analysis of them; however, it is worth considering for a moment the extent to which *Translations* builds on Friel's plays of the 1970s in its exploration of the shifting contours of Irish spaces. After all, even the appearance of *Translations* was a challenge to existing ideas about political and cultural spaces. The play was premiered in Derry's Guildhall, a building then seen by many as a symbol of the Unionist domination of the city. Friel had already made use of this building's symbolic importance when he set the action of his 1974 play *The Freedom of the City* there. In that work, a trio of nationalist protestors takes shelter in the Guildhall after the British Army breaks up a civil rights march. The building is 'regarded by the [Catholic] minority as a symbol of Unionist domination' in Northern Ireland, we're told (Friel, 1984: 117), which means that its apparent 'occupation' is viewed by some sections of the nationalist community as being akin to 'the fall of the Bastille' (118). The judge conducting the enquiry into the eventual murder of the three protestors assumes that their decision to enter the Guildhall must have been a 'carefully contrived act of defiance' (149), since no other explanation for the choice is 'consistent with the facts' (149), as a representative of the British authorities would understand them. Hence, *The Freedom of the City* presents the Guildhall not just as a physical space, but also as a symbol that can be contested and redefined. The staging of *Translations* in that same space – only six years after the premiere of *The Freedom of the City* – must be seen as operating in a similarly symbolic capacity. It was not necessarily an attempt to 'occupy' a space associated with Unionism, but perhaps could be seen as an assertion of the equality of the nationalist and unionist communities in Northern Ireland, or as a symbol of the possibility of reconciliation between both sides in the conflict.

Furthermore, by premiering *Translations* in Derry – instead of Dublin, Belfast, or London – Field Day was also presenting a challenge to the cultural spaces of Ireland and the United Kingdom. Derry City in 1980 was geographically, socially, economically, and culturally marginalized; yet as Gerry Smyth (2001) points out, the establishment of Field Day in that city meant that it became 'for a number of years the cultural-critical capital of the island' (138). As Nicholas Grene (1999) writes, the international status of Friel and the company's co-founder Stephen Rea made the production of *Translations* a 'very significant gesture' which challenged 'the cultural hegemony of Dublin and Belfast' (34).

Translations was also a reconfiguration of imaginative spaces. The play is set in 1833 in a rural Irish 'hedge school', a school for Catholic students – and thus a space that had been branded illegal by the ruling authorities in Ireland. By setting his play in a space that violates the law by its very existence (contrasting strongly with the Guildhall, from which laws are enacted), Friel shows how physical spaces can confer legitimacy. As is well known, the 'translations' referred to in the title are carried out by a British mapping expedition, which is translating Irish place names into English; hence, Baile Beag (in Irish, 'little town'), where the play is set, is 'translated' into English as 'Ballybeg'. So the play is an examination of the role of mapping and education in the extension of colonial power. But there is another, highly theatrical, form of translation at work in the play's use of language: although the audience understands that many of the characters are speaking Irish to each other, all of the dialogue is presented in English. This theatrical device often yields humorous results, but it is also a reflection of a political reality: as a result of the historical situation that Friel is representing on stage, a majority of Irish people no longer understands the Irish language.[2] Hence, Friel must present his dialogue in English. By doing so, he shows that his English-speaking audiences throughout Ireland and his Irish-speaking characters share one characteristic: both are Irish. One purpose of this technique is to suggest that markers of identity, such as language and place names, are not essential characteristics; instead, they should be seen as being subject to constant renewal in and through language. Baile Beag becomes Ballybeg but still occupies the same physical space. The characters in the play speak in Irish, English, and Greek, but adapt each language to their individual needs: work, courtship, education, the exercise of power. This play appears to suggest that, painful as it might be, a civilization can and must develop, even to the point of abandoning one language and taking up another. This is a practical illustration of the argument advanced by Hugh at the play's conclusion that 'it is not the literal past, the "facts" of history, that shape us, but images of the past embodied in language ... We must never cease renewing those images; because once we do, we fossilise' (445). National identity, Friel shows, is not an essence, but a process.

The function of Field Day was not to produce plays that specifically addressed the conflict in Northern Ireland; in its entire repertoire, only Stewart Parker's *Pentecost* (1987) does so directly. Rather, the company used theatrical space as a depoliticized territory in which the cultural assumptions, myths, and stereotypes that underlay the Troubles could be interrogated and demystified. The company did not propose that a single homogenized Irish identity should be regarded as authentic or authoritative; it presented a variety of identities and suggested that Irish spaces could accommodate all of them.

In doing so, the company transcended many boundaries. By using other countries as a context against which to understand Ireland – as in Friel's *Three Sisters* or its 1983 production of Fugard's *Boesman and Lena* – Field Day reconsidered geographical boundaries. It challenged chronological boundaries too, with Thomas Kilroy's *Double Cross* (1986), set during the Second World War, and Friel's *Making History* (1988), set in the early 17th century, being used to interrogate present-day realities. By publishing pamphlets that explored from a critical perspective many of the issues dealt with in the company's plays, Field Day blurred distinctions between art and criticism, between politics and performance. Finally, it transcended linguistic boundaries, as in *Translations* and the company's various adaptations of international classics. Although the company's theatrical output during its most active period (1980–91) was relatively small, it presented its audiences with a variety of viewpoints, so that, as Richtarik (2004) puts it, it portrayed 'alternative visions . . . in the hope of opening up new possibilities for the future' (202).

Friel cannot be credited with all of the achievements of Field Day; as explained below, his decision to present *Dancing at Lughnasa* to the Abbey Theatre shows his ambivalence about many of the company's goals and activities. Nevertheless, I would suggest that the achievement of *Lughnasa* is that it builds on Friel's consideration with Field Day – and especially with *Translations* – of how space and time can be represented. However, it also returns to the themes of *The Mundy Scheme*, asking how an Ireland that was beginning to think once again of its place in the 'global village' might be presented.

Dancing at Lughnasa: time-space compression and narrative

Dancing at Lughnasa is a play that allows audiences to come to terms with the emergence of what could be called 'time-space compression'. The concept of compression was first developed by Marshall McLuhan (1970) to describe the effects of media on global communications; such theorists as Roland Robertson and David Harvey have since developed that idea further to describe the globalization of culture. Robertson (1992) points out that 'globalization as a concept refers to both the compression of the world and the intensification of consciousness of the world as a whole' (8): that is, it does not just transform geographical relations, but also alters the manner in which the world is perceived. For David Harvey, time-space compression is a defining characteristic of postmodernity, a view that Malcolm Waters (2001) elaborates on when he defines it as 'a development in which time can be reorganized in such a way as to reduce the constraints of space, and vice versa. Time-space compression involves a shortening of time and a "shrinking" of space – progressively, the time taken to do things reduces and this in turn reduces the experiential distance between different points in space' (49).

These theorists suggest that globalization does not alter geography: it is obviously untrue that the planet is shrinking. Instead, we are witnessing the development of a *global consciousness*, an alteration of the way in which the world is generally perceived. This alteration could be described as involving the development of a *phenomenology of compression*: the world is not becoming smaller, but our perceptions of space and time make it seem smaller. As Harvey (1989) writes, these processes 'so revolutionise the objective qualities of space and time that we are forced to alter, sometimes in quite radical ways, how we represent the world to ourselves . . . As space appears to shrink to a "global village" . . . and as time horizons shorten to the point where the present is all there is . . . so we have to learn how to cope with an overwhelming sense of compression of our worlds' (240).

This concept is helpful for understanding Friel's play, which attempts to recreate dramatically the sensation of living in a world that appears to be shrinking, as a result of which it is more difficult to cling to old certainties: space, time, memory, truth – even theatrical form. *Dancing at Lughnasa* shows how we can 'cope with an overwhelming sense of compression' – a sense that may not have a basis in physical reality, but which we nevertheless perceive to be true; and it asks us to consider again the ways in which we 'represent the world to ourselves' both in memory and the theatre. 'I know I had a sense of unease', says the play's narrator Michael, 'some awareness of a widening breach between what seemed to be and what was, of things changing too quickly before my eyes, of becoming what they ought not to be' (1999b: 8). *Lughnasa* therefore presents us with an environment in which several forms of communication – some native, others invasive – are competing with each other, breaking down the barriers that we associate with time and space.

One feature of this breakdown of historical and geographical boundaries is Friel's use of narrative. *Dancing at Lughnasa* presents multiple perspectives on one event, exploring the issues of narration and spectatorship while also making use of theatrical form to consider how our perceptions of space and time have been affected by globalization. This is most obviously the case in Friel's use of form: he allows audiences to perceive two different times and places simultaneously, and so the normal boundaries that allow us to differentiate historical and geographical spaces become confused. The first of those spaces is enacted through a naturalistic performance that is set in the home of the five Mundy sisters, with the action taking place in 1936; the other is a narrative delivered directly to the audience by Michael. The blend of naturalism with narrative, and past with present, allows audiences to reconsider their attitudes to a range of issues.

Michael is initially presented as a centralizing authority for the action, who shares the audience's temporal and geographical perspective. He is positioned downstage left in a pool of light as the play begins. He is therefore part of the play but not of the action; he does not interact with the set, and will not look directly at, or point to, any of the characters. Michael states that he is casting his mind back to the summer of 1936, implying that he occupies the same chronological space as the audience, who are encouraged to distance themselves from that era by laughing with Michael's description of music 'beamed to us *all the way* from Athlone' (8, emphasis added). This joke brings the issue of technological compression to the attention of Friel's audiences, who are likely to regard the distance from Athlone to Ballybeg (where the play is set) as negligible.[3]

We soon become aware that there are strange disjunctions between Michael's narration and the action presented on stage: the 'real' past and his recollection of it are shown not to be identical. The audience, for example, sees Father Jack in the opening tableau wearing a 'magnificent and immaculate uniform of dazzling white gold epaulettes and gold buttons, tropical hat, clerical collar, military cane . . . He is "resplendent", "magnificent"' (4). Yet Michael describes him as 'shrunken and jaundiced with malaria' (8). The contrast between Michael's description of Jack and his physical appearance onstage establishes a distinction between the verbal expression of Michael's memories – narration – and Friel's stagecraft. Friel then reveals that the vision of Father Jack in the tableau is taken from Michael's memory of a photograph, which had fallen out of his Aunt Kate's prayer book (17). The photograph of Jack presents him within the iconography of colonialism and Catholicism, highlighting the play's consideration of the relationship between British imperialism and Ireland's Catholic missions to Africa. It also symbolizes the structure of *Lughnasa* itself: the photograph is a visual image leaping incongruously from the pages of a book, acting as an analogy for Friel's representation onstage of the Mundys, which bursts free from the confines of Michael's verbal narrative.

This contrast between representation and reality is developed in the play's opening moments. The first line of the action set in 1936 is, 'When are we going to get a decent mirror to see ourselves in?' (9), an invocation by Friel of a common image in Irish literature: the cracked looking glass. The discussion by three of the sisters (Agnes, Maggie, and

Chris) of their inability to see themselves clearly in the mirror places *Lughnasa* in a tradition that includes Wilde's *Decay of Lying* (1891), Joyce's *Ulysses* (1922), and the second acts of Synge's *The Playboy of Western World* (1907) and Murphy's *A Whistle in the Dark* (1961). The purpose of this intertextual reference is to draw attention to the relationship between identity and perception. Friel opens his play by having his audience watch action, mediated by an apparently unreliable narrator, in which a group of women attempt to see themselves, but cannot do so clearly. This complicated arrangement should alert the audience to the danger of taking theatrical representation as a literal image of reality: we are instead being confronted by an awareness of how reality is mediated, sometimes through multiple layers of representation.

We are therefore constantly aware of a clash between the real and the mediated, most explicitly in Michael's narrative. He tells us at the end of the first act that although his parents Chris and Gerry 'didn't go through a conventional form of marriage, once more they danced together, witnessed by the unseen sisters' (65). His subsequent speech creates the expectation that we will see an informal 'marriage' in the second act. This expectation is unfulfilled, however. Gerry dances with Agnes and Maggie, but not with Chris, in the play's second half. Seeing Agnes and Gerry dance does not signify marriage to Chris: it is at this moment that the insecurity of her relationship with Gerry becomes most clear to her, as is suggested by her spiteful response to Agnes moments later (100). In fact, the ceremony presented in the second act is not one of marriage, but of separation. Father Jack and Gerry both place their hats on the ground, with Jack carefully choreographing the 'symbolic distancing of yourself from what you once possessed' (104). Contrary to Michael's suggestion at the end of the first act, Gerry is in fact turning his back on Chris and Ballybeg.[4]

The audience is thus encouraged to distrust the narrative authority of Michael. After all, he narrates many events that he couldn't possibly have witnessed. Maggie and Kate both discuss their fears for the future very movingly during the play, but their intimacy is predicated upon being alone – how could Michael have overheard them? He observes his parents when they dance, but it is implied by the candour of their comments that he cannot hear them. How can Michael have seen Kate dancing in the garden and the other sisters dancing indoors at the same time? How can a seven-year-old child understand Kate's embarrassment about Austin Morgan, or the nature of the Mundys' concern about their youngest sister Rose? Would Chris have referred to Danny Bradley as a 'bastard' (14) within earshot of her child? There is no plausible explanation for

Michael's knowledge of the events being portrayed on stage: to para-
phrase Frank McGuinness, he seems haunted by memories he could not
possibly possess, but which seem determined to possess him.[5]

To understand Friel's decision to highlight Michael's inability to represent the action authoritatively, the characterization of Agnes and Rose
must be considered. Rose and Agnes are the only characters who appear
in different parts of the stage during the two tableaux that frame the
action. In the first, Rose and Gerry sit on the bench, while Agnes stands
upstage left; in the second, Rose and Agnes change places. This shows
how Agnes and Rose disrupt Michael's narration and the play's action.
Their representation is revealed to be problematic, shifting, and even
unruly, as shown, for example, by Michael's failure to introduce or mention them in his opening monologue. A lack of information is a feature
of the representation of both women, most apparently in Rose's refusal
to explain what happened during her visit to Lough Anna with Danny
Bradley. Agnes's characterization is also full of suggestive silences. She
appears to have strong feelings for Gerry, yet Michael never mentions
them; and her motives for leaving Ballybeg are never mentioned explicitly or interpreted. Her choice of reading material – 'another' novel by
Annie M.P. Smithson[6] (20) – implies that stories of romantic escapism
appeal to her. Little information about either character is presented by
Michael's narrative, or by the action set in 1936. Their dialogue reveals
nothing of their inner life, and their significant contributions to the
plot occur offstage. Friel refuses to give any indicators of the truth about
Agnes and Rose's lives after 1936, only telling us the bare facts of their
impoverishment and death.

Friel's unwillingness to present or speculate about the inner life of
Agnes and Rose is an example of how a 'necessary uncertainty' (to use
a phrase from *Give Me Your Answer, Do!*) informs his later work (Friel,
1997: 80).[7] We must fill in the gaps in Friel's narrative for ourselves, it
seems, just as Michael appears to fill the gaps in his memories of that
summer in 1936.

Lughnasa therefore concerns the role of imagination in the compre-
hension of events. In his final monologue, Michael emphasizes that his
memories are not to be seen as accurate representations of truth. 'There
is one memory of that Lughnasa time that visits me most often; and
what fascinates me about that memory is that it owes *nothing to fact'*,
he states. 'It drifts in from somewhere far away – a *mirage* of sound – a
dream music that is both heard and *imagined*; that seems to be both
itself and its own echo; a sound so alluring and so *mesmeric* that the
afternoon is *bewitched*, maybe *haunted* by it' (107, emphases added).

Lughnasa may invite audiences to consider it a memory play, but it calls into question the relationship between memory and narrative, and asks how we can ever be certain about the authenticity of our recollection of events.

The purpose of this technique is to move the audience's attention from the narrated and spoken words of language to the carnal, physical expressions of ritual and dance. Gerry's fictions, Michael's memories, and Jack's stories and ceremonies may be considered in this context. If the masculine elements of the play are represented by means of verbal discourse, its feminine elements tend to be represented physically. The audience's attention is constantly brought back to the body during *Lughnasa*, with significant differences evident between male and female physicality. Jack's body is 'broken', Gerry's will be maimed, the child Michael's is invisible, the narrator's is extraneous to the action – even Rose's rooster will be killed. This physicality of the women characters contrasts with these images of male degradation and impotence, but that does not mean that those representations should be interpreted as being positive. Friel's emphasis on the female body might be understood in relation to *Philadelphia, Here I Come!* In that play, Friel presents Gar as one character who is performed by two actors, the first portraying Gar's public self, and the second his inner thoughts. Although the action is presented realistically, with the public Gar interacting naturalistically with other characters, his private self is visible only to the audience. The contrast between Gar's public utterances and his private thoughts makes the play very funny, yet the audience will realize as the narrative develops that Friel has been forced to put the private life of Gar on stage because the public man is unable to express himself adequately. Friel's embodiment of Gar's private self is an incarnation of failure, a representation of Gar's inability to reveal himself fully to others.

A similar mode of representation is at work in *Dancing at Lughnasa*. The sisters' use of dance and other forms of body language represents their inability to express themselves within socially legitimated modes of expression. Hence, in the play's dance scene, 'the movements seem caricatured; and the sound is too loud; and the beat is too fast; and the almost recognizable dance is made grotesque' (36). The effect of the dance, the beat, 'this shouting – calling – singing, this parodic reel' (36) means that 'there is a sense of order consciously being subverted, of the women consciously and crudely caricaturing themselves, indeed of near-hysteria being produced' (36–7). The dance thus represents refusal – of order, roles, rhythm, pattern. It is also a refusal of recognizability, the issue about which all five sisters seem most anxious. There is nothing celebratory about this dance; on the contrary, it is an act of defiance made necessary by the sisters' isolation.

In every sense, the Mundys occupy a peripheral position – in terms of discourse, geography, social status, and so on. Where the men speak, tell stories, and lead ceremonies, the women instead express themselves most honestly through dance. They are also geographically isolated. The official culture of the Irish state is beamed to them 'all the way from Athlone' (8); and they are isolated from their own community of Ballybeg. They are also economically marginalized, constantly vulnerable to the risk of poverty: theirs is a household in which three eggs must be made to feed seven people (88), after all. Friel's presentation of these women's lives, and his refusal to allow that story to be mediated successfully by the male presence of Michael, is an attempt to reverse their marginalization.

This explains why Michael's final monologue emphasizes that the dance should be seen as a representation of a failure: 'When I remember it, I think of it as dancing', he says. Dancing *'as if* language had surrendered to movement – *as if* this ritual, this wordless ceremony, was now the way to speak . . . *as if* the very heart of life and all its hopes *might* be found in those assuaging notes . . . *as if* language no longer existed because words were no longer necessary' (107–8, emphases added). The conditional construction of each of these clauses should be noted: Michael's use of dance as the image to describe these things reveals that language in fact *does* exist, and will continue to define the Mundy sisters. Friel's narrator concludes the play by focusing on a dance that the sisters enact not because of a failure of language, but because of social structures that deprive them of access to the language with which they might express themselves more deliberately.

Lughnasa thus becomes a play in which several attempts at communication are made, but none of them adequately. It gives us a radio that always breaks down, presenting a disembodied musical performance to which the five sisters at the heart of the play must respond physically. It gives us the addled ex-priest Jack, whose sentences always fizzle out. It presents us with Gerry, a Welshman who talks like an Englishman, whose repetition of the word 'unbelievable' (47, 48, 49, 54, 77, 99, 103) reveals his own inherent dishonesty. Michael the narrator will try to hold his characters in tableau at the play's conclusion, but those characters will move as he talks; Kate will cry throughout his final speech. And the tragedy of the Mundys is that they may only be represented through memory since, with the exception of Michael, all have died or disappeared: they can no longer speak for themselves.

The play therefore represents the impossibility of narrative control, proposing that any totalizing narrative – imperialism, Catholicism, even Michael's monologue – involves an exercise of power. Friel's response to this situation is to present a variety of voices – and other forms of expression – and to give them all equal value. Friel's unwillingness to allow Michael absolute narrative authority, and the contrast between Michael's memories and Friel's presentation of events, prioritizes the individual's experience over the ideologies associated with transnational phenomena such as multinational industrialization, proselytizing missions, mass-mediated communications, and imperialism. The interdependency of Michael's narrative with the representation of the Mundys therefore disrupts our sense of the opposition between fact and memory, the verbal and the visual, the masculine and the feminine, the religious and the secular, Ireland and Africa. Friel's play can therefore be seen as an early attempt to dramatize the impact of global compression – to show what happens when the world appears smaller, when Abyssinia, Athlone, London, Uganda, and Ballybeg all seem to occupy the same cultural space, when the distance between 1936 and 1990 becomes indeterminate so that, as Harvey puts it, it seems as though 'the present is all that there is' (240). Friel's response is to show that this sense of compression may provoke anxiety, but that it is nevertheless a necessary part of our lives – and that the task of the playwright is to begin the process of imagining new ways for us to represent the world to ourselves.

The reception of *Dancing at Lughnasa*, 1990–99

It is ironic that a play that offers multiple perspectives on one set of events would soon find itself being reduced to one set of meanings by multiple audiences. Why was the play seen in 1999 as a 'vehicle of celebratory nostalgia', as Fricker suggests?

There is one obvious answer: the Ireland of 1999 was considerably different to the Ireland of 1990 – so Friel's play might have been seen as having come from an Ireland that had decidedly been left behind. When *Lughnasa* premiered, Ireland was on the verge of transformation, but the atmosphere that had characterized the 1980s – of economic gloom and political turbulence – remained firmly in place. Kate's fear of losing her job would have resonated with an Irish audience in 1990: unemployment was at that time running at 13.3 per cent after a decade of serious job loss and redundancy.[8] Similarly, the decision of Agnes and Rose to flee Ireland, and their ultimate fate of poverty, alcoholism, and homelessness, was a dramatization of the tragedy of Irish emigration, which in

1990 remained a major part of Irish life: 56,300 people – or 1.6 per cent of the entire population – left the Republic of Ireland in 1990 alone. However, by 1999, Ireland had become a country of net migration, with 47,500 immigrants arriving where only 33,300 had left. Emigration had thus become a memory rather than a reality to be faced. This seemed equally true of mass unemployment, which had dropped substantially, falling from 13.3 per cent in 1990 to a low of 3.9 per cent in 2001.

The representation of Father Jack was also much more likely to shock in 1990 than in 1999. During that decade, a series of absurd or flawed priests would appear on the Irish stage. Father Welsh in McDonagh's *Leenane Trilogy* (1997) and Father Billy in Tom Murphy's *The Wake* (1998) are two prominent examples of an altered attitude to religious authority on the Irish stage, as is the appearance during the decade of the television series *Father Ted*. There are precedents for Friel's Father Jack in the Irish dramatic tradition. Keegan in Shaw's *John Bull's Other Island* (1904) appears to be a prototype for him; Friel himself had created a rather ridiculous priest in *Living Quarters*; and Synge had gently caricatured the priesthood in *The Tinker's Wedding* (1907). But there were few previous instances in Irish culture of a priest like Father Jack, who had rejected Catholicism not for theological reasons, but from a sense of its irrelevance, who recommends having 'love children', and who appears to have had an intimate relationship with his 'house boy', Okawa.

By 1999, however, the status of the Catholic Church in Ireland had altered radically. *Lughnasa's* 1990 premiere occurred only two years before it was revealed that the Bishop of Galway, Eamon Casey, had a son – an initially shocking revelation that would soon seem minor in comparison to subsequent revelations about institutional abuse of children and women by the Irish clergy, whose crimes were covered up by the Catholic hierarchy. So if in 1990, there was a risk of the characterization of Father Jack provoking controversy for appearing to denigrate the Catholic Church, by the end of the decade the reputation of that institution had so deteriorated that any performer playing Jack had to work hard to gain sympathy for his character.

Another taboo challenged by the original production of the play was its morally and ethically neutral presentation of single parenthood. Single-parent families in Ireland in 1990 accounted for 14.5 per cent of all births in Ireland. Yet within Irish discourse, the 'normal' – as well as the legal – family unit remained the traditional heterosexual two-parent married family. Roddy Doyle's novel *The Snapper* (1991) was one of the first mainstream attempts to normalize the phenomenon of single parenthood within Irish culture. Friel's presentation of Chris disrupts notions of normality in a similar way: her unmarried state is rarely mentioned in the play. By 1999, however, single parenthood was considerably less controversial: when figures were counted in 2003, it was revealed that 31.4 per cent of all births in the Republic of Ireland were to single and/or unmarried parents.

Furthermore, audiences in 1999 appear to have seen the play through their memories of *Riverdance*. The choreographer for the 1990 and 1999 productions of *Lughnasa* was Terry John Bates, who explains that for the revival he was forced to add more steps to the dance in the first act: 'There were far more steps the second time because people *were expecting* the energy then. You had to satisfy the audience'. He admits frankly that 'I had to redo it again after *River Dance* [*sic*] again you know. The audience were conscious of *River Dance* – totally' (quoted by Coult, 2003: 195–6).

Also relevant is the 1998 film adaptation. Directed by Pat O'Connor from a script by Frank McGuinness, the film diverged in many respects from Friel's original. The narrator was retained, played by Gerry McSorley (who had appeared in the 1990 premiere), but his function was only to introduce the action in voiceover. This meant that the narrative presented to the viewer was to be understood as reality: not mediated reality, not remembered reality, but reality. It may also have worked against Friel's attempt to provoke the theatre audience to use their imaginations, since in the film many of the gaps in the original narrative are filled. An audience at the play might suppose, for example, that Father Jack sacrificed the rooster that dies at the end of the play; in the film, a fox kills it. Rose's meeting with Danny Bradley is presented, and is shown to end badly, when he frightens her. The dance is moved from the beginning of the action until shortly before its conclusion, presenting it as the culmination of the play's themes. All five sisters dance together, outside and inside the house, which, again, presents the dance as celebratory. Joan Fitzpatrick Dean (2003) has considered the relationship between the film and original play in detail, so I do not wish to do so here. Suffice it to say that although the film may have failed to realize international expectations of what an Irish film should be, it may nevertheless have reinforced audiences' perceptions of the play as being nostalgic and lacking in relevance to Ireland in the 1990s.

Perhaps most significantly, the play focused on a group of Irish women during a period in which the status of women within Ireland was changing considerably. The play premiered six months before Mary Robinson became Ireland's first woman president, and eight months before Garry Hynes began her Artistic Directorship of the Abbey Theatre (in January

1991). The subsequent decade saw the emergence of many Irish women playwrights, the most important of whom is Marina Carr; and there was a general perception by 1999 that the status of Irish women within both theatre and society had improved. This improvement was imperfect, however. Garry Hynes's tenure at the Abbey lasted only until 1993, and although women dominate many areas of Irish theatre, the majority of mainstream productions on the country's largest stages are by male playwrights. The 1990 production of *Dancing at Lughnasa* may have represented a celebration of female physicality, but the mobility of the play internationally contrasted starkly with state attempts to control female movement in Ireland during the decade. Such events as the February 1992 'X Case', in which a 14-year-old girl who had been raped was prevented from travelling from Ireland to England for an abortion (see Holden, 1994), exemplify confusion in Ireland about state control over the bodies of Irish women. If the 1990 dance scene in *Lughnasa* was presented as celebratory, its 1999 revival ought to have been a reminder that much work remained to be done – an issue I return to in Chapter 7 of this book.

Finally, Ireland had become a considerably wealthier country by 1999. An amusing example of the consequences of this can be seen in contrasting responses to one scene. At the opening of the second act of *Lughnasa*, Maggie and Michael talk together in the Mundys' kitchen. Michael says that he is writing a letter to Santa Claus, to which Maggie replies, 'In September? Nothing like getting in before the rush' (68). In the 1990 production, this scene was played for comedic effect, and the audience responded with laughter to the idea of a child thinking of Christmas in early September. In the 1999 revival of the play, this line was again delivered to produce laughter but, on that occasion, none was forthcoming. During the intervening nine years, Christmas had become so commercialized a part of Irish life that the idea of a child thinking of Santa Claus in September was greeted not with amusement but weary recognition.[9]

All of these changes can explain the sense of nostalgia towards Mason's revived production of *Lughnasa*: the 1990 production seemed a relic from an Ireland that had gone forever. That sense of nostalgia is important, however, because it obscures the extent to which the script of *Lughnasa* could have been used to challenge many Irish taboos and problems, both in 1990 and 1999 – about priests, single-parent families, homelessness, unemployment, gender, emigration, and so on. It seems necessary to ask why these challenging aspects of the play went unremarked and unremembered.

Catherine Byrne, who played Chris in the play's 1990 premiere and Agnes in its 1999 'Friel Festival' revival, states that Patrick Mason's *Lughnasa* was intended to be seen as a 'golden production'. 'There's a bleak side to Brian's plays but he doesn't always like that highlighted', she explains. Mason's *Lughnasa* was 'all golden corn and poppies, beautiful lighting; the women were colour-coordinated'. 'But', Byrne adds, 'there's another production of *Dancing at Lughnasa* we haven't seen yet. We haven't seen how dark it is' (quoted by Coult, 2003: 57).

Byrne's comments suggest that the direction and design of this 'golden production' were intended to produce sentimental rather than genuinely emotional responses. The set design by Joe Vanek has now become iconic, presenting a field of corn that dominated the right of the stage, creating the impression of the Mundys' lives being played out against a landscape of abundance. This image worked against Friel's script: while it was visually striking, Vanek's design may have obscured the play's frequent use of images of barrenness, impoverishment, and infertility. 'I had been to Donegal once before [,] prior to starting out on *Lughnasa*', Vanek wrote in 1991. 'I don't recall seeing much in the landscape that would support a towering wheat field. . . . [F]or most of the audience [the set] was seen more as a symbol of harvest, growth and promise, and golden memories of times past, than as a real object in a real place' (Vanek, 1991: 11). The lighting design by Trevor Dawson may have had a similar impact. He used soft yellows and golds in his design, so the overall atmosphere created was of warmth and perpetual sunshine. The playing area was almost entirely open: the walls of the Mundys' house are not presented on stage, and no other structures dominate the space. This openness would have diminished the audience's sense that the sisters' lives were claustrophobic. Furthermore, a set in which none of the structures casts a shadow is unlikely to alert the audience to the possibility that there is an undertone of sadness and loss in the play.

Similarly, the sound design of *Lughnasa* has influenced its reception. The play's director, Patrick Mason, added a number of sound effects not included in the script, the purpose of which was to highlight the similarities between Ireland and Africa. For example, a piece of African chant – tellingly called 'Celebration Dance' – was played at the end of the first act and the beginning of the second to establish a relationship between Irish traditional music and African song. Mason's most influential decision relates to his treatment of the dance in the first act. As Abbey Sound Director David Nowlan explains, a 'major bone of contention for the show' was (as he revealingly terms it) the 'big dance number'. The 'Mason's Reel', Nowlan states, is 'quite a short tune and would have been very, very repetitive. So one of the musicians suggested a reel which is in the same key, called "Miss Macleod's Reel", just to get into the whole excitement of "The Mason's Apron" . . . We did it by doing a lot of bodhran over dubs, making it very, very heavy and percussive'. Furthermore, says Nowlan, 'another part of the brief was that Patrick wanted to give it a kind of African ethnic vibe. Brian quite liked that idea' (quoted by Coult, 2003: 199).

This direction by Mason of the dance scene contrasts strongly with Friel's own stage directions. As we've seen, the movements of the sisters should seem caricatured, Friel writes; the sound should be too loud, the beat too fast, and 'the almost recognisable dance' should appear 'grotesque' (1999b: 36). He states that there should be 'a sense of order consciously being subverted, of the women consciously and crudely caricaturing themselves, indeed of near-hysteria being produced' (36–7). However, as Patrick Burke points out, the intensification of the rhythmic aspects of the dance, when performed, worked against Friel's instructions:

> In its premiere production at the Abbey Theatre, Dublin, and subsequently in New York and London, that dance was generally lauded in terms of the energetically celebratory, an evaluation supported by the *joie de vivre* of the Chieftains' music which, anachronistically and counter to Friel's stage directions, accompanied it. Such an emphasis on celebration tended to ignore the text's emphasis on the ugly aspects of the dance.
>
> (1997: 19)

Some of the performances also affected interpretations of the play. For instance, the role of Kate was performed from 1991 to 1993 by Rosaleen Linehan, a respected actor who nevertheless is known mainly for comic roles. Referring to 'the nature of my temperament', Linehan admitted in 1999 that 'there's a large streak of sarcastic wit' in her personality, which was revealed in her performances of Kate. While *Lughnasa* was on tour in the United States, Friel approached Linehan to discuss this matter: 'Just one thing, Rosaleen', he said. 'I don't write irony'. 'That wiped out the performance for that week!', said Linehan, implying that her portrayal of Kate was 'ironic' for every other week during the production's run (quoted by Coult, 2003: 149).

It is also clear that the play was seen from an early stage as a strong candidate for commercial success on the international stage. The Broadway run of *Lughnasa* was produced by Noel Pearson, who brought to it an entrepreneurial spirit that drove the play to international fame. As Anthony Roche (2006) points out, Pearson later portrayed the move from 'Ballybeg to Broadway' (that is, from the Abbey opening in 1990 to a sell-out run in New York two years later) as an inevitability (645). Pearson had been appointed to the Board of the Abbey in 1987, and acted as Artistic Director between 1989 and 1990. He explains that 'in 1987 I took over the Abbey and [Friel] wrote me a very warm letter and I asked him to give me a play. He gave me *Lughnasa* in 1988 . . . Nobody wanted it [in London]. Nobody wanted it on Broadway, either, at first. An Irish play had not been successful there since [Hugh Leonard's] *Da'* (quoted by Witchell, 1993: 5). The 'golden' quality of the 1990 production may not have been a deliberate attempt to make the play commercially attractive, but those features certainly appealed to audiences in London and New York; Richard Cave (1999) has argued that these features of the production actually became exaggerated due to the audience's response in London (296). In any case, the fact that Pearson knew that 'nobody wanted' *Lughnasa* in London and New York shows that he had obviously explored the possibility of taking the play abroad almost immediately.

Interestingly, the premiere of *Lughnasa* was not especially well received in Dublin, perhaps because the issues that would have been relevant to an Irish audience at that time (homelessness, poverty, emigration) were not presented explicitly. Furthermore, Friel's decision not to offer the play to Field Day, which had produced four of his previous five plays, may have discouraged audiences from reading *Lughnasa* politically. Friel explained his movement away from Field Day as an attempt to prevent his work from being 'associated with institutions or directors': 'I don't want a tandem to develop'. 'Institutions are inclined to enforce characteristics, impose an attitude or a voice or a response. I think you're better to keep away from all that. It is for that reason that I didn't give *Dancing at Lughnasa* to Field Day' (Friel, 1999a: 104–5). This decision was characterized as a *departure* from Field Day (although Friel's resignation from the company did not formally occur until 1994), and hence as a move away from the overtly political work in which he had been engaged since 1980.

This interpretation may also have been influenced by the Abbey's decision to stage *The Glass Menagerie* on its smaller Peacock stage while *Lughnasa* was being premiered. Directed by Friel's daughter Judy, *The Glass Menagerie* was presented implicitly as a blueprint for *Lughnasa*.[10] There are many obvious similarities between the two works. Both involve women living in restrictive, claustrophobic environments.

Both are set in 1936 to the backdrop of the Spanish Civil War, locating a claustrophobic and hemmed-in social setting within a global context. Both involve a male character who represents the 'long delayed but always expected something that we live for' (Williams, 1970: 23). Both are narrated by someone who does not witness many of the scenes he describes. And *The Glass Menagerie* defines a memory play for Friel's purposes. 'In memory', writes Williams, 'everything seems to happen to music' (23), a line that Friel reproduces almost directly in his own play (107). The Abbey's decision to present these two plays simultaneously illustrates its sense of the importance of international work for Irish theatre, both in production and in dramaturgy (an issue discussed in more detail in Chapter 6). That said, the decision to link Friel's new play with Williams's classic might have impeded audiences' willingness to consider the contemporary relevance of *Lughnasa*.

Material in the Friel archive at the National Library of Ireland (NLI) shows that *Lughnasa* was certainly liked when it premiered – there is some interesting fan mail from Bono, among others (NLI MS 37.106.1) – but it was by no means treated as a contemporary masterpiece. Ticket sales were quite good, with total box office takings of about €365,000 for the performances between April and June 1990 (NLI MS 37.106/3). The response from the Irish media was similarly mixed. The *Evening Press* paid most attention to the play's running time, noting with mild disapproval that it didn't end until 10.25 (a mere half-hour before pub closing time). *The Irish Independent* declared that it was a 'many layered sandwich – but it lacks real meat', and the Irish edition of *The Guardian*, damning with faint praise, stated that 'it will be a play loved in Ireland'.[11] Fintan O'Toole (2003b), writing in *The Irish Times*, was generally positive about the play, but criticized Friel's characterization of Father Jack, whom he saw as a 'metaphorical version of a Field Day pamphlet' (95), a line that again emphasizes how audiences were disinclined to consider the political elements of the play.

It wasn't until *Lughnasa* transferred in November 1990 to the Royal National Theatre (RNT) in London that Irish reactions towards the play became more positive. 'The Abbey Stuns the South Bank', declared the *Sunday Independent*, while *The Irish Times* approvingly claimed that London 'raves for Friel Play'. The transfer of the play to Broadway in 1991 cemented its reputation. There was huge excitement in Ireland about the New York run even before *Lughnasa* opened there. The Abbey's Martin Fahy enthusiastically told the media that 'if *Dancing at Lughnasa* gets a good reception from the New York critics, Brian Friel will never again have to buy another Lotto ticket' – a nice reminder of an Ireland where the only way to make a million was by winning the National Lottery or going to Broadway (ATA). Dublin's Lord Mayor hosted a civic reception to celebrate the transfer of *Lughnasa* to Broadway a full nine months before it opened there. The Taoiseach (Irish Prime Minister) Charles Haughey sent a personalized fax to the cast on the Broadway opening night (NLI MS 37). The Irish radio station Radio Telifís Éireann (RTE) Radio 1 dedicated a special edition of its *Arts Show* to the New York production. *Irish Times* readers were invited to enter a competition to win tickets for two to see *Lughnasa* in New York for Christmas 1991.[12] And on 23 November of that year, one month after the play opened in New York – but 18 months after it had premiered in Dublin – a distinctly uncomfortable looking Friel appeared in Ireland's newspapers, seated beside Charles Haughey at the 'People of the Year' awards, at which he'd been one of the winners.[13] This enthusiasm continued for most of the play's Broadway run, with regular media updates telling the Irish public which magazines had interviewed or profiled Friel, and which international celebrities had attended the Broadway production. Put simply, Friel generated far more excitement by bringing *Lughnasa* to Broadway than he had done by producing it in Ireland.

The only person who seemed uncomfortable with this was Friel himself. Accepting his Tony Award for Best Play in 1992, he expressed ambivalence about the reception of his play, reportedly saying that 'success is only the postponement of failure' (quoted by PGIL). His next play, *Wonderful Tennessee* (1993) may, like *Lughnasa*, have evoked the influence of Tennessee Williams, but it also presented a set of characters who were almost completely static to an audience expecting more dance. *Molly Sweeney* (1994) portrays the negative consequences when a visually impaired woman has her sight restored, and thus may be seen as a dramatization of the proposition that success is the postponement of a failure. Crucially, in this play, Friel gives us another dance scene, this time ensuring, through his use of monologue, that no-one will misinterpret his intentions. Molly tells how she found herself on her feet in the middle of her sitting room, calling for music:

And the moment he began to play, I shouted – screamed, 'Now watch me! Just you watch me!'. And in a rage of anger and defiance I danced a wild and furious dance round and round that room; then out to the hall; then back to the kitchen; then back to the room again and round it a third time. Mad and wild and frenzied . . . It must have been terrifying to watch, because when I stopped, the room was hushed.

(Friel, 1994: 31–2)

The appropriate response to a 'wild and furious dance' is, Friel shows, not rapturous applause, but silence.

Give Me Your Answer, Do! (1997) might also be seen as a reaction against – or at the very least as a response to – the perception that *Lughnasa* was a joyful play. Shockingly frank in its treatment of authorial fear about reception, it presents a writer whose child cannot speak for herself, and whose (commodified) work is being evaluated for inclusion in an American archive, with the success of the deal hinging on the author's revelation that he has secretly written two pornographic novels. It cannot be assumed that Friel was commenting directly in these works on the reception of *Lughnasa*, but it is notable that his three subsequent plays diverge from any expectations that might have been generated by its success. It is also noticeable that he showed little interest in the film adaptation of his play, writing to Noel Pearson, 'I really don't care who does the screenplay . . . My crude intention is to sell the film rights to the highest bidder and forget the whole thing'.[14] Finally, we see in one of the notes he wrote for the 1999 Friel Festival a sense of unease about placing his work in others' hands, particularly directors: 'Why do actors place themselves so docilely in the hands of this person?', he demands. 'And why is the playwright asked to entrust the realization of his play in the hands of this interloper who has no demonstrable skills?' (Friel Festival, 1999). In short, throughout the 1990s, we see evidence of Friel being preoccupied by the issue of reception.

I would suggest that this misinterpretation of Friel's play arises because the international success of *Lughnasa* occurred at a period when the performance of Irishness on the international stage was extremely important within the country itself. Ireland's delight with the international success of *Lughnasa* did not happen in isolation, but was part of a growing awareness of the country's status in relation to the rest of the world. For instance, shortly after the premiere of *Dancing at Lughnasa*, the Irish football team took part in the 1990 World Cup, the first for which a team from the Republic of Ireland had qualified. That team included second- and third-generation expatriates, and crossed religious and ethnic divides; its fans believed that they had distinguished themselves for their good behaviour and good humour, which contrasted (they were told) with the hooliganism of their English neighbours. The performance on the world stage of an inclusive and admirable Irish identity created a sense of national confidence, which is encapsulated well by Dermot Bolger's play *In High Germany* (1990) and Roddy Doyle's novel *The Van* (1991). In 1991, Dublin became Europe's 'City of Culture', and the resulting influx of tourists, added to exuberant media commentary, again focused Irish attention on the status of the country abroad. This association of national self-importance with the perception of people abroad dominated the 1990s, and appears to have affected Irish audiences' attitudes to *Lughnasa*. The generally mixed reviews for the play's 1990 premiere were forgotten after it achieved success overseas; its return to the Abbey in 1992 and its subsequent Irish tour were wildly popular. *Lughnasa* toured the world, and Ireland, until 1993. The celebration of the place of Irish culture internationally gained momentum even as *Lughnasa* stepped away from the Abbey stage: Roddy Doyle won the Booker Prize for *Paddy Clarke, Ha, Ha, Ha* in 1994, and Seamus Heaney won the Nobel Prize for Literature in 1995.

This may explain why the revival of *Dancing at Lughnasa* in 1999 was seen as a celebration, not just of Friel's 70th birthday, but also of the international triumph of the play. Furthermore, the revival was Patrick Mason's penultimate production as Artistic Director of the Abbey (a post that he had held since 1994). His directorship had brought the theatre out of deficit and improved the Abbey's status in the wider theatrical community. The 1999 production therefore was not so much a revival as a reprise – a celebration of Friel, Mason, and a transforming Ireland. This celebratory mood was unlikely to encourage a reassessment of the relationship of production to play-script.

The marketing of the 1999 production also reveals a move in theatre marketing towards event-driven theatre. Instead of simply reviving *Lughnasa*, the Abbey, together with the Lyric in Belfast and the Gate Theatre in Dublin, produced a number of Friel's plays over four months, calling it a 'Friel Festival'. There was of course a genuine desire to celebrate the achievement of Friel, but the impetus behind any festival will be celebratory, which explains why, despite the upheavals in Irish society between 1990 and 1999, the two versions of *Lughnasa* were largely indistinguishable. The perspective of audience members at such a festival will usually be retrospective, making it unlikely that they will think of the work as having any direct or immediate relevance to their own lives.

Lughnasa is also an interesting example of an entrepreneurial spirit being used to produce theatre (rather like Michael Colgan's production of Pinter, discussed in the introduction to this book), mainly due to the involvement of Noel Pearson, a man who had a long involvement in Irish theatre when *Lughnasa* appeared, but whose greatest successes have been in cinema. A significant feature of his involvement in the production was that its American production rights were licensed to Ferndale Theatre Productions, a private company owned by Pearson and others. Although the play was billed as the Abbey Theatre on tour, it was in fact a private enterprise, the principle aim of which was not to represent Ireland on the world stage, but to make a profit. This exposed Pearson to the accusation that he had abused his position as acting director of the Abbey for personal gain. The investigations into Ferndale's role in the success of *Lughnasa* by the Public Accounts Committee and the Theatre's auditors and solicitor found that nothing improper had occurred, but it is notable that the financial success of *Dancing at Lughnasa* coincided with a period of financial crisis at the Abbey. The long-term significance of this situation is that it revealed a clash of private interests with the national remit of the theatre, an issue that would continue to arise during subsequent years, especially in 2004 when *Riverdance* director John McColgan's production of *The Shaughraun* appeared at the Abbey, as we will see in Chapter 4.

So if the production history of *Dancing at Lughnasa* is an example of the growing impact of the ideology associated with private business on Irish theatre, then the key concept for an understanding of the reception of the play in Ireland is *mobility*. The play was considered more valuable when it travelled, and was given canonical status within Ireland only when it was endorsed abroad. Irish commentators could not declare the play to be a success until it had been a success internationally, indicating an insecurity about the relative value of Irish critical judgements. Yet the play became mobile only by removing or moderating those aspects of it that might have engaged directly with Irish life. In its 1990 premiere, its humorous and sentimental qualities were emphasized. In both 1990 and 1999, its dance scene was presented as emancipatory and celebratory, rather than as a refusal of order, or an expression of claustrophobia. In order for the play to become mobile, the production first had to divest itself of those elements that might have made it a more substantial and rewarding experience for specifically Irish audiences. Instead, it set about conforming to international audiences' expectations of the Irish play; rather than promoting intercultural exchange, it instead confirmed international expectations, while boosting Irish self-confidence. While this had been a feature of Irish drama in the past, the production of *Lughnasa* provided a model that, throughout the 1990s, companies and playwrights would emulate.

After *Lughnasa*

A consideration of *Lughnasa* reveals continuities and disjunctions in Irish theatre history. The international appeal of the play points to a growth in international opportunities for touring, while the emphasis on the play's more accessible elements suggests that the availability of those opportunities has altered the manner in which plays are produced. Irish awareness of the play's success, coupled with growing awareness of the status of Irish culture internationally, highlights the development of a greater consciousness of the performance of Irishness overseas. The play attempts to chart the reorganization of Irish space, but the production and reception of the play contribute towards that reorganization by prioritizing international over localized responses.

What makes *Dancing at Lughnasa* significant is that its production marks the intensification of these processes from being one element within theatre production, to being the dominant determinant of production and reception. Yet, as the brief discussion of Friel's work from *The Mundy Scheme* to *Translations* reveals, many of the processes associated with globalization have been in existence for a considerable period of time. As discussed in Chapters 3 and 4, it is possible to trace many of the features of contemporary theatre to much earlier periods: to show that the global theatrical marketplace – and the exchange of cultures occurring in it – need to be placed in a historical context.

This consideration of *Lughnasa* thus allows us to identify themes, questions, and problems for consideration in the remainder of this book. First, the contrast between the dramatic qualities of Friel's script and the theatrical elements of its Abbey Theatre productions emphasizes the importance of utilizing a variety of methodologies in the study of theatre: neither textual analysis nor a study of reception offers a complete perspective on the play. Second, the focus within Ireland on the performance of *Lughnasa* overseas shows how international performance occupies an important role within national media. What then is the role of the international in Irish theatre? If globalization promotes deterritorialization, what effect does it have on theatre's relationship to place, especially for national theatres? What is the impact of localization on modes of writing?

The most pressing question to arise from this analysis becomes the subject of the next two chapters. The impact of globalization on the production and reception of theatre requires new ways of thinking about criticism. How then can a theatre criticism that styles itself as national – which Irish criticism currently does – meaningfully address the work of writers whose reputation and reception are now strongly predetermined by global factors? If theatre has become globalized, does that mean that it has ceased to be national?

Part II Globalization and National Theatres

3
Globalizing National Theatre: Sean O'Casey's *The Plough and the Stars*, 1926/1991/2002

In 2006, Ireland's Industrial Development Agency (IDA) – the government body responsible for attracting FDI into the country – announced that Ireland was to be 'rebranded' for the first time in three decades. The new slogan for the country is 'Ireland – knowledge is in our nature', which is part of a promotional campaign on *The Irish Mind* announced in the Agency's 2005 *Annual Report*. 'What is different in Ireland is the way in which we tackle issues, solve problems and seek other new and better ways to meet needs' states the report. That difference, it claims, is 'evidenced in the speed, agility, flexibility and responsiveness of public agencies and private bodies. It requires ambition, vision, cooperation and partnership among many players'.

All of that seems harmless enough, until the report makes a rather alarming claim – that the Irish approach to business 'reflects a mindset and an approach that is innate, and which is likely related to the creativity that has been manifest in the Irish literary and artistic tradition. This is what we will be conveying in our new promotional campaign' (IDA Ireland, 2006: 9). To underline the relationship between Ireland's culture and its economy, the report opens with one quotation from the Irish philosopher and writer Richard Kearney, and another from Gary Hamel and C.K. Prahalad's *Competing for the Future* (1994). Between both is a self-portrait by renowned Irish artist Louis Le Brocquy, which features the slogan 'The Irish mind. The unique resource you will need to bring your knowledge-based business to peak performance' (2).

This proposed rebranding of Ireland as a creative economy provides us with an example of the contemporary relationship between economic and cultural networks, and of how the global and the national interact in both fields. On the one hand, the document seems an obvious response to the challenges of globalization, an attempt to differentiate Ireland from its competitors for FDI (China, India, Singapore, Puerto Rico, etc.) – an attempt, that is, to raise Ireland's profile as one hub on a globalized network of trade and investment. The IDA's campaign is therefore 'national' in two senses: it arises as a result of governmental policy-making at national level, and it presents a vision of the Irish national character as encompassing several 'innate' or essential characteristics. It also proposes a relationship between the national literary/cultural canon and the economy, arguing that the creativity of Le Brocquy and Richard Kearney is not an example of individual achievement, but evidence of an Irish 'mindset and approach' that will, it is implied, be evident in boardrooms, customer service centres, and factory floors throughout the country.

It is often suggested that globalization is rendering the category of nation obsolete, and that it leads to cultural and social homogenization. The IDA campaign suggests, however, that the national – an essential-ized category that is applicable to the life of the state in its entirety – may operate as a mode of differentiating the state in a global marketplace.

While it is probably true that Ireland has produced a disproportion-ately large number of successful writers, artists, and musicians, most of the suggestions put forward by the IDA are nonsense. Many of Ireland's great thinkers and artists achieved success by leaving the country (Joyce, Wilde, Shaw, Beckett), while those who remained at home often achieved an international profile by operating within international cultural frameworks, as in the case of U2. The suggestion that there is an 'innate' Irish temperament seems worryingly essentialist, particu-larly given the increased multiculturalism of Irish society. The use of Ireland's cultural capital as a 'brand' to attract economic investment is therefore founded on a reinvention of Ireland that is based more on how the country is understood abroad than on the realities within its own borders.

This convergence between cultural and economic interests – with the global and national operating as branded categories in both fields – is increasingly evident in theatre around the world. Since the early 1990s, the impact of globalization on theatre has been apparent in such phe-nomena as the growth of international touring networks, the increased mobility across borders of theatre scholars and practitioners, the prolif-eration of information about theatre through virtual and print media, and the development of intercultural performance styles. However, such 'globalized' developments have occurred simultaneously with an appar-ent revival in the fortunes of theatres with a specifically national remit. As discussed in the first chapter, state funding for the Scottish National

Theatre was finally secured in 2003 after many years of lobbying; in New York, it was proposed in the same year that an American National Theatre be built on the site of the World Trade Centre (Pogrebin, 2003). Meanwhile, many existing national theatres are receiving greater levels of public funding and support than ever before, while also attracting higher levels of corporate sponsorship.

The apparently incongruous good health of national theatres during a period of globalization is especially notable in Ireland: it may be the 'most globalized country in the world', but it is also the home of the Abbey, one of the most famous national theatres in the world. During the 1990s, the impact of globalization led many commentators (notably Kearney, 1997) to describe Ireland as both 'post-national' (meaning that it had become globalized) and 'post-nationalist' (meaning that its politics were no longer dominated by the conflict in Northern Ireland). Yet, during the same decade, the Abbey Theatre enjoyed a minor (if short-lived) renaissance under the Artistic Directorships of Garry Hynes (1991–93) and Patrick Mason (1994–99). That renaissance was underpinned by the Abbey's promotion of itself as Ireland's national theatre, a status that allowed it to claim an average of 45 per cent of all available state funding for theatre in Ireland between 1990 and 1999.[1]

To investigate this apparent tension between globalization and national theatre in Ireland, and to explore further the inter-relationship of the cultural, economic, and social development of Ireland since 1990, I will argue that the recent renaissance in national theatre worldwide is closely related to the growth of theatrical and economic networks. To illustrate this, I discuss two Abbey Theatre productions of Sean O'Casey's 1926 play, *The Plough and the Stars*, both of which appeared during the period in question – the first in 1991 and the second in 2002. By doing so, I explore how the role of the Abbey Theatre in relation to the nation changed as the globalization of Ireland and its theatre intensified.

O'Casey's *Plough*, 1926

Together with J.M. Synge's *The Playboy of the Western World*, O'Casey's *The Plough and the Stars* is regarded as one of the definitive Abbey Theatre plays. This status is assured by O'Casey's use of many characteristics closely identified with the Abbey style: provocative political content, linguistic inventiveness, naturalistic acting, the inclusion of characters drawn from the margins of Irish society, and the use of a single household to represent the entire nation. And the play is of course noted for W.B. Yeats's mythologization of the 'riots' that occurred during its first week of performances. However, its lasting significance is that the production reconstituted the role of the national theatre in relation to the newly independent Irish state (Ireland had achieved independence in 1922). It succeeded in doing so in three ways.

First, it established that one function of the Abbey in an independent Ireland would be to analyse the nation's sense of itself. *The Plough and the Stars* was produced shortly before the 10th anniversary of the 1916 Easter Rising, an event presented by many (including Yeats himself) as the foundational event of the new Irish state. O'Casey's representation of that event was both an evaluation of the moral and political legitimacy of the new Ireland, and an attempt to broaden representations of Irish identity to include people already being marginalized in the new order, such as the urban working class and Irish Protestants. So whereas during the Irish Literary Revival, the Abbey's plays had been national insofar as they imagined an Ireland that might someday exist, *The Plough and the Stars* took nation to be a relatively stable category – one that needed to be challenged, broadened, and subjected to a process of continuous renewal.

Second, the production allowed the Abbey to emphasize its importance to – but independence from – the new Irish state. In 1925, the Abbey had become the first state-endowed theatre in any Anglophone country. The subsidy was a recognition by the Irish state of the Abbey's role in the movement towards independence, and an attempt by the state to use the Abbey's cultural capital, international profile, and nationalist credentials as a way of legitimating itself internationally – showing that the IDA's attempt to use Irish writers to brand Ireland was not unprecedented.

However, that recognition also involved the threat of interference from a government whose outlook was becoming dominated by conservative Catholic values. In the months before the production of *The Plough*, George O'Brien – the new director of the Abbey and 'effectively a government nominee' (Foster, 2003: 302) – demanded cuts from O'Casey's play, objecting particularly to the inclusion of a prostitute in its second act. The ensuing dispute between O'Brien and Abbey cofounders Yeats and Lady Gregory became a battle for the artistic freedom of the theatre. O'Brien's argument seemed grounded in the belief that a theatre in receipt of a state subsidy should hold an outlook consistent with the values of that state. Yeats disagreed, arguing that to 'eliminate any part of [*The Plough*] on grounds that have nothing to do with dramatic tradition would be to deny all our traditions' (quoted in Foster, 2003: 305). This statement was a reminder of the theatre's importance to the state, and a challenge to the state's claim to be sole moral arbiter for the entire nation: Yeats was effectively claiming for the Abbey a moral authority that was greater than the authority of the state itself.

Finally, the production of *The Plough* provoked a series of protests that were based on the belief that national theatre is worthy of serious debate and contestation. The Irish tradition of theatre protest has often been misunderstood as riotous behaviour by ignorant philistines, who could always be depended upon to 'disgrace themselves again', in Yeats's memorable formulation. Although they involved moments of violence, the *Plough* 'riots' were occasions of passionate debate about the function of theatre in a national context. These protests reinforced the Irish public's perception that they were entitled to a sense of ownership over the national theatre. That the Abbey's status has remained a subject of incessant dispute in Ireland is, arguably, a sign of the strength of Irish theatre: people feel that it is important enough to become angry about its status and repertoire. So the significance of *The Plough* is not that it provoked riots, but that it configured the category of nation as something that transcends the state – that is, as a concept better realized in artistic production than legislation.

In subsequent years, O'Casey's play lost a great deal of its power: the Abbey's descent into a period of stagnation under the directorship of former Minister for Finance Ernest Blythe meant that many of the principles established by the production of *The Plough* were forgotten.[2] Nevertheless, the play retained its capacity to echo contemporary events. For example, productions of *The Plough* were staged a month after the outbreak of the Second World War, and shortly after its conclusion.[3] One might see such productions as attempts to use O'Casey's critique of political violence to comment upon events in mainland Europe – and perhaps as an attempt to justify Irish neutrality in the Second World War. In 1947, the poet Valentine Iremonger staged a walkout from a revival of *The Plough*, using the status of the play and the history of the Abbey to perform a 'staged event that condensed wider public misgivings about . . . the nature and direction of the Irish state', according to Lionel Pilkington (2001: 143). The outbreak of the Northern Ireland Troubles in the late 1960s led to many productions of O'Casey's Dublin plays (*The Shadow of a Gunman, Juno and the Paycock*, and *The Plough and the Stars*), which theatres in the Republic of Ireland used to indicate their hostility to Republican violence. Again, the national status of the play was used to challenge other expressions of national authority, not only by the British and Irish governments, but also by the IRA.

By the 1990s, however, *The Plough* had been largely sanitized by its classical status, with most productions of the play being presented in commercial venues during the tourist season. As Brian Singleton writes, 'production of O'Casey's plays was trapped in an unchallenged tradition of sentimental accretions . . . something had to be done' (2004: 263). The 1991 production of *The Plough and the Stars* by Garry Hynes at the Abbey was a response to this situation.

Garry Hynes's *The Plough and the Stars*, 1991

The Plough and the Stars was Hynes's inaugural production during her artistic directorship of the Abbey, and it is notable for having provoked unusual levels of media hostility. The first feature of note in this context is the production's treatment of social class. It placed strong emphasis on the poverty of its characters, who were presented on an almost entirely bare stage, in monochromatic costumes, and with shaved heads – a visual image that worked against the tendency to see O'Casey's characters as 'colourful' expressions of working class life in Dublin. This and many other aspects of the play highlighted O'Casey's awareness that poverty was a far greater cause of hardship to his characters than the military conflict dramatized on stage.

The production also challenged existing images of Anglo-Irish violence. Before the action began, the stage was draped in a large Union Jack; at its conclusion, the flag was again drawn across the stage, this time covering the body of Bessie Burgess, the Irish Protestant whose son is fighting in the First World War while rebellion is underway in Dublin. This framing device can be seen as a statement about Ireland being under imperial rule (literally), with the outburst of insurrection being fully contained by the end of the action.

Republican violence is treated in a similarly harsh manner, however. In Hynes's production, Nora's miscarriage arises directly from the actions of her husband Jack, who throws her across the stage in response to her demands that he stop fighting in the Rising (see O'Casey, 1998: 87). Political violence in this production is thus evaluated in terms of gender, with both British and Irish militarisms presented as arising from various forms of male inadequacy – and all of the victims of that violence being female. This, added to the emphasis on Bessie Burgess's Protestantism, made the production very relevant to ongoing debates about the Troubles, which had entered a particularly brutal period when Hynes's production opened, as I discuss in more detail below.

Finally, the production insisted that *The Plough* should not be seen exclusively as an element of Ireland's heritage, but rather as a statement of where the nation found itself in 1991. Particularly controversial in this context was Hynes's staging of the play's second act, which takes place in a bar while, offstage, a figure representing Padraic Pearse addresses a crowd. In this part of Hynes's production, the back of the stage was dominated by a large mirror, in which the Abbey audience could see themselves. Suddenly, a member of the audience rose and began to speak while the action was underway, leading the other spectators to realize – after some moments of uneasiness – that what they were seeing on stage was not intended to be understood as a mirror. Rather, it was meant to represent a window from the bar, opening out to a public arena in which a large crowd was being addressed by a speaker. The audience, therefore, was put into the world represented onstage; they were watching a historically significant event, while seeing themselves represented in it. The disruptive nature of this act evoked memories of the riots that interrupted the premiere of *The Plough* in 1926, while also making it difficult for the Abbey audience to imagine that the people represented by O'Casey were different from themselves.[4]

The production was the subject of intensive media debate. Playwright and columnist Hugh Leonard was particularly critical of the production, attacking what he called its 'Brechtian' elements; he also criticized Hynes's decision to hire Fintan O'Toole as a literary adviser for the production, referring to him as her 'grisly guru'. Leonard also attempted to shame the production by referring to how his English guests had not been able to understand the action – before admitting that he had formed his opinion of the production based only on its first two acts: he had left at the interval (Leonard, 1991). This controversy damaged the production initially, but positive word of mouth meant that the final weeks of its run almost all sold out.[5]

We therefore see that Irish theatregoers in 1991 believed that national theatre was worthy of serious discussion and debate, the occurrence of which ultimately encouraged audiences to make up their own minds about the production. Much of that debate focused on the play's relevance to contemporary events, including the changing role of women in Irish life, the ongoing conflict in Northern Ireland, and fears about the erosion of Irish sovereignty caused by the impending transformation of the European Community into the European Union (the Maastricht Treaty was due to become part of Irish law on 1 January 1992, causing some anxiety within Ireland). So we see evidence of an interesting form of national theatre, formulated to address the concerns – and challenge the assumptions – of a specifically Irish audience.

Ben Barnes's *The Plough and the Stars*, 2002

The Abbey did not produce *The Plough* again until 11 years later, in November 2002 (the longest previous gap between productions had been eight years).[6] Much had changed during that period: as stated in previous chapters, economic development gave rise to prosperity in Ireland, while widening the gap between rich and poor. Another major change in Irish life during that decade was the development of the Peace Process. At the beginning of the 1990s, the Troubles seemed intractable: the early years of the decade were among the worst of the entire conflict, with 81 deaths in 1990, and 96 in 1991, the year in which Hynes's *Plough* appeared.[7] However, secret talks between the IRA and the British government were underway at that time, leading to the development of the Peace Process, which resulted in the Good Friday Agreement of 1998. By enshrining the notion of 'parity of esteem' in the legislation of both Northern Ireland and the Irish Republic, the Peace Process established that there could be no single, homogenous Irish identity: a person living in Northern Ireland could identify as Irish, British, or both.

The 2002 production of *The Plough and the Stars* presented an opportunity for the Abbey to use the national status of the play as a way of analysing and responding to contemporary social arrangements, as Hynes had done in 1991. The poverty of the characters might have been used to challenge Irish complacency about its newfound economic prosperity. The treatment of Bessie Burgess might have allowed for an exploration of the changing demography of Irish society. And the play's treatment of militarism might have allowed audiences to reflect upon the changing status of politics in Northern Ireland, as well as Irish involvement in the emerging 'war against terror'. Put simply, the national status of the play might have been used to provoke many new modes of enquiry into the transformed Ireland. Despite the existence of these opportunities, however, the play as directed by the Abbey's then artistic director Ben Barnes was firmly in the style of a 'heritage' production, with the theatre's national remit being fulfilled not on stage, but in a range of ancillary activities of civic merit, such as international touring and outreach.

The production therefore seemed entirely lacking in relevance to contemporary events. Its meaning was generated not by the audience's interaction with text and performance, but rather by the use of cinematic and musical cues: traditional Irish music was used to instruct the audience on the appropriate emotional responses, while also authenticating the action as recognizably 'Irish'. Similarly, spotlighting and freeze-framing were used to underscore key moments, signalling directorial reluctance to trust audiences' ability to draw their own conclusions (a charge that could, in fairness, also have been made against Hynes). While Hynes's production had emphasized its characters' poverty by using an almost empty and colourless set, Barnes's filled the stage with expensively constructed images of destitution. The front rows of the auditorium were removed, replaced by layers of rubble and detritus, while the crumbling tenement building in which most of the action takes place dominated the stage, impressively revealing how much money the theatre had spent on design. In scale and substance, the set created an uneasy tension between medium and message.

The production was accompanied by a similarly impressive array of supporting materials and events, coordinated by the theatre's outreach and education department. While the Abbey routinely engages in outreach activity, it invested an unprecedented level of funding in support of *The Plough*: a resource guide and DVD were produced to accompany the production, both of which featured interviews with the creative team and background information about O'Casey and the play. While such material undoubtedly has value – and while outreach is important[8] – it is notable that the effect of these materials was to present the meaning of the play as stable, as something that can be consumed by audiences. Essays by Martin Drury and Christopher Murray in the book, and interviews with Barnes on the DVD instruct audiences on how they should receive the play, highlighting themes and key features. A significant element of that process was an emphasis on the historical context of the play: the publication and DVD highlight the accuracy of accents and settings in Barnes's production, suggesting that he and his team aimed to communicate more about Ireland's past than its present or future. Barnes wanted to 'find a way of placing the play firmly in its historical context of the 1916 Rising' (Abbey Theatre, 2002: 49), while voice director Andrea Ainsworth speaks about how 'I got several recordings of the accent [from RTE archives]. We also talked with older people who had grown up in Dublin' (78). This emphasis on historical accuracy re-imagines the Abbey's functions as being akin to a museum's.

Thus, the production appears to have been designed to appeal to theatregoers' sense that they were purchasing an 'authentic' experience. With its high production values, expensive design, and the inclusion of many of Ireland's leading actors in its cast, the production was presented as a lavish spectacle that compared favourably with other forms of cultural output available at that time. This is because, during the period between 1991 and 2002, there was an increased drive in government policy and economic literature to see art forms like theatre as 'creative industries' – as social entities that contribute to economic performance both directly and indirectly. This meant that the value of theatre was increasingly being constructed in economic terms, and that managers like Barnes, whose theatres were in receipt of a state subsidy, were being called upon to produce work that could be measured in terms of its contribution to state activities, such as tourism, education, and the attraction of FDI.

There is a growing literature on the importance of creative industries, but for the present purposes I want to draw on one of the most straightforward – from Richard E. Caves. Caves (2000) suggests that theatres and other producers of art must now conduct their businesses using models that apply across all forms of culture, rendering distinctions of genre, form – or indeed between avant-garde and kitsch – obsolete. He suggests that the 'creative industries' operate according to seven principles, all of which function independently of aesthetic criteria and judgements. He points out that the demand for creative products is uncertain, and thus involves higher levels of risk than might be the case in other industries: a food manufacturer can reasonably assume that people will be hungry, but the likely success of a theatrical show is difficult to predict. Second, he suggests that creative workers tend to identify themselves more with their work than people in other industries do, which results in theatre practitioners receiving lower wages than workers in other industries. Creative products require a 'diverse range of inputs' and are differentiated relative to each other: hence, people are more willing to pay for an Abbey Theatre play than one at a fringe venue because of the relative status of each product, even though both may have cost the same to produce. Creative products are also 'vertically differentiated': the input of a director may be of greater value than that of a writer, but the presence of a star actor may be more important than both. Creative products require unusual levels of temporal coordination, requiring unusual levels of organization between the many different participants. Creative products must also be durable: they should be able to last long enough to produce a return on any investment. And ideally, they should produce a profit for the people who have made an input into them (2000: 2–17).

Caves argues that these seven principles are applicable to all forms of culture, and that distinctions of genre and form no longer apply. Rather, theatre is an industry that involves multiple inputs and high levels of risk. Interestingly, in only one of Caves's seven examples is the issue of artistic value relevant: the payment of actors and other practitioners, who are told that their involvement in 'art' should be compensation for the financial insecurity attendant upon their profession.

This emphasis on measuring theatrical output in relation to economic and social factors became a feature of the Abbey's management under Barnes's Artistic Directorship (2000–05). For example, he attempted to differentiate the Abbey from other forms of culture. One of his earliest decisions was to raise ticket prices, not from a need to increase funding, but because he believed that audiences found the Abbey's products too cheap (see White, 2000: 12); this was affecting the theatre's ability to present itself as offering attractive corporate entertainment. Barnes argued that the value of the Abbey would be determined by its relative expense in comparison to other forms of entertainment.

Furthermore, his approach is an example of the rise of event-driven theatre internationally, a phenomenon whereby audiences do not purchase access to a play, but instead consume the experience of *having been to* the play. Michael Colgan explains how, as a theatre producer, he sets out to give audiences an 'experience'. 'I don't think audiences will sit down for two hours anymore unless you give them a reward', he says. 'And the reward you give them is by telling them that they have been to an *Event*. When you *Event* something, you've a much better chance of getting them to sit through even five hours of theatre' (cited in Chambers *et al.*, 2001: 87, emphases in original). So just as business people now use theatrical techniques to provide their customers with an 'experience', theatre producers draw on the same philosophy, branding their products as 'events' – as experiences that are unique, unusual, different to the simple experience of watching any old play in any old theatre.

The creation of media-driven 'events' has been an element of theatre marketing since *Look Back in Anger* was premiered in 1956, but recent years have seen an intensification of this process. The Royal Court in London has pioneered this kind of marketing. When Jez Butterworth's *Mojo* premiered there in 1995, the Court claimed it was the first debut of a young writer on their main-stage since *Look Back in Anger*, implying that Butterworth's work had the potential to equal the quality of John Osborne's, that the play was epoch-making, and that the Court was bravely supportive of 'cutting-edge' new writing. However, this claim was not based on research but on the fact that 'no one at a script meeting could think of any previous instance' of this happening, according to Aleks Sierz (2001: 236). Dominic Dromgoole interestingly discusses how Stephen

Daldry, artistic director at the Court for much of the 1990s, approached the issue of marketing:

> Over tea with Stephen Daldry, before he took over the Royal Court, we discussed what was out there. 'We're living in a Golden Age,' I said. 'Are we?' he asked sceptically. 'Fuck knows,' I replied, 'but if we start saying it often enough, people should join in.' We did, Stephen with his genius for PR most persuasively, and they did. Is it a Golden Age? Well, of course.
>
> (Dromgoole, 2001: vii)

Dromgoole's suggestion is that the creation of a theatrical fact is possible by saying something 'often enough'. That might seem crass, but it is certainly accurate, as the financial and critical success of new, heavily marketed writing in Britain during the 1990s shows: those plays were (tellingly) seen as valuable because they were 'experiential', as Aleks Sierz (2001) suggests.

That move towards 'eventing' sometimes led to the circulation of erroneous or misleading information. For instance, the visit of Can Themba's *Le Costume* to Dublin in 2001 was described as a major event because it was directed by Peter Brook, with the marketing adding that, 'amazingly, [Brook's] work has never been seen in this country' (eircom Dublin Theatre Festival, 2001: 10). This was incorrect since, although it played to mostly empty houses, Brook's production of Dürrenmatt's *The Visit* toured to Dublin in 1958. One of the reasons that first visit has been largely forgotten was that clerical opposition meant that very few people saw the production. As Brook amusingly explains in *The Shifting Point*, 'the box office manager explained to us that business was bad because Catholic opinion was shocked. "It's the coffin," he said gloomily' (1987: 36).

That event was significant for Brook's career because the Dublin production was seen by an influential American businessman who encouraged Brook to bring his play to New York. It also sheds interesting light on Irish theatre in the 1950s, showing that, although they were poorly attended, many interesting productions took place in Dublin at this time. The need to brand the production of *Le Costume* as an event meant that this information was not publicly discussed. Irish theatre-goers may have valued their visit to *Le Costume* more for believing it was Brook's first production in Dublin – but perhaps they understood its significance less.

The distinguishing characteristic of the theatrical 'events' that have been staged globally since the mid-1990s is that they do not require social or political significance for their value, but proclaim themselves as events in order to attract audiences. The making of a DVD and book for Barnes's production of *The Plough* is one example of an 'eventing' strategy; another is the production's inclusion in the theatre's 'abbeyone-hundred' centenary programme (discussed in detail in the next chapter), as part of which it toured to London in 2005.

The production was generally successful during its Dublin run: if it failed to provoke the excitement that Garry Hynes's 1991 *Plough* had generated, so too did it avoid that production's controversial response. It was well attended by audiences, and was revived in 2003. Reviews for the production were generally positive, though none was unreservedly enthusiastic. Fintan O'Toole (who had resigned his post at the Abbey after Hynes left in 1993) saw Barnes's *Plough* as 'a forceful, persuasive mainstream production of a great play' but was disappointed that it had failed to rise to the challenges laid down by Hynes in 1991 – though, given his own involvement in that production, it is not surprising that he found Barnes's disappointing. The production generated a mixed response in London, receiving positive reviews from such critics as Michael Billington and Benedict Nightingale, though Paul Taylor in *The Independent* was scathing. 'The only thing that this touring revival . . . is likely to provoke is incredulity', he wrote. 'How can they have made a play that is so bursting with tragicomic, unregenerate humanity feel so remote and unengaging?' (Taylor, 2005: 40).

I would suggest that Barnes's production should be seen in the context of the impact of globalization on theatre generally, and in particular on the Abbey Theatre. The use in *The Plough and the Stars* of a range of authenticating markers allowed the production to be branded as Irish, a status that made it recognizable to audiences throughout the world, facilitating international touring and enhancing access to the theatre for tourist visitors to Ireland. We also see a shift away from a desire to comment on Northern Ireland – as Hynes's *Plough* did – and towards a presentation of Ireland for global consumption, a movement away from the post-colonial that would have lasting consequences.

Global theatre networks, branding, and reproducibility

It is necessary to consider the practices of branding and 'eventing' theatre in the larger context of the globalization of culture, and to consider the existence of theatrical networks in which high-profile productions now circulate. Major arts festivals (such as those in Avignon and Edinburgh) emerged in the late 1940s as a means of restoring cultural values and a sense of shared civilization in the wake of the Second World War. The processes of globalization have contributed to a subsequent festivalization of the performing arts industry, transforming festivals into the preferred sites for the promotion and consumption of high-end cultural products. The West's major festivals and arts venues – and the people who participate in them (including artists, producers, promoters, audiences, and the media) – now constitute a global network in which numerous elements circulate: not just cultural products, but finance, ideas, and cultural power.

Another context for the increased mobility of performing arts products in the contemporary era is the impact of mass-media entertainment such as cinema. Walter Benjamin had argued that 'there is . . . no greater contrast than that of the stage play to a work of art that is completely subject to, or like the film, founded in mechanical reproduction' (1992: 223). In older art forms such as painting and theatre, Benjamin argued, 'the presence of the original is the prerequisite to the concept of authenticity' so that 'the original preserved all its authority'. In a theatrical context, authority and authenticity were vested in the presence of a live audience and performers, whereas in film, 'man has to operate with his whole living person, while forgoing its aura. For aura is tied to presence: there can be no replica of it'.

A theatrical performance cannot be mechanically reproduced, as Benjamin observes. However, the contemporary commercialization of theatre, such as we can observe on Broadway, in London's West End, and in Las Vegas – and the advent of global touring networks which allow productions to circulate for lengthy periods of time to a variety of audiences – depends on the live theatre product being as easily 'reproducible' as in cinema. This is achieved through the processes of branding, which removes the site of authenticity and authority – the production's 'aura' – from the live performance, and makes it conceptual: the authenticity of a cultural product is now grounded in the recognizability of its cultural sources. In a branded cultural product, audiences do not experience a performance, but identify with a concept – with the Irishness of the Abbey Theatre, or a Le Brocquy portrait, or a U2 album. A theatrical performance cannot be reproduced, and thus is resistant to the centralized management required for mass-mediation. But a brand may be controlled centrally, and reproduced infinitely without (necessarily) losing its authenticity.

Global theatre networks create opportunities for theatre companies to earn large amounts of money, but those opportunities also give rise to financial risk, as was mentioned in my discussion of Caves's definition of the creative industries. These risks are exacerbated by the fact that the reception (and hence the financial success) of theatre is generally dependent on unpredictable factors, such as reviews, performances by actors, and so on. So another function of branding is to ensure (as much as possible) against such risks. Because branding attempts to determine the reception of a play in advance, it is a way of facilitating the secure mobility of a theatre product through global networks.[9]

This explains the emphasis placed by producers on brand over performance. If a show is internationally distributed, then actors, sets, and performances must eventually change. A brand can be used everywhere, however. The relationship of branding to theatre is explored in more detail in the next chapter, but for the present it is sufficient to state that globalization creates the conditions under which it becomes possible to think of theatre as a mass-mediated form of entertainment, with the brand a form of manageable reproduction that is not mechanical but *conceptual*.

So the use of branding, corporate sponsorship, and similar developments has facilitated the transformation of theatre into a creative industry. This leads to what Chin-Tao Wu has termed the 'privatisation of culture', whereby funding for theatre is moving away from state subsidy and towards corporate sponsorship. Wu states that companies are now using the cultural capital of art as part of their own marketing strategies. It might be inferred that corporate sponsorship would promote conservatism, yet Wu's research indicates that 'the mythological cult of artistic personality and the strong association between avant-garde art and innovation within the paradigms of modernism have provided the business world with a valuable tool for the projection of an image of itself as a liberal and progressive force' (2002: 125). Wu also discusses how companies involved in controversial industries such as cigarette manufacturing and oil exploration have demanded that museums, galleries, and theatres that receive their sponsorship should lobby on their behalf in political matters (185–94). The role of the state in this context is to promote work with obvious social utility: governments are not always enthusiastic about funding art, but they will fund activities that are consistent with state concerns. The 2002 Abbey Theatre *Plough* exemplifies this, with its emphasis on international touring, educational outreach, and other activities that can be related directly to economic output. And, in order to ensure that corporations will see the production as a viable form of entertainment for its clients, the Abbey increased the cost of tickets. We have an interesting reversal of roles here, whereby corporations are willing to sponsor art for (something like) art's sake, while state agencies insist that theatres must have discernible civic utility – preferably of a kind that can be measured in economic terms.

This suggests that the two globalized networks under discussion – the economic and the cultural – are beginning to converge in many respects. Just as the IDA uses the cultural capital of Ireland's writers to 'brand' the nation as a site for investment, so the production of Irish theatre has been influenced by the importation of strategies first developed by corporations and state entities competing within a global network.

What we see, therefore, is a transformation between 1991 and 2002 of the conception of national theatre in an Irish context, whereby the Abbey has moved from the pinnacle of a vertical network of Irish theatres and cultural organizations, to being one hub on an international horizontal network. The 1991 *Plough* was created on the basis that the Abbey Theatre was related to, but independent of, the state: its function was to draw on the best elements of Irish theatre (all of which were positioned below it on a vertical network) as a means of critiquing the state. There were connections between state and the national theatre at this time (principally in relation to funding), but these involved limited interactions, such as the transfer of funds from the state to the theatre. In contrast, the 2002 *Plough* shows that the national theatre had become one hub on a state-run network, operating in tandem with – and governed by similar ideologies to – such institutions as the IDA, tourism agencies, educational agencies, and so on. The Abbey also operates within a global theatre network where it must compete against other national and international theatres, its success in doing so determined by the dominance and success of branded versions of Irish identity.

This move from being part of a vertical network to occupying a position on several horizontal networks has led to a transformation in the cultural authority of the Abbey Theatre. By operating at the summit of a national network, the Abbey in 1991 had an influence on the development of Irish culture and society: Hynes's production was controversial because she used the status of the Abbey to communicate and raise troubling issues. Yet in 2002, we see an Abbey Theatre that is simply one of a number of government agencies engaged in activities of social, civic, and economic utility; it is, furthermore, only one of countless national theatres occupying an international stage, each of them promising various forms of experiences branded as authentic by their use of nationalized stereotypes. The 2002 *Plough* may suggest that national theatres are thriving because the concept of nation is now regarded simply as a brand that can function on the international network, and that the national theatre is just one hub of a state network.

This issue is complicated by the increasing similarities in the composition, maintenance, and reproduction of economic and cultural networks. In a network of societies competing for FDI, Ireland uses the cultural capital of its literary tradition to differentiate itself: the increased flow of capital to this hub on the economic network is thus aided by investors' familiarity with, and faith in, branded versions of the Irish as creative. Hence, we see how culture is used to attract investment capital into Ireland: the Irish brand facilitates the mobility of funds into and out of the country. Similarly, the transformation of theatre into a creative industry has seen the emergence of forms of theatre that operate according to the ideologies underpinning global capitalism: privatization, liberalization, competition, and so on. This creates interesting areas of overlap between cultural and economic networks. The cultural capital of the Abbey Theatre can be used to differentiate Ireland's place in the economic network for capital flow, which means that culture is being used for economic ends. This also benefits Irish theatres: a promotional campaign such as the IDA's 'Irish Mind' will inevitably promote not just the country but also its culture, to the benefit of both. Similarly, the Abbey's success abroad promotes the IDA's aims, providing one more example to potential investors and customers of how Irish citizens 'tackle issues, solve problems and seek other new and better ways to meet needs' (IDA Ireland, 2006).

More significantly, however, that success also promotes the ideologies associated with global capitalism. The success of the Abbey abroad can be presented to Irish citizens as evidence of the value of cultural competition, branding, and other values associated with multinational corporations. The appearance of the Abbey on international touring networks is not just evidence of the strength of Irish culture, but also a way of suggesting that the country's economic policies can produce benefits. The economic and cultural in an Irish context are separate networks, but the rhetoric and ideology underpinning one is used to support the other, creating fascinating interdependencies and shared values. In such a situation, it becomes difficult to see how the Abbey's history of independence may be protected.

The possibility of providing such a theatre is made difficult because the meaning and status of the terms 'national' and 'nationalist' are being re-evaluated because of globalization. This issue has been explored in an Irish context by Richard Kearney in *Postnationalist Ireland* (1997). Kearney suggests that the country will become more 'post-national' due to the combination of regionalization with federation within the supranational structures of the European Union. Irish people will, he argues, tend to identify themselves more closely with their own localities; simultaneously, they will consider themselves to be part of a political configuration that supersedes national boundaries: as citizens of the European Union, they may consider themselves at 'home' in Krakow as much as Connaught. The national will thus become irrelevant to the political, cultural, and economic lives of Ireland's citizens – in theory, anyway.

Kearney, like John Hume before him, sees the integration of a regionalized Ireland into the European Union in generally positive terms, viewing it as a necessary step towards the resolution of conflict in Northern Ireland. There have been many positive consequences of both regionalization and European integration: as is discussed in Chapter 6, the liberalization of many of Ireland's laws was enabled by the capacity of Irish citizens to appeal to the European courts. Yet such processes may also involve an erosion of Irish sovereignty. European legislation may have had a positive impact upon Irish life, but the European legislature is generally regarded – throughout the EU – as undemocratic and distant from the people it purports to represent. Similarly, the presence of multinational companies in Ireland (brought about by the relaxation of several national trade barriers) may have increased employment in the country, but it also means that the Irish economy has become dependent for its stability on events occurring outside its own borders, over which it has little or no control: international conflict, the price of oil, events in the international exchange markets, and so on. Insofar as sovereignty exists on a national level in Ireland, it tends to involve the management of the input of international capital into the country. Taxation – not to mention investment in housing, infrastructure, education, and culture – tends to be focused most on the need to maintain Ireland's international 'competitiveness'. So, as Castells remarks, 'nation states will survive but not their sovereignty' (1998: 335): the purpose of the Irish government is therefore to manage state services and to promote the Irish 'brand' internationally.

Globalization has eroded national sovereignty, but it has also tended to discredit nationalism. The homogenizing effects of globalization can produce localized expressions of powerlessness and resentment, which have in some cases been realized in a rise in ethnic nationalism. Kearney points out that 'legitimate nationalism is the expression of a normal need for *identification* (by others as much as ourselves)', which he contrasts with 'regressive nationalism', a term that describes the efforts of those who refuse to accept, or to mourn, the inevitable passing of the nation state (184). 'Legitimate nationalism' might thus be exemplified by such developments as the devolution of political power to Scotland and Wales in Britain, while 'regressive nationalism' might describe the rise of the National Front in England. However, the rise of ethnocentric nationalism, especially after the Cold War, has tended to discredit nationalism generally. The post-Cold War era may have been initiated by the collapse of a wall, but it was characterized by an alarming outbreak of ethnic conflict. Civil war in the former Yugoslavia, the Rwandan genocide, and indeed the Northern Irish conflict were all seen as examples of the consequences of unchecked ethnic nationalism. A result of this phenomenon was that nationalism has become discredited as irrational, anti-modern, regressive, and inherently monocultural.

David Lloyd points out the need for caution about uncritically accepting such representations. 'The displacement of irrationality onto nationalisms is an ideological convenience of a historical moment in which a further effort of homogenising rationalization is taking place globally in the name of the New World Order', he writes. 'At such a moment, when the violence of the nationalist and patriarchal states is literally beyond reason, and when the irrationality is conjoined with the profound economic rationality of transnational capitalism, there are sound pragmatic reasons to adhere to a nationalism as a minimal defence against homogenization' (1999: 36). Lloyd's comments imply that to devalue nationalism is also to devalue the concept of nation. This may have the positive outcome of focusing attention on the need to resist the spread of exclusivist ethnic nationalisms. It also facilitates the spread of global capitalism, however: if nationalism is characterized as inherently irrational, then the erosion of national sovereignty must therefore seem rational. To position nationalism as irrational may be to imply that resistance to globalization is anti-progressive, reactionary, and irrational.

This discussion allows a refocusing of the consideration of the place of national theatre in a globalizing world. As Lloyd states, there can be 'sound pragmatic reasons' for using the national to defend against global homogenization. The Abbey Theatre in 1904 was established to resist the homogenizing tendencies of a transnational ideology: namely, colonialism. As nations again face homogenization and integration into a transnational system over which their citizens have little influence, the purpose of national theatre might be to act as a site of cultural expression and, perhaps, of resistance. This may be one explanation for the current high status of national theatres throughout the world. The RNT in London has, for example, achieved impressive levels of commercial and critical success by producing work such as David Hare's *The Permanent Way* (2003) and *Stuff Happens* (2004), each of which makes use of a state subsidy to challenge government policy at both national and international levels.

It may also be the case that national theatres are thriving because the concept of nation is now regarded as largely obsolete, at least insofar as theatre is concerned. The production in 2002 of Barnes's *Plough* implies that this is more likely to be the case, in Ireland anyway. This is not to suggest that education and outreach activities, or international touring, are of themselves bad things – quite the contrary. But there is no evidence in Barnes's production of tension between the goals of the national theatre and the interests of both the Irish state and the corporations that sponsor much Irish economic activity. Rather, the production seems to support the goals of the Industrial Development Agency – promoting a representation of Irish identity that is homogenized, regressive, and essentialist – but also recognizable on international cultural and economic networks. We see that old divisions between the economic and the cultural are becoming redundant, as both become organized into networks that operate in similar and often overlapping ways.

At present, we see two modes of national theatre jostling with each other for dominance. The first is a national theatre that presents national identity as a globalized brand – a commodified abstraction – that may be diffused internationally, while at home it exists not to challenge state policy, but to enact or promote it. The second is a national theatre grounded in notions of citizenship – one that assumes that theatre practitioners share experiences and concerns with local audiences, even when these experiences exist only to be rejected or evaluated. These two productions of O'Casey's *The Plough and the Stars* – not to mention the original 1926 production of the play – show that, despite globalization, the category of nation still has value. The question, however, is this: will that value be construed mainly in civic terms – or economic ones? This question informs the development of the next chapter, in which I consider further the issues of branding, asking whether globalization represents a new departure for theatre.

4
Globalizing the Brand: Dion Boucicault's *The Shaughraun*, 1874/2004

'Selling Out' at the Abbey Theatre, 2004

On 19 November 2003, Ben Barnes launched the Abbey Theatre's 'abbe-yonehundred' programme for 2004 – a year-long celebration of the the-atre's centenary which aimed to commemorate the past while pointing new ways forward for Irish drama. The theatre was badly in need of a new sense of direction after going through a somewhat depressed period since Barnes began his tenure as Artistic Director in 2000. There had been artis-tic problems: productions such as *Barbaric Comedies* (McGuinness, 2000), *Hinterland* (Barry, 2002), and *Ariel* (Carr, 2002) had provoked contro-versy due to their content, but each of the three was attacked on aes-thetic grounds also. Only Eugene O'Brien's *Eden* (2001) had achieved both critical and commercial success under Barnes's stewardship, while many of the other new Irish plays produced during his time there had been met with disappointment or apathy. There were political problems too. Barnes had been publicly attacked for his handling of negotiations with the government over the development of a new building for the Abbey, with Taoiseach Bertie Ahern pointedly describing Barnes's pro-posal to move the theatre to a new site in Dublin's Docklands as 'deeply disappointing for the [Abbey's] local community – and to me' (*Irish Times*, 2001). The announcement of the centenary programme was an opportunity for Barnes and the Abbey to move on, to rearticulate the theatre's significance in a way that would not only attract new audi-ences, but also generate public and governmental support.

Considered from that perspective, the centenary programme appears not to have achieved its goals. Throughout the year, the Abbey failed to generate sufficient levels of enthusiasm from its audiences, prospective sponsors, or the media – and so, by the summer of that year, the whole programme looked set to unravel. Attendance figures from January to May 2004 were considerably lower than the theatre's management had predicted, and the Abbey's fundraising committee had failed to meet its expected targets. The resulting sense of crisis led to an announcement in September 2004 that up to one-third of the theatre's staff would be made redundant, while there were many calls for the dismissal of Ben Barnes from his post. This situation was exacerbated by a leaked email from Barnes to members of the international theatre community, in which he criticized the Theatre's Board, while attempting to defend himself. It was also announced that two productions planned for the final quarter of the year (Paul Mercier's *Smokescreen* and a revival of Lennox Robinson's *Drama at Inish*) would be cancelled due to financial problems.

Although the programme for 2004 was well publicized (a glossy brochure outlining the year's productions was widely distributed), it failed to capture the public's imagination. This may have been due to its conservatism: as a statement by the Abbey of its achievements during the previous century, the programme sent out confusing messages. Barnes's unwillingness to risk new drama on the theatre's main-stage during 2004 was unusual for an institution that prides itself on a tradition of nurturing new writers. Its choice of productions also provoked some controversy. Although it included acknowledged Irish classics such as Marina Carr's *Portia Coughlan* (1996), Yeats's *Purgatory* (1938), *The Playboy of the Western World*, Tom Murphy's *The Gigli Concert* (1983), and McGuinness's *Observe the Sons of Ulster* (1985), the programme also featured *I Do Not Like Thee Doctor Fell* (1979), the first play by Bernard Farrell, a well-known Irish playwright who happened to be on the Abbey Theatre Board when the 'abbeyonehundred' programme was announced. Farrell's comedies of middle-class Dublin life have been among the most popular Irish plays of the 1980s and 1990s and, as Christopher Murray points out in *Mirror Up to Nation*, the popularity of *Dr Fell* suggests that 'there is something at the core of the play which answers to the anxieties of many Irish people' (1997b: 240). Nevertheless, its inclusion in a programme that purported to represent the best of a century of theatre-making was questionable.

The messages conveyed by the theatre's omissions were also criticized. Only two of the full productions in the 'abbeyonehundred' programme – Paula Meehan's Christmas play for children *The Wolf of Winter* and the revival of Carr's *Portia Coughlan* – were by female authors, both of whom were being produced on the Abbey's Peacock stage, a smaller space used for experimental work and new writing. Although full productions by Yeats and Synge featured, the only work by the theatre's third figurehead, Augusta Gregory, was a staged reading of *Spreading the News* in September 2004. And only three of the year's full productions were directed by women: Lynne Parker directed her uncle Stewart's *Heavenly Bodies*, Lorraine Pintal directed *The Burial at Thebes*, and Andrea Ainsworth directed *The Wolf of Winter*.

Also criticized was the theatre's omission of plays in the Irish language, its failure to undertake meaningful Irish tours, and many other features of its artistic policy. Finally, the theatre's management of the centenary programme itself was criticized, both during the summer of 2004 when it was forced into the unplanned rearrangements of its line-up mentioned above, and from September 2004 onwards, when the theatre's management structures were subjected to intense media scrutiny.

Most of the criticisms of Barnes's programme seem to have been grounded in a belief that, as a national institution, the theatre confers value on dramatists and their works by including them in the national repertoire. The 'abbeyonehundred' programme was not simply a collection of plays; it was, as an act of public memory, a statement of what Ireland, as a nation in 2004, valued from its past. This explains the disappointment many felt about the lack of work in Irish or by women writers from the centenary programme. To be fair, it should be stated that the Abbey produced three plays by women in 2003, and produced four well-regarded plays in the Irish language under the artistic directorship of Patrick Mason.[1] Nevertheless, the exclusion of both from the centenary programme seems a serious oversight – one that both reveals and reinforces many of the prejudices of Irish society.

The construction of the centenary programme, however, implied that the theatre's immediate priority was simple financial survival, rather than national self-representation. The Abbey entered its centenary year with an operating deficit of €800,000, which, by the end of 2004, had risen to more than €2 million. Financial necessity probably explains the production of Farrell's *Dr Fell*, as well as the lack of new writing and the theatre's unwillingness to invest funds in Irish-language drama and in substantial levels of touring. Economics may also explain the one controversy that seemed genuinely to surprise the Abbey's management: the media's sceptical response to Barnes's decision to produce Dion Boucicault's 1874 play *The Shaughraun*, directed by John McColgan, as its major summer offering.

In part, this scepticism arose because McColgan had never before directed a professional piece of theatre, though he had been responsible for *Riverdance*. Commentators noted that McColgan was chair of the Abbey's fundraising committee, and that he had himself donated large

amounts of money to the theatre – believed to be in the region of
€400,000 (see McKeon, 2004a). McColgan vigorously defended his right
to direct the production on the popular Irish television programme *The
Late Late Show*, which dedicated a special edition to the Abbey in January
2004. Yet the controversy persisted.

Even if we ignore the Abbey's decision to give its lucrative summertime
slot to a first-time director who was also the theatre's chief fundraiser,
the inclusion of Boucicault in the Abbey's centenary programme is
puzzling. When the Abbey was established, melodrama was very popular in Dublin: the week before the Abbey's inaugural production on
27 December 1904, Dublin's Queen's Theatre had staged *The Shaughraun*.
And, as Chris Morash points out, 'on the same December night' as the
Abbey's first performances, 'across the Liffey almost two thousand people
were howling for the informer's blood' in another Irish melodrama, J.W.
Whitbread's *Sarsfield*, which was also staged at the Queen's (Morash,
2002: 129). Dublin audiences in 1904 were familiar with, and fond of,
Boucicault. *The Shaughraun, The Colleen Bawn* (1860), and *Arrah-na-Pogue*
(1864) had been revived every year in Dublin during the 1890s, according to Stephen Watt (1991), and were the most popular of the many Irish
melodramas produced at that time. However, the foundation of the Irish
Literary Theatre in 1897 and the Abbey in 1904 was an attempt to offer
Irish audiences something different from, and better than, these melodramas. 'We will show', wrote Yeats, 'that Ireland is not the home of buf-
foonery and of easy sentiment, as it has been represented, but the home
of an ancient idealism'. The Irish people are 'weary of misrepresentation'
by such writers as Boucicault, Yeats claimed (quoted by Gregory, 1965: 9).
This hostility to melodrama persisted throughout the theatre's earliest
years: even in the 1920s, Sean O'Casey stated that when he began working for the Abbey he 'instinctively kept firm silence about Dion Boucicault,
whose works he knew as well as Shakespeare's' (1963: 105).

Stephen Watt points out that 19th-century Irish melodrama has been
undeservedly neglected, while Nicholas Grene explains how the authenticity of the Abbey's representations of Irish life would soon become as
controversial as Boucicault's (1999: 5–50). O'Casey was not the only
Irish writer to have admired Boucicault, whose influence is evident
in plays by Synge, Beckett, and others. Furthermore, although some
Abbey personnel, such as Hugh Hunt, continued to express reservations
about melodrama, it became a part of the theatre's repertoire from the
1940s onwards, notably in the work of Louis D'Alton. *The Shaughraun*
was itself produced at the theatre for the first time in 1967, was revived
in 1975, and produced again in 1990 (ATA). And a production of

The Colleen Bawn directed by Conall Morrison in 1998 was one of the Abbey's greatest successes under Patrick Mason. There was, therefore, a tradition of Abbey productions of Boucicault before 2004, many of which combined popular appeal with critical success.

So it is not necessarily a problem that the Abbey included Boucicault in its centenary programme. After all, any institution must move beyond the ideals of its founders, and the Abbey could not have survived for a century without doing so. Indeed, Yeats and Lady Gregory probably would have disapproved of many of the plays that later became popular at the theatre they founded and, as we saw in the last chapter, Garry Hynes's *The Plough and the Stars* was successful partially because it departed so radically from the original text. Yet the historical significance of the Abbey is not that it provided an alternative to Irish melodrama, but that it built upon that form to enrich and broaden the range of Irish drama. It did so thematically, as for example with Synge's transformation of the wake scene from *The Shaughraun* in *The Shadow of the Glen* (1903). And it did so institutionally: by contesting the Irishness of Boucicault's characters, the Abbey reinvested 'authority in new and different versions of Irishness', which became the basis for the theatre's subsequent output (Grene, 1999: 8). The return of Boucicault to the Abbey's repertoire in the 1960s was thus a *progression*. The theatre was not abandoning its principles, but building on them to find new ways of performing and staging Irish work.

Barnes and his staff seemed aware of these continuities in their construction of the 'abbeyonehundred' programme. While *The Shaughraun* was performed on the theatre's main-stage, Stewart Parker's play about Boucicault, *Heavenly Bodies* (1986), was produced in the Peacock, with a revival of *The Playboy of the Western World* following both. This programming established a relationship between Synge and Boucicault and, with the production of Parker's play, the theatre showed the relevance of that relationship to the contemporary tradition. This was an important statement by the Abbey of a sense of its place in Irish dramatic history. It was, as a national theatre, reaching back to a tradition that predated its own foundation, while also bringing Parker's play, which had never before been professionally produced in Ireland, into its own repertoire.

These continuities were apparent only in the theatre's programming, however. The Abbey's 2004 production of *The Shaughraun* was notable in that it seemed to have been conceived without any reference whatsoever to the previous century's work.[2] Twentieth-century productions of Boucicault at the Abbey tend to be notable for directors' employment of such distancing devices as music, tableaux, and the utilization of frames in stage design, all of which emphasized that Boucicault's claim to represent an authentic Ireland had been superseded. McColgan's production was, however, conceived without any apparent sense of distance between the source material and its performance. Audiences were encouraged to boo and cheer at the action by a pre-performance announcement, which meant that part of the attraction of *The Shaughraun* was that it reproduced the ethos of a 19th-century melodramatic performance: thus, the production from 27 December 1904 being commemorated was not *Cathleen ni Houlihan*, but the Queen's *Sarsfield*.

Furthermore, McColgan imported into the production many contemporary mass-mediated images of Irishness that *do* purport to authenticity, including scenes of traditional Irish dancing taken directly from his own *Riverdance*, a show that is regarded as emblematic of contemporary mass Irish culture. The blend of a play from 1874 with the sensibility of *Riverdance* implied that, for McColgan, there was no difference between Boucicault's representation of Irish culture and his own, making the two men seem like contemporaries. The positioning of *Riverdance* beside Boucicault used the international popularity of the former to validate the latter. It is strange that the Abbey, during its centenary year, played host to a confluence that seemed to ignore its contribution to Irish culture during the previous 100 years.

The success of the production surprised some commentators: Helen Meany (2004), for instance, queried McColgan's presentation of 'ersatz Irishry' (12). In an interview with RTE Radio's *Rattlebag*, McColgan dismissed these criticisms as 'academic snobbery', pointing out that the production was selling out most of its performances, and that it was likely to transfer abroad. McColgan's view of *The Shaughraun* appears to have been shared by the management of the Abbey. The consensus appears to have been that financial gain and international exposure should be the primary determinants of the production's success. The production generated the theatre's 'highest box office returns in fourteen years', according to Fiona Ness (2004), which is a substantial achievement. However, it is disappointing that criticisms of the production on the grounds of aesthetics and authenticity were not only ignored, but also dismissed as irrelevant. 'I never had a doubt in my mind that John McColgan was the right person to direct *The Shaughraun*', said Ben Barnes, referring to the commercial success of the play. 'The theatre has been vindicated and I have been vindicated' (quoted by Ness, 2004).

Such remarks didn't stop observers from expressing concern about a possible conflict of interest, particularly when it was announced that

McColgan's Abhann Productions – the producers of *Riverdance* – would tour *The Shaughraun* in the United States from 2006.[3] Just as Noel Pearson was accused of using the Abbey Theatre to 'test-run' *Dancing at Lughnasa* before its Broadway production, it now seemed that McColgan would move from being a fundraiser for the theatre to being awarded the rights to tour *The Shaughraun* internationally.

Should the Abbey have produced *The Shaughraun*? It would be wrong to suggest otherwise: the problem for the theatre is not that it achieved great commercial success with a Boucicault play, but that it was incapable of drawing upon – or at least using the production to show an awareness of – its own century-long repertoire to achieve a similar or greater success. This gives rise to questions about how far the national theatre has progressed since the 1897 manifesto. Once again, we see an Irish theatre that values commercial success and international endorsement over artistic integrity, while a community of critics express alarm at the misrepresentation of Irishness, both at home and abroad. Although these issues have been part of Irish theatre throughout the 20th century, their resurgence at a time when the Abbey ought to have been asserting its role as Ireland's national theatre is surprising. To progress this discussion, I will relate this case to a consideration of how globalization has affected theatre business in general.

Locating globalized theatre

The growth of opportunities for international touring – coupled with audiences' and critics' heightened access to global media – has altered the way that many plays are produced and received. It is possible when analysing these developments to note five general tendencies in the globalization of world theatre. This grouping is necessarily formulaic but, to varying degrees, each of the following characteristics may be found in theatre productions that are designed specifically for international diffusion:

- First, globalized theatre tends to involve the use of branding to manage risk.
- Second, it succeeds not because it is universal, but because it stimulates a reflexive response from audiences.
- Third, its mobility provokes anxiety in local audiences.
- Fourth, it facilities the emergence of a globalized discourse about theatre.
- Finally, it inhibits intercultural exchange.

Branding and nationality – a brief discussion

The issue of branding has already been discussed briefly. The economies of scale involved in international theatre productions bring large financial rewards, but also present financial risks. As a way of offsetting these risks, production companies often use instantly recognizable markers that encourage audiences to visit a production without necessarily knowing anything about the play being produced. They instead go to the theatre to consume an element of it that they are already familiar with in some ways – its authenticity, its national origins, and other examples that I will discuss below.

The issue of branding is discussed and defined in considerably more detail in the rest of this book. To sketch briefly the way that nationality becomes part of the branding process, I want briefly to use the example of how plays from England are marketed for their sophistication, as was especially notable during the 2003 Broadway season. During that year, Vanessa Redgrave's performance in *A Long Day's Journey into Night* and Simon Russell Beale's appearance in *Uncle Vanya* and *Twelfth Night* were widely praised, with Ben Brantley of the *New York Times* declaring (apparently without irony) that Beale's 'posture alone makes two trips to the Brooklyn Academy a necessity for connoisseurs of acting' (2003). The thematic complexity of the many English plays produced or toured in America during that year is also noteworthy. Peter Nichols's *A Day in the Death of Joe Egg* is about a couple raising a disabled child; Nicholas Wright's *Vincent in Brixton* is about Van Gogh; *Continental Divide* by David Edgar is an anatomization of American politics since the 1960s; and *Humble Boy* by Charlotte Jones includes astrophysics among its themes. American theatregoers' admiration for the acting of Redgrave and Beale – together with the thematic complexity of these four plays – offers an indicator of the kinds of English work being exported to, or produced in, the United States since the turn of the century. Those productions typically included refined, elegant acting best appreciated by 'connoisseurs', and a plot that cites – but does not elaborate upon – such weighty themes as astrophysics or modern art. This may be seen as an example of theatre being driven by branding: audiences do not pay to encounter something *new* or unfamiliar, but instead to have their presuppositions about English drama confirmed.

Reflexivity

A second tendency is for plays to be received 'reflexively'. That term requires careful definition. The notion of reflexivity has been described by Ulrich Beck (1997) as a key component of modernism; it dominates debates about methodology in the social sciences, and it also has an impact on culture. But how is it relevant to theatre?

Put simply, a reflexive act is one that refers back to itself. In the study of literature and the arts, debate about reflexivity has tended to focus mainly on the issue of artistic creation: as Lawson puts it, 'the writer discusses the role of the author, the artist includes his own easel in the painting, the film-maker films the making of the film' (1985: 10). So, a consideration of reflexivity in literature has tended to involve discussion of metafictional or metatheatrical strategies, usually in relation to ideas about postmodernity. What, though, about the role of the audience? To an extent, the issue of reception can be related to Roland Barthes's notion of reader response: the meaning of some texts is determined not by authorial intention but by the reader's interpretations. However, although Barthes's theories are useful, I do not think that terms like 'readerly' or 'writerly' are appropriate to theatrical reception: as we'll see throughout this book, the determination of the meaning of a play arises from much more than the interplay of linguistic signifiers.

My suggestion instead is that theatrical 'reflexivity' is a mode of reception, whereby an audience's enjoyment of a theatrical production is determined by that audience's capacity to relate the action to their own preoccupations and interests, as those preoccupations and interests are determined locally. I must distinguish here between plays that can stimulate a reflexive response and theatre that is universal or homogeneous. Writing about what he terms 'McTheatre' (that is, theatre for a mass-mediated audience, such as the Broadway and West End mega-musicals of Andrew Lloyd Webber), Dan Rebellato states that the problem with such work is 'not that it is everywhere but that it is everywhere the same' (2006: 108). The point, however, about theatre that can be received reflexively is that its reception is everywhere *different*: the meaning of a play is not so much determined by authorial intention as audiences' willingness to interpret the play in relation to individual and/or communal concerns. Miriam Bratu Hansen explains how reflexivity functions in relation to early cinema, which, she claims:

> Succeeded as an international modernist idiom on a mass basis . . . not because of its presumably universal narrative form but because it meant *different things to different people, both at home and abroad.* We must not forget that these films, along with other mass cultural exports, were consumed in locally quite specific, and unequally developed, contexts and conditions of *reception.*
>
> (Bratu Hansen, 2001: 335)

Mobility

The growth of a global touring circuit has led to the emergence of a number of plays that do not attempt to be universal or local, but instead attempt to make themselves sufficiently open to interpretation to be understood in different ways by different audiences. For example, the international success of Friel's *Translations* is not due to its representation of a universal situation: the play is a success because it allows for a multiplicity of interpretations. It allows people in such cities as Prague and Barcelona to explore their own different linguistic histories, and their relationships to other, dominant linguistic traditions nearby. On the other hand, audiences in places where language is generally less contested might respond to the play's exploration of the instability and flexibility of identity. The strength of the play (as is the case with many of Friel's works) is not that it presents a universal situation, but that, to borrow Hansen's phrase, it 'means different things to different people' or, as Nicholas Grene writes, that audiences everywhere 'loved it, though for significantly different reasons' (1999: 35).

To varying degrees, directors preparing plays for international tour seem conscious of the need to facilitate this kind of response. This can be done in simple – perhaps even crude – ways. Peter Brook confessed that his production of *The Mahabharata* wasn't above ingratiating itself to the local audience. 'Coming into a city the actors rapidly learn a bit of the text in Spanish or whatever the local language is', he explained. 'In a play, particularly in a comic play where you can talk directly to the audience, even a few phrases of the language of the country make a great difference in one's relation with the audience, because the audience know that you are interested in them, that you are trying to make contact with them' (quoted in Delgado and Heritage, 1996: 52–3).

Brook's emphasis on language is interesting – but it is one not shared by many other directors. Increasingly we are seeing plays that attempt to facilitate reflexivity by emphasizing non-verbal language and signs, such as spectacle, music, celebrity casting, special effects, and marketing. Moretti's analysis of the recent success of Hollywood action movies offers a model for what is happening in theatre:

> Stories travel well because they are largely independent of language . . . This relative autonomy of the story-line explains the ease with which action films dispense with words, replacing them with sheer noise (explosions, crashes, gunshots, screams); while this brisk dismissal of language, in turn, facilitates their international diffusion.
>
> (Moretti, 2001: 92)

To varying degrees, directors preparing plays for international tours seem conscious of the need to facilitate reflexive responses. The diminution of localizing references and the promotion of reflexivity allow companies to capitalize on opportunities for touring and joint production.

This may lead to conflict because, as theatres increasingly desire mobility, local communities will need theatres to be firmly focused on their immediate environment – due particularly to the loss of 'meaning generation' that can occur in small communities as a result of globalization (as I discussed in relation to *Stones In His Pockets*). The growth of global touring means that theatre companies may now determine their success not by the satisfaction levels of local audiences, but by their ability to tour overseas – which means that local audiences may feel neglected.

Theatre – a globalized discourse?

Fourth, discourse about theatre is globalized, but not internationalized. With the globalization of media, Irish newspapers may easily report upon the success of plays like *Dancing at Lughnasa* on Broadway, but rarely report on comparable developments in American drama – and, as we'll see in Chapter 6, are sometimes dismissive of American plays on Irish stages. Such reportage is thus not directed towards the promotion of links between American and Irish culture, but exists merely to give Irish audiences a broader perspective on issues that are of local importance.

Globalization and intercultural exchange

Finally, international touring tends to inhibit rather than promote intercultural exchange. As Patrice Pavis writes:

> [O]ne may say that contemporary theatrical or choreographic production has become international, often for simple economic reasons: in this way artists and producers stand a much greater chance of making a profit, since their productions can be understood everywhere without adaptation. This may seem to justify them, but it also risks reinforcing national stereotypes. There is a great temptation to produce immediately exportable productions . . . But the internationalization of festivals and productions and the cosmopolitanism of certain groups . . . do not necessarily result in an intercultural experience.
>
> (Pavis, 1996: 5)

This claim can be illustrated by considering again the Brian Friel/Simon Russell Beale production of *Uncle Vanya*, toured with *Twelfth Night* by the

Donmar Warehouse to the Brooklyn Academy of Music in 2003. The play is adapted by an Irish writer from a Russian text, produced in London by a British director who had recently won an Oscar, before touring to New York. The production thus moves freely from one cultural centre to another with a set of instantly recognizable selling points. As such, it is an almost perfect blend of internationalization, commercialization, and mobility – three key features of globalization.

Yet it would be wrong to exaggerate the level of cultural exchange that occurs during this process. No specialized knowledge of British society or culture was required of American audiences to appreciate the play, nor was such knowledge imparted. American audiences were not asked to consider their relationship to Ireland, Britain, or Russia; nor were members of the original London audience encouraged to compare Britain under Tony Blair to pre-revolutionary Russia, or to consider their place in the analogy between pre-independence Ireland and Russia. It would be insulting to those audience members to assume that none of them independently reached such conclusions. Nevertheless, *Vanya* also shows that, despite the rhetoric of borderlessness that accompanies globalization, the production's mobility took place as a result of the exchange of a great deal of capital, but very little culture. The mobility of the production may have mitigated against the exchange of culture.

Each of these five characteristics is explored in more detail later. None of them is a feature of every production that is successful globally; but they are all features of the contemporary theatrical landscape. What I want now is to place these features in a historical context, showing how much of what we think of as resulting from globalization has in fact been part of theatre throughout its modern history.

The Shaughraun – branding Irishness

My suggestion in this section is that *The Shaughraun* appeared in the Abbey's centenary programme mainly because it is well suited to the global theatre network, because it presents Irishness as a commodified abstraction, which can be understood as a precursor to, or a prototype of, a theatrical Irish 'brand'. While the genealogy of the Irish brand is discussed in more detail in Chapter 8, I would argue that, through globalization, the historic 'otherness' of Irish drama has been reconfigured to correspond to an internationalized branding of Irishness as a consumable commodity. This process has been underway for several decades in the marketing of Irish popular music, international tourism, food, clothing and drink production, and, most notably, in the spread of the 'Irish' pub (see Graham, 2001, for a detailed discussion of these issues).

This commoditization of a nationalized abstraction is, unlike the Nike logo or the Intel Pentium noise, not a copyrighted brand owned and controlled by a centralizing authority, so it is difficult to define precisely. But it is possible to identify a number of characteristics in plays marketed internationally as 'Irish', all of which are present in the works of Boucicault too.

The first element of the branding of Irishness evident in Boucicault's plays is his representation of Irishness as *other*, an issue that has been considered at length by Nicholas Grene in *The Politics of Irish Drama*. The representation of Irishness in literature has most often involved a presentation of Irish identity as grounded in a predominantly rural, Irish-speaking, Catholic society – but it always did so within a literary tradition that was part of an urbanized social structure. That is, representations of Ireland were always presented for an audience presupposed to be homogenized, metropolitan, and inherently different to the Irish being presented in the text. This gave rise to many tensions. The conventions of British writing were dependent on a sense of shared values between audience and author, who might both understand the notion of truths that could be 'universally acknowledged' (even ironically), and on an accepted sense of 'realism' that was dependent on those values. Such conventions simply could not be made to fit to Ireland. The country lacked any of the stable bases that writers in more industrialized countries had depended on. Language in Ireland was in a difficult state: Irish was in decline, yet there was no consistent version of English capable of being taught or learned. Hence, the majority of Irish characters speak a language that requires frequent annotation and explanation, and so they are perpetually marked out as different. Ireland also lacked the industrialized urban areas that could stimulate a psychological novel such as Dickens's *Great Expectations* (1861), Hugo's *Les Misérables* (1862), or Dostoevsky's *Crime and Punishment* (1866). This meant that Irish writing in the 19th century had to operate on two levels, with a central 'Irish' narrative, sometimes of a mythic, symbolic, or romantic kind, framed by a more conventional narrative that provides for readers and audiences some kind of interpretative and moral anchor. One example of such mediation is the editorial and glossary to *Castle Rackrent* (1800), which sanitize and explain the Irish narrative. Another is the contrast between the Standard English used to narrate 19th century Irish novels, and the Hiberno-English used to represent dialogue within the same books.

A similar process occurred in Irish theatre. To be viewed from inside Ireland, a play's action must be meaningful to an Irish audience; to be successful abroad, the central 'Irish' narrative must be framed or mediated in a way that will provide an interpretative framework for an urbanized, cosmopolitan audience lacking in specialized knowledge of Ireland. In *The Politics of Irish Drama*, Grene describes this process as involving the use of 'stage interpreters', such as Molineux in *The Shaughraun*: characters whose interaction with Irishness does not just provide comic effect, but also fulfils an interpretive and mediative function for non-Irish audiences. The use of otherness in this way facilitates the international diffusion of Irish writing: it allows non-Irish cultures to address reflexively their own concerns, without having to merge or mix with Irish culture itself. That is, Irishness acts as a deterritorialized space in which audiences may explore local preoccupations (as mentioned above in relation to Friel's *Translations*). This was true in the time of Boucicault, and remains true for the reception of many Irish writers at present.

A second feature of Boucicault's Irish drama is that it presents Irishness as undisciplined but not transgressive. That indiscipline can exist in many forms. It may be linguistic, so that Irish speech is received not as a language in its own right, but as a mild deviation from standard speech, whether that speech is American or English. Irish speech is always represented typographically as a form of deviance. 'Conn nivir did an honest day's work in his life – but dhrinkin', an fishin', an' shootin', an' sportin' an' love-makin', says Mrs O'Kelly in *The Shaughraun* – the spelling of her words as unruly as the behaviour she describes (1987: 271). This indiscipline may also be moral. When asked if he will reform, Conn famously replies, 'I don't know what that is, but I will' (326), suggesting that he can be subjected to moral discipline without necessarily understanding it. This duality is perhaps best encapsulated in Conn's declaration that 'it goes agin my conscience that I did not crack the skull of that thief when I had him fair and asy under my foot. I'll never get absolution for that!' (303). This emphasis on indiscipline has persisted, both thematically and formally, in Irish drama.

A third feature of Boucicault's work that has persisted is its conflation of 'authenticity' with an absence of industrialization and urbanization so that, to borrow Victor Merriman's phrase, the work on stage is received as 'nature' to the audience's 'culture' (1999: 315). All of Boucicault's Irish villains share one characteristic: their upward mobility. His heroes, in contrast, occupy stable social categories, tending either to be gentry or peasant, usually in idealized form. Conn's simplicity exemplifies this: uneducated, unsophisticated, and uninitiated into the moneyed classes, Conn is naturally inclined towards generally moral behaviour. The running joke in *The Shaughraun* about Molineux's desire to categorize 'you Irish' can thus be seen as an example of a need to reduce the Irish to abstractions, with an emphasis on primitive or 'natural' characteristics. This desire might explain why most Irish drama happens in the least populated parts of the country: an Irish *character* would have to occupy a society, but an Irish *type* need only occupy a landscape. Such representations may thus be understood as indicators of audiences' desire for escapism, with 'Ireland' being offered as a reassuring counterpoint to the world to which audiences will return when they step from the theatre to the urbanized, prosaic, and commercialized space of Broadway, the West End, or theatreland in any city's downtown (including the cities of Ireland itself).

This emphasis on Irish authenticity persists. For instance, Irish speech is considered more authentic than other forms of English. As recently as 2004, the English dramatist Rebecca Linkiewicz could explain her decision to set her play *The Night Season* in Sligo (the same setting as *The Shaughraun*) in terms of the naturally poetic quality of Irish speech. 'Despite having some Irish blood in her background, the playwright has never lived there', Victoria Segal tells us, stating that Linkiewicz freely admits that 'she wanted to use Irish voices to facilitate her lyrical language, aware that the same words in an English accent might sound 'flowery'' (2004: 9). Irish speech is thus considered available for any playwright who wishes to add a layer of credibility to otherwise 'flowery' material. Linkiewicz, together with the play's director Lucy Bailey, went on a so-called 'fact-finding' mission to Sligo before she wrote the play for a production at London's RNT.

Similarly, Michael Hasting's *Calico* (2004), which concerns the relationship of Samuel Beckett with Lucia Joyce, uses a stage-Irish speech to represent the Irish identity of some of its characters – notably Nora Barnacle, whose speech is inflected with Irishisms, including an unusual tendency to refer to potatoes. 'Poor old Him has this potato-brain mud woman who's only good for one thing', she says, speaking of her husband (2004: 48), while she later encapsulates her fear of poverty by asking, 'how long will this bag of potatoes last?' (54). The actors playing Lucia and Giorgio Joyce delivered their lines in Irish accents in *Calico's* production at the Duke of York's Theatre in April 2004, yet the historical figures upon whom these characters were based had been raised outside the country. Language is used as a form of national identification: to be Irish means to speak in an Irish manner.

Next, Boucicault's Irish work is typically received as reflexive rather than universal. This means that his Irish plays will not promote one theme that everyone agrees upon; instead, their themes will be sufficiently vague for audiences to relate the action to their own lives and localities. In this sense, we can see how the Good Friday Agreement made use of a tendency in Irish literature towards creative ambiguity – to overcome difference by allowing people to read into a text whatever they expect to find there. For example, in *The Shaughraun*, Boucicault only ever states that Robert is a convict, but no explicit statement is made about whether he is guilty of the crimes for which he was convicted. Hence, those who want to believe that Robert is an Irish nationalist hero will be fully enabled to do so. Simultaneously, those predisposed to assume that he has been wrongfully convicted, and would never willingly have participated in the Fenian movement, will be enabled to believe that to be the case. Another example of reflexivity in Boucicault is his distinction between law and justice, particularly in the presentation of Robert's status as a subject of British law. By escaping from prison, Robert, ironically, disqualifies himself for release; by surrendering, he entitles himself to freedom. To a 19th-century British audience, the contrast between legality and justice will represent the persistently disorderly and uncontrollable behaviour of Ireland within the United Kingdom: the implication might be that the path to Irish peace lies in surrendering to British laws. For an Irish audience, however, that contrast might serve as evidence of the arbitrary and inherently contradictory nature of the system of control that attempts to govern their lives.

It is therefore not the case that Boucicault's plays have one 'correct' meaning that might alienate any potential audience, but that they invite many interpretations, none of which may necessarily be privileged. Boucicault allows his audiences to discover in his plays whatever is that they wish to find there. He could legitimately claim to be acting on behalf of Irish republican prisoners (writing a letter in support of jailed Fenians to the British press when *The Shaughraun* appeared in London), while taking the congratulations of Queen Victoria, whose favourite play was *The Colleen Bawn*. His *The Poor of New York* would become *The Poor of Liverpool*; his *Octoroon* could have a happy ending added for an English audience. Boucicault, in other words, was as alert to the consumption as the production of his plays, and was always happy to make changes to his globalized product to meet the demands of local audiences.

A fifth feature of Boucicault's commodified Irishness is that it is arbitrary: it is not dependent for its currency on any form of Irishness that actually exists. His Irish plays are set in many different parts of the country. *The Colleen Bawn* takes place in Limerick, but manages to have the Lakes of Killarney – approximately 100 kilometres away – for a back-drop. *The Shaughraun* takes place in Sligo, but an early scene is set on the Blasket Islands, implying that they are off the coast of northern Connaught, near Sligo, when they are about 170 kilometres away, off the coast of Kerry. Boucicault is presenting Ireland as a collection of picture-postcards, using internationally identifiable images of Irishness as part of his scenography, without any regard for geography – an early example of the separation of ideas about Irishness from the physical spaces that gave rise to those concepts in the first place. Similarly, the Irish speech in Boucicault's plays is generic: it admits of no regional variations or individual inflection. It is, simply, an invented speech that allows for verbal extravagance, exoticism, and the use of harsh language that would not be censored.

The arbitrary quality of what is and is not considered 'Irish' persists. Not all Irish plays will be marketed for their Irishness, as Dublin's Gate Theatre has shown in its international tours of work by writers such as Pinter.[4] Similarly, not all plays marketed as Irish are from Ireland, so that McPherson's *The Weir* (1997), Barry's *The Steward of Christendom* (1995), and McDonagh's *The Cripple of Inishmaan* (1996) were all received as Irish when they toured to New York, despite the fact that each of the three was a British production.[5]

Finally, the Irish brand is commodified. Its value is not innate but is instead established in relation to other brands, and that value can there-fore rise and fall. Boucicault's plays went out of fashion, and were briefly rehabilitated in Ireland in 2004. Similarly, in 2003, Simon Russell Beale's posture was considered a more marketable aspect of the Donmar Warehouse production of *Uncle Vanya* than Brian Friel's script. A decade earlier, however, Friel was being held up as an example of precisely the kind of work to which the British theatre should aspire (see Billington, 1992: 10).

These features of Boucicault's presentation of Irishness do not appear in every Irish play, but they do offer a way of understanding many of the important debates in recent drama worldwide. Although it is possi-ble for an Irish play to do good business overseas without having its Irishness emphasized, plays that actively challenge audiences' precon-ceptions about 'Irish' work will usually be received with hostility, as has been shown with the US premiere of Marina Carr's *On Raftery's Hill* (see Sihra, 2004). Furthermore, these characteristics are so strongly associ-ated with Irish drama that audiences expect to find them in every play branded as Irish – sometimes with the result that they misunderstand what they are seeing. As mentioned already, *Philadelphia, Here I Come!* presents its audience with a disruption in form, whereby Gar is performed by two actors, one portraying his private thoughts, while the other enacts his public persona. Writing about its 1966 New York premiere, however, John Harrington states that the pre-publicity for the play 'overwhelmed [the play's director Hilton] Edwards's intentions'. 'The work intended to broaden expectations for Irish plays, because of its successes, inadvertently narrowed them', writes Harrington. 'The kind of praise *Philadelphia* received always referred back to the Irish play familiar in New York and deplored by Hilton Edwards'. Even the one negative review for the play in New York 'built its verdict on the established conventions of the Irish play', writes Harrington (1997: 153–4).

For all of these reasons, it makes sense that the Abbey would choose to produce Boucicault in 2004. In an environment in which it is expected to 'compete', without appropriate levels of state subsidy, the Abbey must maximize its profits and audiences. This explains its desire to brand itself, with the compound word 'abbeyonehundred' an attempt to create a corporate identity for a body of work, so that the experience being offered to audiences is not one play, but a year of theatrical productions that should be consumed in their entirety. It also explains the theatre's production of Boucicault, whose work is an example of low-risk theatre with mass – and probably international – appeal. The Abbey has chosen to accommodate itself to the opportunities presented by globalization – *not* by developing new Irish theatre that might have global value, but by reverting to a tried and trusted formula for appealing to international audiences. Its positioning of Boucicault at the centre of its centenary thus signals a surrender of sorts to pressures associated with the need to be competitive. To be successful means to be *financially* successful; to be financially successful will most often require the ability to compete on the global, rather than the national, stage. The Abbey thus reclaimed a businessman/artist whose invention of a mass-mediated popular theatre has again become useful. As we shall see in Chapter 8, the relationship between colonial and global constructions of identity reveals much about the relationships between theatre's past and present.

Concluding comments

The crisis of the Abbey Theatre in 2004 may be seen as arising from a combination of many factors associated with globalization. The promotion of the ideology associated with global capitalism has transformed the Abbey into a 'creative industry' that must compete with other forms of entertainment. Government unwillingness to provide sufficient funds to the theatre has led it to seek private and corporate sponsorship, and to produce work that may exploit the opportunities available for profit on a globalized theatre circuit. The inclusion of *The Shaughraun* in the Abbey's centenary programme arises from a desire by an entrepreneur – John McColgan – to produce a globalized Irish theatre product with a proven record of accomplishment. The financial success of McColgan's production reveals the Abbey's historical confusion between having national and popular success: sometimes a successful national theatre is one that irritates its patrons beyond endurance, as we saw in Chapter 3. The criticisms of the Abbey's centenary programme reveal, however, that an appetite exists for a theatre with a national remit, but shows also that such a national theatre should be grounded in a civic rather than an ethnic or essentialist conception of its role in relation to the nation. This discussion also reveals that the concept of the 'national' remains viable within theatrical discourse. The purpose of the next chapter is to explore the place of 'nation' within critical discourse in more detail, by considering the career of Martin McDonagh.

Part III   Globalization and Cultural Exchanges

5
Globalizing Authorship: Martin McDonagh, 1996/2003

A psychopathic killer is on the loose. Bodies are turning up in strange places. The police are developing elaborate theories but getting nowhere. And the killer has been given a catchy nickname – 'The Pillowman'.

To those familiar with Martin McDonagh's works, this passage might seem a loose description of his 2003 play *The Pillowman*. It is, however, a sketch of an episode from Salman Rushdie's 1999 novel *The Ground Beneath Her Feet* in which a serial killer called Cyrus Cama is responsible for murders in Mysore, Bangalore, and Madras. Unable to 'stand the anonymity' brought by his nickname, Rushdie's Pillowman sends 'a boastful letter to all the relevant police chiefs, incriminating himself while insisting that he would never be caught by such duffers as they' (136). He is later captured and incarcerated, but proves popular with his guards.[1]

There are obvious differences between McDonagh's play and Rushdie's novel, as well as some interesting parallels. The most amoral moments of violence in *The Pillowman* are performed by Michal, who acts out his brother's grim tales of infanticide, apparently unaware of the moral consequence of doing so. He is caught rather easily by the police and, unlike Rushdie's character, lacks the mental capacity to take responsibility for his actions. And although he displays some pride in his achievements – 'I'm getting quite good at it', he tells Katurian – he cannot be described as boastful (McDonagh, 2003: 49).

What both texts have in common is their characters' need to be recognized for their achievements: Katurian is willing to sacrifice his life in the hope that his stories will survive, while Cyrus Cama appears to view incarceration as an acceptable price for being recognized as the killer that he is. And there is of course the use of the same name – the Pillowman – in texts that in both cases focus on actions that are 'profoundly disordered, utterly immoral and highly dangerous' (Rushdie, 1999: 137).

When confronted with these details, it is possible to form erroneous conclusions about who is influencing whom here. Rushdie's novel appeared four years before McDonagh's play premiered in London, so one might assume that McDonagh's use of the 'Pillowman' name is an example of his tendency to quote gleefully from a wide range of cultural sources or, as Chris Morash – borrowing from Baudrillard – puts it, to produce 'copies that have forgotten their originals' (2001: 269). Yet McDonagh told Fintan O'Toole (2006: 44) that his play was written in 1994 and we also know that *The Pillowman* was first performed by Druid Theatre in a reading in Galway in 1997 – long before Rushdie's novel appeared.[2] It is reasonable to assume that Rushdie was not borrowing from McDonagh's text, given that its existence was not widely known until 2003; and it is impossible that McDonagh was quoting from Rushdie. We can only conclude therefore that both authors, writing around the same time, happened to use the same name – which appears nowhere else – in stories that describe similar events. That is, the affinity looks like a strange, but interesting, coincidence.

This resemblance points to the difficulty of dealing with such issues as influence, intention, and intertextuality in a globalizing theatre culture – issues that become problematic when we attempt to consider McDonagh's place in the Irish dramatic tradition. We know that McDonagh borrowed the title of *A Skull in Connemara* (1997) from Beckett's *Waiting for Godot* (1955), and *The Lonesome West* (1997) from Synge's *Playboy of the Western World* (Beckett, 1986: 43; Synge, 1982: 65). The first play in *The Leenane Trilogy*, *The Beauty Queen of Leenane* (1996), shows traces of both Tom Murphy's *Bailegangaire* and Beckett's *Endgame* (1956), while *The Pillowman* bears some interesting resemblances to Garry Mitchell's *The Force of Change* (2000), another text written after McDonagh's play, but published before it. However, McDonagh has refuted suggestions that he was influenced by the Irish dramatic tradition when he wrote *The Leenane Trilogy*, and has tended to reject attempts to link his work with that of other Irish writers. McDonagh explains that, although his work can be compared to Synge's, that writer did not influence his composition of the Leenane plays:

[a]s soon as I started writing the first scene [of *A Skull*], I realized it was completely fresh for me and I wasn't harking back to anything I had seen or read. I can see similarities now. I read *The Playboy of the Western World* and the darkness of the story amazed me. I thought it

would be one of those classics that you read in order to have read, rather than to enjoy, but it was great. At the time, though, I didn't know it at all.

(quoted by O'Toole, 1997a: 1)

Notwithstanding McDonagh's denial of having been influenced by Synge, he has been compared to that writer more frequently than to any other (cf. Richards, 2003; Lanters, 2000; Vandevelde, 2000).

Arguably, Synge is such a strong presence in McDonagh's work due to the influence of Garry Hynes on his writing. Both at the Abbey and at Druid, Hynes has had an enormous impact on the development of contemporary Irish playwriting.[3] She has commissioned and directed many of the most significant plays in the contemporary Irish repertoire, including Murphy's *Bailegangaire* and Carr's *Portia Coughlan*. Questions about McDonagh's work should thus include a consideration of Hynes's influence on his writing. Contrary to Richard Eyre's assertion that McDonagh had 'sprung from the womb a fully-fledged playwright' (quoted by Bradley, 1997), Hynes did not just discover McDonagh but developed him too – working with him to cut scenes and lines from his original scripts, which developed through many drafts (see Ross, 2003). For example, *The Lonesome West* originally involved only three characters, two brothers and a female character from England; it was only in later drafts that the female character became Girleen, while Father Welsh was added.[4] Questions about the impact of Synge on McDonagh might start with Hynes, whose reputation is founded on her productions of *The Playboy of the Western World*.

As McDonagh acknowledges when he states that 'I can see similarities now', the comparison of his work to Synge's is certainly valid – but comparison to other authors is also possible. For example, a feature of four of McDonagh's six produced plays is the reappearance of characters who are presumed dead by the audience: Mairtin in *Skull* (1999: 118), Billy in *The Cripple of Inishmaan* (1996: 61), the mute girl in *Pillowman* (2004: 95), and Wee Thomas in his 2001 play *The Lieutenant of Inishmore* (56). There is certainly a parallel between these reappearances and the 'resurrection' of Old Mahon in Synge's *Playboy of the Western World*, particularly in the case of Mairtin in *A Skull in Connemara*. Yet we could also compare this feature of McDonagh's plays with elements of other cultural forms – with, for example, the surprising return of apparently dead characters in soap opera (such as Harold Bishop in the Australian serial *Neighbours*, 'Dirty' Den Watts in the BBC's *Eastenders*, or Bobby Ewing in the American show *Dallas*). It might also be compared to a scene in

Quentin Tarantino's *Reservoir Dogs* (1992), in which Mr Orange (a character presumed to be unconscious by the audience) shoots Mr Blonde. Yet, whereas McDonagh denies being influenced by Synge, he has often spoken of his indebtedness to Australian soap and Tarantino.

Just as critics have shown themselves generally unwilling to explore the influences that McDonagh himself acknowledges, so too have they ignored his desire to avoid being categorized as an Irish dramatist. Only Merriman (2004) has attempted to broaden analysis of McDonagh's works into a non-Irish context. But he does so as a mode of negative criticism, suggesting that the *Leenane Trilogy* offers 'a kind of voyeuristic aperture on the antics of white trash whose reference point is more closely aligned to the barbarous conjurings of Jerry Springer than to the continuities of an indigenous tradition of dramatic writing' (254). Most other critics attempt to define McDonagh's importance in national terms – to consider his place in the Irish literary canon or to present him as an example of the British style of *in-yer-face* theatre (as in Sierz, 2001: 219–25). Yet McDonagh resists the attempt to categorize himself as either Irish or British:

> I always felt somewhere kind of in-between . . . I felt half-and-half and neither, which is good . . . I'm happy having a foot in both camps. I'm not into any kind of definition, any kind of -ism, politically, socially, religiously, all that stuff. It is not that I don't think about those things, but I've come to a place where the ambiguities are more interesting than choosing a strict path and following it.
>
> (quoted by O'Toole, 1997a: 1)

So the attempt to relate McDonagh's works to nationalized categories tends to lead to frustration. For Mary Luckhurst (2004), he is a turncoat Irishman, 'selling out' to the British – a 'thoroughly establishment figure who relies on monolithic, prejudicial constructs of rural Ireland to generate himself an income' (40). Quoting from a selection of McDonagh's media interviews, Luckhurst presents the anti-Irish responses to *The Lieutenant of Inishmore* from the British press as evidence that the playwright is deliberately 'forging speech patterns and representations that build on prejudicial constructs [in Britain] of the Irish as little more than boneheaded buffoons' (38). Many others have attacked McDonagh on similar grounds, and the debate about whether his work has value – or whether it can be seen as 'really' Irish (whatever that is) or 'actually' English – continues to polarize scholars of his work.

In provoking such responses as these, McDonagh's work can indeed be related to other Irish plays: for example, Luckhurst's critique of

The Lieutenant seems eerily similar to Brendan Behan's self-referential response to similar attacks on his own work in *The Hostage* (1958):

SOLDIER: Brendan Behan, he's too anti-British
OFFICER: Anti-Irish, you mean. Bejasus, wait till we get him back home. We'll give him what for for making fun of the Movement.
SOLDIER: [To the audience] He doesn't mind coming over here and taking your money
PAT: He'd sell his country for a pint.

(Behan, 1978: 204)

The accusation that McDonagh is 'selling out' to the British – or, as Behan has it, 'coming over here and taking your money' – means that his work can be located not in an Irish literary tradition, but rather in an Irish *critical* tradition, in which scholars express concern about the reception of Irish plays abroad. In such criticism, there is a tendency to conflate authorial intention with audience response, to assume that if a playwright's works are received in ways that give rise to national stereotyping, the author must be deliberately 'cashing in' on the existence of such prejudice.

In part, this confusion between intention and reception arises because scholars place excessive weight on comments made by or attributed to McDonagh in press interviews – which are frequently full of inaccuracies, exaggerations, omissions, and inconsistencies. For instance, Mimi Kramer, writing for *Time Magazine* in 1997, reported correctly that the performance in the West End of *The Leenane Trilogy* and *The Cripple of Inishmaan* made McDonagh 'the only writer this season, apart from Shakespeare, to have four plays running concurrently in London' (71). This report transformed quickly into the downright silly assertion that McDonagh was the first playwright *since* Shakespeare to have four of his plays running in London, a claim first made by Sean O'Hagan which has appeared subsequently in many outlets (32). Moving from inaccuracy to inconsistency, it is also notable that many different dates have been given for the composition of McDonagh's plays. For example, Liz Hoggard reports that McDonagh wrote *The Lieutenant of Inishmore* 'after the failure in 1996 of the first IRA ceasefire' (12). Yet (as I discuss below) Dening (2001) suggests that its composition predates that of *The Cripple of Inishmaan* (12), while O'Toole claims that the play was written in 1994, simultaneously with McDonagh's five other produced plays (2006: 44). When readers are confronted with such obviously exaggerated claims – or with so many apparently contradictory statements by

McDonagh – they seem to have concluded that the writer himself might be something of a fraud.

This problem, however, appears to arise from the conditions under which theatre journalism is commissioned and received in the mass media. Many (though of course not all) of the writers commissioned by newspaper editors to interview McDonagh seem to know little about drama, often characterizing him as 'the perfect playwright for People Who Dread Theatre' (Hoggard, 2002: 11). The presentation of McDonagh in this way may, as Luckhurst argues, have helped to market his plays. Perhaps, however, it also reveals the attitudes of commissioning editors to theatre which, in the case of McDonagh, reveals a tendency to focus on those elements of the medium that are assumed to be of interest to a non-theatregoing audience: violence, the deliberate provocation of controversy, iconoclasm, and an air of not taking oneself too seriously. In any case, it reveals the need to be cautious about using McDonagh's media interviews as a way of interpreting his plays.

Furthermore, it is surprising, given the intensity of debate that surrounds his work, that critics have been reluctant to explore McDonagh's statements about the writers and artists who actually have influenced him. This neglect may arise because, at the beginning of his career, McDonagh sometimes spoke dismissively of others' work. For instance, Richard Eyre reports that when McDonagh was asked what he thought of the 1997 opening of David Hare's *Skylight*, he replied 'well, I didn't write it so it's crap' (364) – a comment that encapsulates well the tone of his remarks at that time.[5] Critics' objections to this (apparent) arrogance may explain their unwillingness to take McDonagh more seriously. Certainly, his dismissal of other writers has tended to overshadow his discussion of those dramatists whom he admires. He spoke in his first interviews about his indebtedness to Mamet and Pinter; he told Fintan O'Toole that his use of the 'Irish' voice in his first plays arose from a deliberate decision to disguise the influence of those two writers (1997a: 1). At that time, he also referred to his high regard for such plays as Mamet's *American Buffalo* (1975), Pinter's *The Birthday Party* (1958), Shepard's *True West* (1980), and Tracey Letts's *Killer Joe* (1993), and the influence of such texts may certainly be found in *The Leenane Trilogy*. In 2001, McDonagh spoke frankly about the influences he had drawn on for *The Lieutenant of Inishmore*, describing that play as 'much more in the Joe Orton tradition than in any tradition of Irish drama' – a statement that seems accurate if the play is considered in relation to Orton's *Loot* (1965). And throughout his career to date, he has spoken of how his writing has been informed by his admiration for others' work: for the films of Tarantino, Martin

Scorsese, John Woo, Sam Peckinpah, and Terrence Malick; for Australian soap opera; for the music of the Pogues, The Clash, Nirvana, and the Sex Pistols; and for the fictions of Nabokov and Borges.

What is notable about McDonagh's range of influences is its eclecticism. He reads Argentinean fiction, saying of Borges that 'it's from him I began to appreciate the importance of telling a story' (*Galway Advertiser*, 1996: 23).[6] He enjoys independent cinema from the United States and Hong Kong. He moves easily from Pinter to Kurt Cobain to *Neighbours*. In citing such influences, he is far from unusual: the popularity of his works arises partially because audiences share a similarly broad range of cultural interests and are conversant with the wide range of forms from which he quotes.

Of course, Irish writers have always pointed out the importance of international culture to their work (an issue that I will explore further in the next chapter). McDonagh could be seen as different from other Irish dramatists in that his work crosses more easily the boundaries between high and low cultural forms, but again he is not unusual in this respect. Mark O'Rowe draws liberally from Asian cinema in such plays as *Made in China* (2001) and *Howie the Rookie* (1999); his 2007 play *Terminus* features a running gag about the Bette Midler romantic comedy *Beaches* (1988). McPherson's *The Weir* (1997) and *Shining City* (2003) are dependent for their impact on audiences' enjoyment of old-fashioned ghost stories, and appeared in a period when supernatural plot twists were being made popular by such filmmakers as M. Knight Shyamalan in *The Sixth Sense* (1999). Brian Friel makes extensive use of popular American song in his works, notably in *Dancing at Lughnasa* and *Wonderful Tennessee*; and as I've already shown, both plays reveal the influence of Tennessee Williams. To consider these writers' work in an exclusively Irish context is to overlook many features of their drama, both in terms of its composition and audiences' familiarity with the internationalized cultural forms from which these authors draw.

The difficulty for scholars who attempt to come to terms with such elements of McDonagh's work is that existing analysis of it is grounded in a national literary model. As such, the methodology presupposes a stable 'Irish' tradition in which McDonagh's plays may be located – and further assumes that inclusion in that tradition should be determined by literary value. How, then, can we accommodate such issues as the influence of Tarantino, Pinter, and Mamet – or the impact of 'low' cultural forms such as soap opera – on McDonagh's work? One solution might be to see McDonagh's work as part of a 'world' literary tradition, but again this gives rise to problems. McDonagh may be considered in relation to a vast array of other writers, from Synge to Borges to Rushdie – and no doubt, the list of other writers who might also be considered is a long one. However, there is an obvious impracticality in studying his writing without regard for literary or national boundaries. 'What can one make of such an idea?' asks Claudio Guillen (1993), describing the possibility of studying world literature as 'unattainable in practice, worthy not of an actual reader but a deluded keeper of archives who is also a multimillionaire' (38). As the overlap between *The Pillowman* and *The Ground Beneath Her Feet* indicates, a consideration of McDonagh's work in an international context can at best alert us to interesting coincidences. Furthermore, notions of a world literary system make the same presupposition as national literary systems: that inclusion in the canon or system is determined by notions of physical space and an author's ability to meet predetermined criteria about literary or artistic worth.

I suggest, then, that the debates created by scholars' attempts to categorize McDonagh in terms of a national literary canon arise because of a clash between the assumptions underlying literary criticism on the one hand, and the globalized quality of much contemporary cultural production and reception on the other. In other words, we are attempting to use a nationalized discourse to analyse work that has transcended national boundaries. Work by such playwrights as McDonagh needs to be understood not in relation to an international or world literary system, but instead in terms of a globalized framework, grounded in national traditions but engaging with ideas from other cultures. Doing so allows us to consider more fully the issues of hybridity, intertextuality, and aesthetic value in McDonagh's plays, while also pointing us towards new ways of understanding the works of other dramatists, both Irish and international. To make this case, I want to consider McDonagh's drama in relation to some of the influences he has himself cited, considering how a criticism that styles itself as national – as both Irish and British dramatic criticism currently does – may be used to understand the work of such globalized writers as McDonagh.

'Everybody Needs Good Neighbours': McDonagh and soap opera

When considering the national qualities of McDonagh's work, it seems appropriate to begin with the issue of setting. All of McDonagh's Irish plays are set in identifiable locations – in Leenane, a small town in the north of County Galway, and on the Aran Islands, which lie off the coast of the same county. The setting of *The Pillowman* is by comparison quite vague. 'Kamenice', Werner Huber (2005) notes, 'is a very common place-name in the Slavonic settlement areas of East Central Europe. Thus, we find, for example, Česká Kamenice (in Bohemia, Czech Republic), and also Saska Kamenice (in Saxony, where the German form is "Chemnitz")' (2004: 285). It is possible, therefore, to relate the settings of each of the plays to existing locations. McDonagh has stated, however, that his decision to choose such settings has largely been arbitrary. Speaking to Penelope Dening (2001) about the composition of *The Lieutenant of Inishmore*, he claims that play was set on the Aran Islands only because 'for plot purposes, [he] needed "a place in Ireland that would take a long time to get to from Belfast". Inishmore fitted the bill. Three Aran Islands prompted the idea of a trilogy' (12). This decision about the setting of *Inishmore* in turn led to McDonagh's *Cripple of Inishmaan* and the as yet unproduced *Banshees of Inisheer*.

The arbitrary manner in which these places were chosen implies that, for McDonagh, plot rather than setting is of primary importance: he is not trying to provide an authentic representation of the places he portrays, but instead chooses locations that are appropriate to the stories he wants to tell. Hence, in the case of Leenane, we are told that (as is true in almost every Irish town) there is a church and graveyard, but we are given no sense of their location in relation to the homes of the characters, or to other places in the town. Similarly, we are told that Father Welsh 'drowned himself in the lake last night' (1999: 177), which seems rather unusual, given that the largest body of water in or near Leenane is not a lake, but Killary Harbour, an area of great natural beauty that dominates Leenane but which is never mentioned in *The Trilogy*. We learn even less about the real world from McDonagh's presentation of the Aran Islands in *Cripple* and *Lieutenant*. The running joke in the latter play about Davey's pink bicycle (4) presumably arises from McDonagh's knowledge that cycling is the principal mode of transportation on Inis Mór, but there are few accurate references to the local geography – to the prehistoric forts, the stone walls, or the windswept character of foliage and shrubbery. The plotting of *Lieutenant* also reveals a marked lack of interest in geographical accuracy. Padraic arrives on Inishmore at night, meeting Mairead by 'moonlight' (McDonagh, 2001: 32), after which Donny and Davey go to sleep at five in the morning, or 'early blue dawn' (36). Padraic does not arrive at his father's house until seven hours later, at 'twelve noon', according to the stage directions (38). Given Padraic's concern for his cat, one would assume that he would go immediately to his father's house. Yet, because the entire island of Inis Mór is just less than 12 kilometres in length, it seems strange that it takes Padraic at least ten hours to travel there from the island's harbour (the entire journey from Northern Ireland to the Aran Islands could be completed in about seven hours).

And of course, there is never any reference in either of the published *Aran Islands* plays to Irish, the first language of the islanders. The language used by McDonagh's characters also fails to display any of the regional variations that would be evident in the speech of people from different parts of Ireland. Although we are told that Christy, Brendan, and Joey 'all have Northern Irish accents' in *Lieutenant* (27), this is not evident in the script, and was not made evident in its premiere production for the Royal Shakespeare Company (RSC) in 2001.

This lack of geographical authenticity is also evident in *The Pillowman*, which offers us no insight into the kind of society that Katurian lives in. We're told that it is a totalitarian state, but it is unclear what form of totalitarianism is in operation. The references to the city's Jewish Quarter do not provoke any of the expressions of anti-Semitism that might be expected in a fascist European state (26) and, because the power of the 'Little Jesus' story arises from its breaking of religious taboos, it seems unlikely to be a communist country. What seems most likely is that the decision to set the play in a totalitarian state arose simply from McDonagh's desire to raise the dramatic stakes, by making the possibility that Katurian will be executed for his writing seem credible – another example of his prioritization of plotting over place.

There is little reference to contemporary politics in any of McDonagh's plays: we get brief allusions to the Yugoslav civil wars of the early 1990s in *The Lonesome West*, but have no sense of how politics function within the Ireland being presented onstage. This absence of political awareness is notable in *The Lieutenant of Inishmore*, a play that ostensibly attacks certain strands of Irish political thought while making no reference to any of the figures actually involved in Irish terrorism. The only real people referred to in the play are victims of the Northern Ireland Troubles. McDonagh includes 'jokes' in his play about the Guildford Four (33), wrongly convicted of involvement in terrorism; he also invites us to laugh at the victims of the Bloody Sunday shootings by the British Army in Derry in 1972 (28). And his characters allude to four victims of IRA violence: Timothy Parry and Jonathan Ball, the children (aged twelve and three respectively) killed by the 1993 IRA bombing of Warrington, England; and Stephen Melrose and Nicholas Spanos, two Australian tourists shot dead in The Netherlands in 1990 when they were mistaken for off-duty British soldiers by the IRA.[7] That the deaths of these people are used for humorous purposes, while their murderers – and their apologists – are satirized only in general terms, reflects poorly on McDonagh, and reveals how the politics of *The Lieutenant of Inishmore* relate only superficially to the conflict in Northern Ireland.

This discussion reveals that taking McDonagh literally can lead only to absurdity: the places that he uses may all be found on a map, but local knowledge of these places is not displayed by the author, required of the audience, or communicated by the plays – a feature apparent in the Irish plays of Boucicault. To require of McDonagh's work such features as authenticity and accuracy in the presentation of political and social facts is to miss the point of his works entirely. McDonagh's Leenane, Inishmore, and Inishmaan should not be thought of as being similar to O'Casey's or McPherson's Dublin, Friel's Ballybeg, Mitchell's Belfast, Carr's midlands, or Murphy's Tuam. Rather, the function of place in McDonagh's works is to aid international audiences' understanding of the plays. This, I argue, is not an example of McDonagh's indebtedness to Irish drama, but rather an example of how his works may be considered in relation to soap opera.

Much has been written of McDonagh's interest in this form of television. 'We'd get up at 12:00, 1:00', John McDonagh told the American media in 1998, describing the lifestyle he shared with his brother in their London home in the early 1990s. 'We'd have breakfast; we'd watch Australian soap operas on the television; and then he'd go to his room, and I'd go to mine, and we'd twiddle our thumbs, and maybe we'd write something, and then come down and have something to eat at 6:00, and start watching television again' (NBC News 1998). Comments like these have often been quoted in discussion of McDonagh's work, used as evidence to support the claim that the playwright learned his dramatic craft not from the great authors of world theatre, but from watching such Australian soap operas as *Neighbours* and *Home and Away*. Do these claims have any validity?

McDonagh's plays reached Australia at a time when that country was undergoing a growth in cultural self-confidence: like Ireland, it was becoming more aware of itself as occupying a role on the global stage, and culture was an element of its attempt to come to terms with this development. Hence, media coverage, both of the original 1998 Druid production and the 1999 touring Sydney Theatre Company production directed by Garry Hynes, focused more on what the plays might be saying to Australia, than on what they might be saying about Ireland. The Irish origin and setting of the plays were certainly considered, but when the question of authenticity arose, it was treated as if the reader would understand that the plays are self-evidently inauthentic. One report of the visit of the touring production to Canberra encapsulates this well, telling readers that 'of course it's not an Ireland that exists any longer', and that 'one might argue that *The Beauty Queen of Leenane* is actually a post-modern play written about the stage Irish more than the real people' (Eccles, 2000: A.12).

Considerably more attention was paid to McDonagh's use of Australian soap opera. In an article headlined 'Aussie Soaps: McDonagh Comes Clean', Joyce Morgan asked a question that was preoccupying the Australian press at that time: 'did he really learn to write plays by watching *Neighbours*?'. The answer proves inconclusive. Morgan states that while he was in Australia, McDonagh was 'amused to keep hearing the rumour that he learned how to write plays by [watching] Australian soap', but 'acknowledges there's a spot of truth' in the rumour. 'I was unemployed for a long time and when you are unemployed in England all you do is watch soaps ... and most of them are Australian', McDonagh stated. 'Hey,' he asked. 'You don't know when they're on here, do you?' (27). Hynes was also asked for her views on the subject. 'Australian soaps entertain a lot of people, otherwise they wouldn't be as popular as they are', she told the Sydney *Daily Telegraph*. 'Martin entertains people, so the connection is quite apt really'. This might seem a rather weak link, but later in that interview, Hynes states that 'Australian soaps have made a very big contribution to these plays, and to the writer generally' (quoted by Chisholm, 1997: 45). This 'contribution' was underlined when Maggie Kirkpatrick – best known in Ireland and the UK for her role in the Australian soap *Prisoner, Cell Block H* – starred in the 1999 touring Australian production of *The Beauty Queen* directed by Hynes. So while Irish critics worried about Australians taking McDonagh literally, in Australia, his plays appear to have become part of that country's debate about how its own cultural exports play out for overseas audiences.

A number of studies of soap opera in Britain, Australia, and the United States have been published in recent years, appearing mostly in the field of cultural studies – with the result that scholarship in this area has tended to explore the relationship of the genre to such issues as gender (see Blumenthal, 1997; Brundson, 2000; and Mumford, 1995), ethnicity (Gillespie, 1994), and social class (Seiter *et al.*, 1991). As yet, few studies have attempted to explore the relationship between soap opera and literature. Where comparisons are made, the tendency is to state that soap opera draws on such literary forms as melodrama (see Ang, 1985) and the 19th century realist novel (Hobson, 2003: 28), but little work has appeared suggesting that the influence might work in the opposite direction – that literature might draw on soap operatic conventions. I suggest, therefore, that McDonagh's plays and Australian soap opera function in similar ways when they leave their national cultures for the global market.

All of the major international soaps are set in broadly identifiable geographical locations. *Eastenders* and *Brookside* are set in the English cities of London and Liverpool respectively, *Neighbours* takes place in Melbourne, and is one of the most successful soaps of all time is *Dallas*. The function of these settings is not to represent a place that its inhabitants will recognize as their own, or to perform a localized culture for audiences living elsewhere. Rather, these locations give audiences a sense that the stories being presented are credible, because the action is situated in an ostensibly authentic setting that will be recognizable to them. That recognizability is not provided by viewers' knowledge of the real locations of London, Liverpool, Brisbane, or Dallas, but instead by the programme-makers' inclusion of local markers that are understood both nationally and internationally to refer to those places. Just as McDonagh (following Boucicault) provides picture-postcard presentations of Ireland that had no purchase on geographical realities, soap-makers provide landscapes or cityscapes that conform to outsiders' expectations, as seen in the use in *Coronation Street* of an iconic row of terraced houses to represent the north of England, in *Eastenders* by the use in the titles of a map of London, or in the perennially good weather of *Home and Away's* Summer Bay and *Neighbours'* Melbourne. Likewise, accent tends to be of a generic regional variety (London speech in *Eastenders*, the Texan tones of J.R. Ewing in *Dallas*), using a homogenized form of English peppered with easily understood local slang and pronunciations, ensuring that the dialogue is both localized and easily understood across regional and national boundaries.

The use of settings that are simultaneously recognizable and exotic or 'other' accounts for the popularity of soap opera across national boundaries, a phenomenon related to the genre's capacity to allow viewers to identify selectively with characters, themes, and storylines without needing localized knowledge. Dorothy Hobson claims that this makes soap opera a 'universal form', but I think her description of it makes clear that she's referring to the capacity of the genre to facilitate the kinds of reflexive response I described in Chapter 4:

Audiences bring their own experience, knowledge, preferences and understanding to every television text they watch. They interpret the text according to what they choose to take from it and this may change according to their own circumstances and experiences. . . . [V]iewers always highlight areas which have interested them and discuss the programme in a way which is driven by their specific interest. . . . This is not just a negotiated reading or a polysemic understanding, but rather an active choice of what aspects of the programme they wish to take. They subconsciously edit out stories and themes that are not of interest, and they see in every work aspects which are of interest to themselves.

(Hobson, 2003: 166–7)

This process of selective identification is enhanced by the emphasis on storytelling in the genre. Soap tends to involve occasionally outrageous plotting, with the return of characters presumed dead a relatively regular phenomenon, which, as mentioned above, is also a recurrent feature of McDonagh's writing. Such storylines function within the genre by the creation of rules of internal credibility, which is aided by the relative stability of character development, whereby the moral parameters of the soap environment are delineated by the consistency of characters' responses to the events presented. Characters in soap opera thus tend to represent single character traits (the lustful villainy of J.R. Ewing in *Dallas* or Dirty Den in *Eastenders*, the down-to-earth decency of every soap's patriarch or matriarch), or to embody a single issue of social importance (homosexuality, single parenthood, drug abuse, etc). The movement of soap opera plotting is thus not teleological, as is the case in drama or prose fiction, but circular: since soap can be continued indefinitely, it is essential that its primary characters remain relatively unchanged – their circumstances may alter but their character traits must remain firmly in place.

We can see many of these features in the work of McDonagh. As stated above, his work reproduces many of the staples of soap opera plotting: unrequited love (between Billy and Helen in *Cripple* and Girleen and Father Welsh in *The Lonesome West*), domestic discord (between Mag and Maureen in *Beauty Queen* and Coleman and Valene in *The Lonesome West*), and unfulfilled ambition (Tom's desire to be promoted within the Irish police in *Skull*, Billy's trip to Hollywood in *Cripple*). Similarly, McDonagh's action is centred on the development of plot rather than character, with the result that none of the people he presents ever changes. Valene and Coleman, and Ariel and Tupolski will continue to bicker; Billy will resume life on Inishmaan (perhaps with tuberculosis), as will most of the surviving characters in Leenane. The reference in *The Lonesome West* to the brutal behaviour of the under-12s' football team suggests that the population of the town is trapped in a cycle of eternal recurrence, with the children behaving much as the adults do (168). And, no doubt, Wee Thomas will not wait long after the conclusion of *The Lieutenant of Inishmore* before setting off on another 'two-day bender chasing skirt the length of the island' (48). The only alterations to the circumstances of the characters arise through death (as in the case of Mag and Father Welsh in *The Leenane Trilogy*, Mad Padraic in *The Lieutenant of Inishmore* and Katurian and Michal in *The Pillowman*) or emigration (as with Mairead in *Lieutenant* and Pato in *Beauty Queen*). And, most importantly, McDonagh's Ireland relates closely to the Melbourne of *Neighbours* or the London of *Eastenders*. The place being presented does not correspond to geographical, political, or social realities. Instead, it is presented to affirm audiences' presuppositions about those locations.

An excellent example of how those presuppositions can vary from place to place is the contrasting responses of audiences in Leenane and Inishmore – two places that McDonagh himself presents as interchangeable – to *The Beauty Queen*. During the first scene of the play, Mag and Maureen debate the merits of the Irish language. Irish, says Mag, 'sounds like nonsense to me. Why can't they just speak English like everybody? . . . Where would Irish get you going for a job in England? Nowhere' (14–15). Mac Dubhghaill (1996) explains that Mag's statement exposes a 'deeply-felt conviction, held in many Gaeltacht communities, that Irish is of no value' (12). This feeling, he suggests, is 'not often articulated openly in public, for fear of jeopardizing the community's chances of getting any grants that might be going' (12). The expression of this sentiment on the Aran Islands is thus breaking a taboo: it means that someone 'on stage [is] saying what many privately feel, and the audience [in Inishmore] is loving it' (12). When the play was performed in Leenane itself, however, the audience was silent during the same scene, because, Mac Dubhghaill claims, Mag's opinion came as 'an unwelcome reminder in an area where the decision to abandon Irish as a community language is still uncomfortably close' (12).

This example shows how the notion of a homogeneous 'Irish' response to any play is problematic. It is also a reminder that Druid Theatre actually brought McDonagh's work on tour around Ireland – a process that is a key element of branding productions for international consumption. This is an excellent example of how Irish theatre often derives its authenticity from its relationship with real physical spaces, but achieves success from its ability to travel freely from those spaces.

A further example of this phenomenon is the variety of international responses to *The Lieutenant of Inishmore*. Premiered in early 2001, the play

was initially controversial because of its treatment of animals; but attitudes towards the play changed markedly after the 11 September 2001
attacks on the United States. The play's treatment of terrorism resonated
with audiences struggling to come to terms with Britain's role in the
emerging 'War against Terror'. *The Lieutenant's* London run coincided
with the posting of tanks at Heathrow Airport, the posting of British
troops to Afghanistan, and the passage of strict anti-terrorist laws
through the British parliament. The play was presented as a way for
British audiences to come to terms with the threat of terrorism, by
laughing at it. Wilson Milam, the director of the RSC production, recalls
seeing 'American tourists milling around after performances shortly
after 9/11 . . . They would talk about how it was a marvellous thing for
them to see. That it did help them to go through their own experience
and come out with a viewpoint of what was valuable in life' (quoted by
Crawley, 2003: 2–3).

By September 2003, *The Lieutenant* had been translated into 28 languages and produced in 39 countries (Crawley, 2003: 1), where it was
frequently received as an explicit commentary on the 'War against
Terror'. For example, in December 2003, Mehmet Ergen directed his own
translation of the play in Turkey, only weeks after a series of devastating
terrorist bombs in Istanbul. The reception of the play was therefore conditioned by Turkish audiences' actual confrontation with terrorism. As
Susannah Clapp writes, 'some of the cast thought they should cancel [the
production]. They had all heard about people picking up body parts in
the streets; the play ends with body parts strewn over the stage' (2003:
14). Similarly, in September 2003, Australia's Company B produced *The
Lieutenant* at the Belvoir Street Theatre in Sydney. One context for the
production was, undoubtedly, the terrorist bombings of a Bali nightclub
frequented mainly by Australians in 2002. However, the director of the
play, Neil Armfield, included *The Lieutenant* in a season that addressed his
conviction that Australia's political direction under John Howard was
'shameful'. While *The Lieutenant* was being performed, Armfield wrote
that, in Australian society, 'we're being taught values that don't seem to
represent good parenting – where is the sense of the primacy of tolerance,
understanding, sympathy, generosity? . . . We've been yoked to the pre-
emptive assertion of power, and it doesn't seem the right way to go. It's
about fear, not trust' (quoted by Low, 2003). This reference to the 'pre-
emptive assertion of power' appears to be an allusion to Australia's participation in the 2003 invasion of Iraq, suggesting that the reception of
The Lieutenant in that country was conditioned by Armfield's critique of
his government's militarism in Afghanistan and Iraq.

The productions in Istanbul, Sydney, and London appeared within 18 months of each other, but provoked a variety of responses. Audiences in Istanbul must have seen the play in relation to the atrocities carried out within a very short distance of the theatre itself. Conversely, audiences in Sydney were invited to see the play in the context of Armfield's protest against the foreign policy of the Australian government. McDonagh says that *The Lieutenant* was written from a position of 'pacifist rage' and that it is a 'violent play that is wholeheartedly anti-violence' (quoted by O'Hagan, 2001: 24). It is revealing that the play was presented in Istanbul mainly in the context of terrorist violence, whereas in Australia it was presented as a condemnation of state violence.

This variety of interpretations is an example of the reflexive quality of McDonagh's works, which are successful not because they are universal or local, but because they are sufficiently open to interpretation to be understood in multiple ways by different audiences. To that extent, they can be compared to soap opera, viewers of which 'interpret the text according to what they choose to take from it and this may change according to their own circumstances and experiences', as Hobson (2003) puts it (167). It should be noted that this feature of McDonagh's plays might also be observed in other cultural forms to which he has referred – notably Hollywood cinema.

Shallow graves or gravely shallow? McDonagh and 1990s cinema

The relationship between McDonagh's work and cinema has received some attention to date, focused principally on the intermediality of *The Cripple of Inishmaan*, which makes extensive reference to Robert Flaherty's 1934 documentary *Man of Aran*. Robin Roberts (2003) argues that McDonagh's play, together with *Stones In His Pockets*, 'use[s] the US film industry to represent the corrupting and dangerous influence of American media on Ireland' (111). Although this is an intriguing argument about the play, it doesn't explore McDonagh's consideration of how Irish filmmakers and actors (and Irish playwrights) might be complicit in the media representation of their country.

In contrast to Roberts, Werner Huber (2002) sees *The Cripple* as an example of how 'McDonagh metaphorically and rather cynically uses *Man of Aran* as a general emblem of the "crisis of representation" and as a broadside targeted at various images of Ireland'. He goes on to suggest that the play should be seen as an example of meta-cinema (14) – that is, he sees the play's main achievement as formal rather than thematic. While Roberts and Huber draw different conclusions, both make clear that *The Cripple of Inishmaan* can be seen as an attempt by McDonagh to use theatre as a means of commenting on the composition and reception of films about Ireland.

The film that appears most closely to resemble McDonagh's works is, interestingly, not one he has mentioned in any interviews: the 1994 British movie, *Shallow Grave*, directed by Danny Boyle. This film appeared shortly before *The Beauty Queen* premiered and was released during the period when most of McDonagh's plays were composed, if we are to believe the statements made by McDonagh to O'Toole in his 2006 *New Yorker* interview. Like *The Lieutenant of Inishmore*, *Shallow Grave* features intensely disturbing scenes of dismemberment, with the mild-mannered accountant David presented in Boyle's movie with his 'right arm . . . moving briskly back and forth accompanied by a vicious sawing noise' (45). Similarly, in *The Lieutenant*, a character named Davey will, together with Donny, 'hack away' at body parts, turning them into what McDonagh calls 'sizeable chunks' (55). As in *The Pillowman*, *Shallow Grave* features a pair of police officers investigating murders, who act to 'disconcert and destabilise' their suspects with 'asinine nonsense' (82). There is also a similarity between McDonagh's plays and this film in terms of setting and accent: *Shallow Grave* is set in Scotland, offering occasional moments of local colour that are not relevant to the plot (men in kilts, a traditional dance); and it features characters who will be broadly recognizable to middle class audiences throughout the West – an accountant, a doctor, and a journalist, each of whom speaks in a homogenized but mildly accented form of English. In a similar fashion, McDonagh's plays also present characters speaking in an English that is non-standard but easily understood, and who also occupy broadly recognizable social or familial roles – as shopkeepers, a priest, a pair of warring brothers, a dysfunctional mother and her daughter, and so on.

I would suggest, however, that the principle impact of the film on McDonagh's work has been in the area of reception, particularly in Britain. Together with Irvine Welsh's novel *Trainspotting* (1993) – which was adapted first as a play (1994) and then as a film also directed by Boyle in 1996 – *Shallow Grave* was instrumental in creating the trend in British culture for darkly humorous but intensely violent works of fiction. It also helped to cultivate audiences for the new wave of so called *in-yer-face* dramatists that emerged in Britain from 1996 onwards, one of whom was, as Aleks Sierz (2001) argues, McDonagh himself.

The resemblance of McDonagh's work to this British film is important because the area to which McDonagh's works are most frequently compared is the genre of gangster movies, particularly those from the United States. Some interesting overlaps emerge. For example, in a 2004 episode of the television Mafia serial *The Sopranos*, two members of Tony Soprano's crew travel to a farm in rural New Jersey to dig up the corpse of one of their victims, who was murdered many years before. The pair brings the remains to an outhouse where, using wooden mallets, they smash the victim's bones into powder before placing them in a sack and dumping them in a river. This moment recalls McDonagh's *Skull in Connemara*, which features an almost identical set-up, with two characters 'battering the shite' out of skeletons before 'eas[ing] them into the lake' (1999: 103). This similarity demonstrates how readily McDonagh's works may be compared to the genre of American films and television focusing on gangsters (particularly the Mafia) whose ethnicity as well as their behaviour marks them out as different from mainstream American society. McDonagh has often cited Scorsese and Tarantino as influences – though he has not elaborated much on how their impact can be found in his work. He has, however, spoken about the resemblance of his work to the films of Tarantino:

> I suppose I walk that line between comedy and cruelty [which is evident in Tarantino's films] because I think one illuminates the other. And, yeah, I tend to push things as far as I can because I think you can see things more clearly through exaggeration than through reality. It is like a John Woo or a Tarantino scene, where the characters are doing awful things and, simultaneously, talking about everyday things in a really humorous way. There is a humour in there that is straight-ahead funny and uncomfortable. It makes you laugh and think.
>
> (quoted by O'Hagan, 2001)

McDonagh's comments on the similarity between himself and Tarantino offer a way of thinking about his own works. Tarantino's earliest films, *True Romance* (1993) and *Reservoir Dogs*, can provide a template for analysing McDonagh's plays, particularly in relation to the self-referentiality of Tarantino's movies and his use of cultural forms that are regarded as either aesthetically or geographically peripheral.

Reservoir Dogs opens with a discussion of the meaning of a song by a popular cultural icon – Madonna – and posits a number of possible meanings for her early hit 'Like a Virgin'. It's 'all about a girl who digs a guy with a big dick', says Mr Brown in the film's opening line (3). This discussion of a woman's sexuality quickly moves into consideration of other women: of Vicki Lawrence, the 'cheatin' wife [who] shot Andy', and of the waitresses serving the gang of criminals their pre-heist breakfast. 'Waitressing', says Mr White, 'is the number one occupation for female non-college graduates in this country. It's the one job basically any woman can get, and make a living on' (10). This comment contrasts interestingly with the discussion of Madonna that has just concluded.

The movement in this scene is from the cultural to the social: from the representation of a woman as a sexual agent in Madonna's song to a discussion of the grim realities of life for women not unlike those described in Madonna's earliest work: the urban working classes. By making the opening scene of his film move along this arc, Tarantino instantly highlights to his audience two important themes. The first is the extent to which any form of culture – the pop song, in this case – can be a subject of debate, analysis, and multiple interpretations. The second is the manner in which the representation of people in popular culture diverges strongly from their social roles, particularly insofar as gender and social class are concerned. The film is, after all, centred on the idea of interpretation of performances – of the credibility of under-cover cop Mr Orange's performance as a gangster – and it draws attention to the need for audiences to relate cultural representations to their sources in society. Tarantino thus uses this opening scene to provide audiences with the interpretative tools needed to understand his film and appreciate it fully.

McDonagh's works operate in similar ways. His use of *Man of Aran* in *The Cripple of Inishmaan* provides audiences with an extended tutorial in how to interpret Irish culture. For example, the audience is moved by the apparent death of the play's protagonist Billy, whose last words are given in detail:

> Mam? I fear I'm not longer for this world, Mam. Can't I hear the wail of the banshees for me, as far as I am from me barren island home? A home barren, aye, but proud and generous with it, yet turned me back on ye I did, to end up alone and dying in a one-dollar rooming-house, without a mother to wipe the cold sweat off me, nor a father to curse death o'er the death of me, nor a colleen fair to weep tears o'er the still body of me. A body still, aye, but a body noble and unbowed with it. An Irishman!
>
> (McDonagh, 1997: 52)

This scene includes many examples of stage-Irish stereotypes, such as Billy's irregular speech patterns, the references to banshees, and his nobility in the face of death. Yet audiences are being primed to receive this inauthentic representation as if it were an integral part of the plot of *Inishmaan*: McDonagh appears to assume that they will react emotionally to the action's sentimental qualities. Those audiences are then embarrassed by the realization that what they had taken to be reality was a screen test for a Hollywood movie, and that Billy was not only unsuccessful in his attempts to gain the part for which he had been auditioning, but contemptuous of the lines he had been speaking:

> It wasn't an awful big thing at all to turn down Hollywood, with the arse-faced lines they had me reading for them. 'Can I not hear the wail of the banshees for me, as far as I am from me barren island home' . . . 'An Irishman I am, begora! With a heart and a spirit on me not crushed for a hundred years of oppression. I'll be getting me shillelagh out next, wait'll you see'. A rake of shite. And had me singing 'The Croppy Boy' then.
>
> (McDonagh, 1997: 63)

McDonagh is neither creating nor exploiting images of stage-Irish characters in this passage. Rather, he is highlighting his audiences' willingness to accept such images uncritically. This is an example of how his theatre demands of audiences that they apply more rigorous attention to their reception of mass-mediated cultural products, such as the Hollywood film for which Billy auditions.

Similarly, *The Lieutenant of Inishmore* draws repeatedly on existing modes of representation of Irish terrorism. The serious intent of *In the Name of the Father* (Sheridan, 1993) is undercut as McDonagh proposes that it might be a suitable date-movie for Padraic and Mairead, while Padraic's assertion that 'there's no boy-preferers involved in Irish terrorism' (33) can be read as a reference to Neil Jordan's *The Crying Game* (1992). The play also alludes to Irish rebel songs, to the presentation of republicanism on the Irish stage, and to media representations of terrorism in the UK. As such, *The Lieutenant* can be seen as offering audiences an opportunity to consider the validity and authenticity of previous representations of terrorism: the play, therefore, is again a tutorial of sorts on how culture might be understood.

This didactic pattern may also be identified in McDonagh's other works. As has been observed *ad nauseam* by critics, *The Leenane Trilogy* draws on existing modes of theatrical representation of the Irish to focus on issues of interpretation and analysis – about who killed whom, about the meaning of words such as 'unbear' in *The Lonesome West* (183), about whether 'splinter group' is one or two words in *The Lieutenant* (45), and about how Ireland is understood by American tourists. *The Pillowman* considers the issues of intention and responsibility in relation to artistic production, contrasting Katurian's (apparently disingenuous) assertion that 'the only duty of a storyteller is to tell a story' (7) with the way that his actions are motivated by many different senses of duty (particularly towards his brother).

Another similarity between McDonagh and Tarantino lies in the area of idiom and cultural influence. Tarantino's use of the word 'nigger' in his films has brought a large amount of criticism his way, notably from Spike Lee, who used part of his film *Bamboozled* (2000) to satirize a scene in *Pulp Fiction* (1994) in which a character, played by Tarantino himself, uses that epithet several times. The objection to Tarantino's films doesn't arise from his usage of African-American idiom specifically, but because it is often presented as a way of expressing sentiments that are violent, aggressive, or misogynistic, implying that there is an association between the acts themselves and the manner in which they are articulated. Hence, Jimmy, the character played by Tarantino, gives us the following rant:

> What's on my mind at this moment isn't the coffee in my kitchen, it's the dead nigger in my garage . . . Now let me ask you a question, Jules. When you drove in here, did you notice a sign out front that said, 'Dead nigger storage?' – Answer the Question. Did you see a sign out in front of my house that said, 'Dead nigger storage?' . . . You know why you didn't see that sign? . . . 'Cause storin' dead niggers ain't my fuckin' business!
>
> (1999: 146–8)

The gratuitous and callous manner in which these comments are uttered – and their delivery by Tarantino himself – suggests strongly that the epithet is being included solely for the purposes of provocation.

Yet Tarantino has countered such accusations. 'The word "nigger" is probably the most volatile word in the English language', he states. 'Should any word have that much power? I think it should be de-powered. But that's not my job. I don't have any political agenda in my work. I'm writing characters' (quoted in Keough, 1998). Tarantino thus presents himself as a storyteller, whose first duty is not to anyone's 'political agenda', but to his own plotting and characterization ('the only duty of a storyteller is to tell a story'). His use of African-American slang might also be compared to his inclusion of cultural forms that are regarded as in some respects marginal in his films: Blaxpoitation pictures, pulp fiction, Hong Kong martial arts films, and others.

McDonagh has been attacked on similar grounds. Merriman (2001) sees his work as presenting a range of 'theatrical freaks' to present a version of rural Ireland as a 'benighted dystopia' (59), and argues that the purpose of these presentations is to allow middle-class audiences to avoid facing their responsibilities for the genuinely marginalized members of Irish society. That critique is persuasive but, rather ironically, it only works if we assume that all Irish theatre audiences are middle-class people living in urban areas: as the analysis of audience response in Leenane and the Aran Islands above shows, writing about one 'Irish' audience is as much an act of homogenization as anything that McDonagh is doing. The 'caricaturing' of Irish people referred to by Merriman is principally in the area of speech, with the backwardness of McDonagh's characters being represented by an inarticulacy that is closely related to their Hiberno-English idiom. A case in point is Pato's speech of exilic longing in *Beauty Queen*: 'when it's there I am, it's here I wish I was . . . But when it's here I am . . . it isn't there I want to be, of course not. But I know it isn't here I want to be either' (1999: 22). In performance, this speech can be quite moving – but its pathos is communicated precisely by its simplicity, by Pato's inability to express with elegance thoughts that are complex and deeply felt. And, while this inarticulacy can be found in all of McDonagh's Irish plays, it is present in *The Pillowman* only in the speech of Michal, which could support the suggestion that McDonagh's plays seem to portray Irishness and mental disability as interchangeable categories.

For McDonagh, the use of Irish speech was a simple matter of aesthetics:

> I wanted to develop some kind of dialogue style as strange and heightened as those two [Mamet and Pinter], but *twisted* in some way so the influence wasn't as obvious. And then I sort of remembered the way my uncles spoke back in Galway, the structure of their sentences. I didn't think of it as structure, just as a kind of rhythm in the speech. And that seemed an interesting way to go, to try to do something with that language that wouldn't be English or American.
>
> (quoted by O'Toole, 1997a: 1)

His presentation of Irish speech as a 'twisted' form of English or American diction gives his plays the rhythm that he desired. Just as Tarantino denies that his use of African-American diction has any function within a 'social agenda', McDonagh similarly sees his use of Hiberno-English as a simple matter of storytelling. A difficulty arises from the disparity between authorial intention and reception, however: once Tarantino and McDonagh's works encounter an audience, they enter a social forum in which their use of idiom becomes problematic. As discussed above, however, the issue of accent and social marginalization is also a feature of soap opera, and of films other than American heist, Mafia, and gangster movies.

The discussion of *Shallow Grave* above reveals that the resemblance in McDonagh's work to particular cinematic styles is not (as has been suggested) to the genre of gangster film; nor is it exclusively a matter of him and Tarantino both using postmodern pastiche in their works. Rather, all three forms discussed thus far – 1990s cinema, McDonagh's plays, and the soap opera genre – have in common their ability to travel across international boundaries with ease, despite their use of regional or marginal idioms, settings, and forms. How, then, do these three forms function within a global context? And how did McDonagh's work make the transition from the national to the global?

Core and periphery in global culture

Literature and other 'high arts' have tended towards internationalization since the 19th century or earlier. The concept of a world literature (*weltliteratur*) was originally mooted by Goethe, and developed by Marx and Engels: the avant-garde, as well as the educated elite, of most countries have always tended towards the cosmopolitan. The impact of globalization on literature is manifested in the deterritorialization of the relationship between core and periphery in literary production. Pascale Casanova (1999) and Franco Moretti (2001) both argue that the current world literary system should be distinguished from those that existed in previous eras because it is founded upon a relationship of core and periphery: that it is a unitary system, but comprised of unequal parts. As Moretti writes, the system is '*one* and *unequal*: with a core, and a periphery (and a semiperiphery) that are bound together in a relationship of growing inequality' (56). In the area of theatre, Rustom Bharucha (2000) also argues that globalization involves an unequal relationship between core and periphery. He focuses on countries in the developing world, pointing out that the transfer of cultural productions in the West is governed by copyright, and involves authorship and (usually) the payment of royalties. He contrasts this with the 'cultural piracy' that has led to aspects of peripheral cultures being assimilated into the core.

While the insights of Bharucha, Casanova, and Moretti are useful, they may be used to obscure the extent to which the relationship between core and periphery is no longer simply geographical or physical. Although, as Bharucha shows, geography remains an influence on the distribution of power, core and periphery are also formed within national boundaries. Examples of 'cultural piracy' thus include the commodification of African-American urban youth culture by US multinationals (not to mention its usage by Tarantino and others), or the assimilation of feminist rhetoric into mass entertainment (see Gilroy, 1999: 242–78; McNair, 2002: 113–28). Core values are much the same throughout the globalized world, but peripheries may differ from one locality to another. The formation of core and periphery hence operates on a cultural and conceptual level, with one of them always privileged on a deterritorialized basis.

One of the principle causes of the formation of core and periphery is the impact of *mobility* on the production of culture. The relationship of core to periphery should be understood in terms of the mobility of cultural and conceptual spaces. The social 'core' of a globalized society is defined by mobility, the periphery by stasis. Globalization thus involves an increase in the movement of people across national boundaries, but the relative status of business executives and tourists on the one hand, and displaced peoples, economic migrants, and asylum seekers on the other varies considerably, notwithstanding the way in which they all exemplify the imperative to be mobile. Refugee, tourist, and executive may share ethnicity, gender, level of education, religion, and nationality. The inequality between the three exists in their *entitlement* to move across national boundaries. Mobility thus is the 'most powerful and most coveted stratifying factor' in contemporary society, as Zygmunt Bauman puts it: 'The freedom to move, perpetually a scarce and unequally distributed commodity, fast becomes the main stratifying factor of our late-modern or postmodern times' (2001: 3).

The relationship between core and periphery – and the differences between globalized and geographical networks – can be seen in the Table 5.1 overleaf. Some of the examples given therein need to be explained in detail. McDonagh's works can be seen as operating within the core of the global network because they are so mobile. In contrast, other forms of Irish dramatic writing occupy the periphery of the network because they are immobile. Examples of the latter category include (*inter alia*) plays in the Irish language and, perhaps, the works of Tom Murphy, which depend for their impact on audiences' appreciation of a range of references that are specific to Ireland. I would suggest that McDonagh's work achieves such mobility because of its use of

Table 5.1   Core and periphery in global theatre productions

	Mobility	Phenomenology	Branding	Examples
Globalized core (conceptual)	Moves freely across cultural boundaries	Reflexive: audiences relate experience to their own preoccupations	Presents itself as 'authentic'	McDonagh's plays, soap opera, Tarantino's films
Globalized periphery (conceptual)	Rooted in one geographical location by language or local references	Communicative: meaning conveyed from production to audiences	Depends on pre-existing relationships with audiences	Plays in Irish language, plays about local politics
Geographical core (physical)	West End, Las Vegas, Broadway, international festivals. 'Global cities'	Audiences purchase access to an 'event'	The experience is the commodity	*The Leenane Trilogy* in the Royal Court, McDonagh on Broadway
Geographical periphery (physical)	Rooted in space	Serves local needs	Identity is related to place	Tour of *Leenane Trilogy* to Leenane and Aran Islands for authentication

a cultural idiom that is geographically peripheral – rural Irish speech and the Irish setting – to achieve recognizability across national boundaries. McDonagh's construction of Irishness operates as a commodified abstraction – or a brand – that can operate globally, being received reflexively, and selectively, by international cultures. This allows us to understand better the notion of hybridity in his works: he combines techniques that allow for cross-national mobility (received notions of Irishness, an emphasis on plot rather than setting, stable characterization, reflexivity) with the authenticating characteristics of Irish settings and idioms. In a similar fashion, Tarantino's works are mobile because of his use of the same techniques, with authentication being provided by reference to a range of decontextualized pop culture references. And soap opera, as mentioned above, uses the imagined spaces of Melbourne, London's East End, or Dallas to anchor stories that are received selectively by audiences internationally.

Work by writers such as McDonagh should be seen not as local or national – or even as international in the sense that Goethe envisaged world literature – but instead as functioning according to a globalized model. That model encourages audiences to respond to his plays' universal qualities and dilemmas (the desire to be elsewhere, inter-familiar strife), while receiving his usage of Irish idiom and setting as markers of authenticity that 'brand' the experience. In a similar fashion, Tarantino's movies also make use of the authenticating markers of peripheral cultures (Kung Fu films, soul music, Blaxpoitation movies) as a way of providing a geographical rooting for plot-driven tales that have such universal qualities as a focus on father-son relationships, 'true romance', the revenge quest, and so on. And soap resembles both in its ability to use plot to encourage audiences to identify themselves with imagined communities. This is not to suggest that the national, the local, or indeed the international have become obsolete as categories of literary analysis; on the contrary, the rise of globalized cultural forms makes it essential that suitable levels of attention are paid to peripheral cultural forms. I suggest instead that the emergence of global networks of mass communication – the internet, cinema, international news corporations, and the international theatre network – has resulted in the emergence of new forms of culture which use specific strategies to transcend (rather than cross) national boundaries. McDonagh's work is one of the strongest examples in contemporary theatre of this new kind of culture.

These alterations in the construction of culture – and their increasing interdependency with economics – allow us to understand better the relationship between McDonagh, Australian soap, and Tarantino. All three draw on cultural forms that are geographically peripheral – either in terms of regional speech, social marginalization, or geographical isolation – but present them within frameworks that may be internationally diffused. That means that there is now a divergent relationship between the cultural core and geographical periphery: artists who can offer what might be called a 'tourist's gaze' on peripheral cultures – working class London, rural Ireland, or the subcultures of Los Angeles – can achieve an international success that places them at the core of cultural production. As we have seen, these presentations have consequences for local cultures. In order to broaden this analysis further, I want to consider how theatrical traffic might move in the opposite direction, and therefore, in the next chapter, consider the interflow between the Irish and American stages, using as an example the strange case of Tony Kushner's *Angels in America*, produced in Dublin in 1995.

6
Globalization and Cultural Exchange: *Angels in America* in Dublin

I concluded the last chapter with an attempt to model the flow of global culture. That model is necessarily limited, since it involves using spatial terms to describe processes that are deterritorialized. So this chapter aims to refine that model, and to clarify some of the terms that I have been using by considering how culture is exchanged within globalized networks by giving some tangible examples of their mobility. I will explore three different forms of cultural exchange: international exchange (movement from one country to another), intra-societal exchange (movement from the margins of a society to its centre), and global exchange (the consumption of a global product by local audiences). I root this discussion in a case study: the Abbey Theatre's 1995 production of *Angels in America Part One*. I wish to explore whether, as an American play appearing on an Irish stage, the Abbey's production involved an *international* exchange. But I also consider how its appearance was one part of a process, initiated by the director Patrick Mason during the 1990s, of bringing homosexual voices from the margins to the centre of Irish theatrical discourse. I will conclude by contrasting those forms of exchange with the increased importance of global (rather than international) practices in theatre. This reveals the value of intercultural exchange as it is carried out in and through theatre – and shows how that value is being eroded by the deliberate flattening of difference that occurs through globalization.

I should state from the outset that I am not specifically referring to the genre of intercultural theatre, defined by Lo and Gilbert as a 'hybrid derived from an international encounter between cultures and performing traditions' (2002: 36) – works such as Lepage's *Dragon's Trilogy* (1985), Brook's *The Mahabharata*, and (to a certain extent) *Riverdance*. Nor am I specifically interested in discussing what Pavis terms 'cultural collage', an 'unexpected or quasi-surrealist encounter of cultural debris' from different national and regional formations (1996: ix) – productions like Robert Wilson's version of *Woyzeck* (2000) for the Betty Nansen Theatre, which blended a Danish script with a design that recalled German Expressionism, and songs written in English by Tom Waits and Kathleen Brennan. And finally, although my use of the term 'intra-societal exchange' might seem to involve (or be similar to) multicultural theatre, I am not referring specifically to that either. That genre can be understood as involving the staging of an exchange between different cultural formations within one society, a performance that (as Lo and Gilbert put it) functions 'within a statist framework premised on ideals of citizenship and the management of cultural/ethnic difference' (37). The point, however, is that multicultural theatre tends to involve the presentation of different cultures within one theatrical space: multicultural theatre literally *performs* multiculturalism. What I am interested in is the relationship between an audience that is dominated by one set of cultural values and a performance that represents *other* cultural values.

Central to this discussion is an awareness of how the 'international' (rather than such nationalized categories as the Irish, or the English, the American, and so on) functions as a conceptual category within national frameworks. To describe a play, film, or other art form as 'international' is simultaneously to mark it as different (because it is not part of the nation) without necessarily seeing it as 'other' (since the international may encompass much that is also present in the nation). The international should therefore be distinguished from the global. An 'international' play is one that presupposes that the conditions of reception will involve an exchange between nations, whereas a global production is one that transcends national boundaries, coming from everywhere and nowhere simultaneously.

This definition gives rise to some difficult questions. How do audiences form expectations when they choose to attend an 'international' play? How are cultural differences managed and explored by producers, practitioners, and audiences? Has globalization increased or reduced opportunities for intercultural dialogue? And how is the reception of theatre from particular cultures affected by the trend within academic criticism to see the marginal (or the liminal) as offering the possibility of liberation? By raising such questions, I want to consider how cultural difference is deployed for economic as well as artistic motives, arguing that we have much to gain from intercultural exchanges, whether they exist within national, local, or international frameworks. Those opportunities are threatened by many of the processes associated with globalization, however.

My decision to discuss this issue in relation to *Angels in America* is based on many considerations. The most important is that it was the only new international play produced on the main-stage of the Abbey Theatre between 1990 and 2005; a fact that itself tells us much about how a period of globalization will not necessarily lead to greater levels of cultural exchange. This gives rise to many other areas for consideration. It is often assumed, for instance, that globalization and Americanization are similar and in some ways identical processes, yet we see in the Irish reception of *Angels* an indifference to American culture when the country was warmly embracing American investment, economic policies, and business practices. It is also important to see *Angels* in the context of the 'queering' of the national stage in Ireland during the 1990s, a discussion of which allows for a consideration of how other kinds of cultural exchange can be transformative. I am suggesting, therefore, that cultural exchanges in the global era need to be seen not simply in terms of unequal transfers within hierarchical structures (between, for example, the developing world and the West). Rather, drawing on my analysis of Martin McDonagh's work, I will consider how localities can benefit from the 'outsideness' of other cultures, while also explaining why theatre producers will seek to make their global products seem *familiar* rather than *other*.

Angels in America at the Abbey Theatre, 1995

Rather like the plays of Martin McDonagh, Tony Kushner's *Angels in America Part One: Millennium Approaches* has been received in many different ways throughout the world, which means that it would be reductive to define its meaning for international audiences solely in terms of Kushner's intentions. Writing about it in 1994, John M. Clum called it the 'most talked about, written about and awarded play of the last decade or more' (313) – a statement that (one assumes) is not actually based on documentary research, but which captures well the impact that *Angels* has had on scholars, journalists, and audiences since it first appeared in 1991. Sarah Kane's *Blasted* (1995) would probably strike most observers today as the 'most talked about' play of the 1990s, but the appearance of *Angels* is also an important event in recent theatrical history. Like *Blasted*, it is as frequently noted for its reception as its content: it was a commercial hit in the normally conservative Broadway environment, but it was also greeted with protests in many countries owing to its treatment of homosexual characters and themes (see Bennett, 1997: 109, 111, 117).

The play is deeply concerned with issues of cultural exchange, using the setting of New York as the 'melting pot in which nothing melted' (Kushner, 1992: 1) to call for the creation of new spaces: for the development of a social space that will allow individuals to express and explore multiple identities, while avoiding the normalization of one particular set of values. This theme is underlined by the fact that the play itself resists categorization. Do we see it as an American play? As queer theatre? As a Broadway hit? A counter-cultural polemic? And can it be all of these things at once? Can it be seen as mainstream (as an example of commercial theatre and/or American culture) without losing the iconoclastic power generated by its queer perspective on political, religious, and theatrical conventions?

The answers to these questions about definition will necessarily be different from place to place – and perhaps they will also differ from one audience member to another. But they are an example of how the play (like so many others discussed in this book) has achieved success through its ability to allow audiences to respond reflexively to it, rather than as a result of its expression of one specific message or meaning.

Those issues of definition are particularly relevant when we consider the play's Irish debut at the Abbey Theatre in June 1995. Perhaps surprisingly, its Irish production was neither successful nor controversial: it was instead generally ignored. The play's failure in Ireland has been the subject of much discussion, but no convincing explanation for its reception has yet been advanced. It received universally positive reviews, so it certainly wasn't a critical failure. The problem is that Irish audiences mostly stayed away from it, so that it achieved an overall seat occupancy of only 31 per cent throughout its run, in a year for which the average attendance at the Abbey Theatre was 65 per cent of capacity. When considered in relation to loss of revenue, out of a possible 23,864 seats, the Abbey only sold 7488 – or, out of a possible box office take of €300,000, it took in slightly more than €86,000.[1] With the production's large cast and expensive visual and sound effects, these figures were seen as disastrous. A production of *Perestroika*, the second part of the play, had been scheduled for 1996, but it was cancelled at short notice, to be replaced by *Macbeth* – a considerably less risky venture, owing to its presence on the Irish Leaving Certificate examination that year. As of 2008, Irish audiences still await the national premiere of *Perestroika*, and there has been no subsequent professional staging of *Millennium Approaches*.[2]

So what went wrong? Two explanations have been advanced. The first is that the play's commercial failure is evidence of negative Irish attitudes towards homosexuality – it is worth remembering in this context that homosexuality in Ireland had only been decriminalized in 1993, after all. Patrick Mason, who directed the production, is cautious in his assessment of its reception, but reaches a strong conclusion. 'It's all the subject of speculation', he acknowledges. 'The critics all were encouraging about it; they all said how important the play was and how good the acting was'. However, he claims that anecdotal evidence suggests that Irish audiences stayed away because of their belief that the play is, as Mason puts it, 'about queers' and is therefore 'not about us' (by which, presumably, he means Abbey audiences). Audiences believed that the play 'wasn't about Ireland, [that] it's nothing to do with us, [because] it's about AIDS', Mason complains.[3]

The second explanation is that Irish audiences just aren't interested in unknown work from other places – that the country is happy to export its plays, but has no desire to import them. Referring to the 1995 production of *Angels in America* and a commercially disastrous 1996 Abbey production of Pirandello's *Six Characters in Search of An Author*, Fintan O'Toole argues that 'well directed, well acted, well designed performances of great plays have met with a depressing degree of indifference' in Ireland. The failure of Pirandello's and Kushner's plays to attract an audience has, O'Toole claims, been matched by a disappointing response to 'practically every well staged international classic on the Dublin stage in the last few years' (1996: 10). Ireland, O'Toole would later argue, thus seems to operate a 'huge cultural trade surplus' (2003: 12).

However, the documentary evidence available on this issue doesn't really support either of these explanations – so it is very difficult to agree with Mason that the play's lack of popularity is evidence of Irish homophobia, or with O'Toole that it should be seen as arising from cultural insularity. That, of course, is one of the limitations of documentary evidence: it would be obviously absurd to suggest that an absence of documentary evidence means that homophobia doesn't exist. Likewise, if audiences are apathetic towards foreign work, they are unlikely to commit that apathy to print or leave some other material trace of it. And of course there are problems with anecdotal evidence too. Mason may be correct in blaming his audience for the failure of *Angels* – but then, one might point out that he would, wouldn't he? He was the director of the play and, as artistic director of the theatre, made the decision to programme it in the first place.

So what use is the evidence that actually is available to us?

Angels was due to open at the Abbey in May 1995, but technical difficulties caused a week-long delay, which meant that it wasn't until 5 June that Irish audiences first saw it. Although some controversy had been expected, there was only one major objection to its production, four days before its delayed opening, when Brendan McGahon, a TD (Member of Parliament) for the Fine Gael party, declared on RTE Radio's *Sunday Show* that 'homosexual practices are an unnatural and disgusting act . . . and the majority of people around the country agree with me. Liberals and left-wing trendies in Dublin 4 may well support homosexuality but they are totally out of touch with the opinion of ordinary people'.[4] The stupidity of these comments appears to have consolidated opinion in favour of the play, with the other panellists on the radio show, and many members of the public, criticizing the TD's attitude (though some listeners to the radio show also phoned in to express their support for McGahon's outlook).

After the play's opening, some discomfort with its theme was apparent in the response of critics, but no writer was openly hostile. Gerry McCloskey's *Sunday Times* review is typical of responses. 'Homosexuals have no power; Roy Cohen has power. Therefore he is no homosexual', notes McCloskey, offering a succinct exposition of the play's treatment of how 'labels' confer authority. However, his review continues with the statement that Cohen's 'predilection for buggery does not, as it were, enter into it' – a rather cheap schoolyard gag that suggests an inability or unwillingness to discuss homosexuality with any seriousness (1995: n.p.).

Most other reviews were very positive. Emer O'Kelly's *Sunday Independent* review situated the play's treatment of discrimination in an exclusively Irish context. 'This was the week when we had a Traveller family referred to on national radio as an "inferior people"', she began, drawing a parallel between homophobia and Ireland's treatment of other marginalized groups. *Angels in America*, according to O'Kelly, is an 'extraordinary, troubling . . . kaleidoscope of an American play' that 'has to, must be seen'. By producing the play, Patrick Mason had 'spectacularly fulfilled the brief of a National Theatre Artistic Director in bringing the play to Ireland', she argued (1995: 18).

Perhaps the best example of the critical response to the production is an exchange between Gay Byrne, radio presenter, and Fergus Linehan, Arts Critic for *The Irish Times*. Speaking on Byrne's very popular morning programme on RTE Radio the morning after the production's premiere, Linehan stated that *Angels* was a 'brilliant play'.[5] 'I couldn't forget [it] when I was going to sleep last night', he said. 'It is an epic play and, as you know, it is three-and-a-half hours long. Apart from that, it is an unforgettable play and wonderfully performed'.

Byrne agreed. 'Wonderfully performed, wonderfully produced', he said. 'But I think that people should be warned – well . . . it is only fair to tell them that it is a polemic about homosexuality written by a very left wing Marxist man called Tony Kushner in America, and people would be outraged by the theme of the play, by the language in the play. I think a lot of people would be outraged'.

'Well I suppose very conservative people', Linehan conceded, arguing that the play was not just about homosexuality, but that 'it is about really the whole meaning of life, I suppose . . . you know, without being too heavy. Because it is very, very funny'.

'Very, very funny', said Byrne quickly – and then, after a short pause, added that 'the theme of homosexuality will outrage some people and the language in it will outrage some people'. Lest his audience think that Byrne was himself outraged, he stated that 'my *own* reaction was that anybody who's interested in theatre at all, direction, production, lighting, acting, whatever, anybody who's in the drama movement or the musical movement really should go to see it for the technicalities alone. . . . They [the cast] are all wonderful and it is a very, very outstanding play . . . I was thinking to myself', Byrne concluded. 'Ernest Blythe must be ballistic in his grave . . . Five years ago it probably couldn't have been done, ten years ago certainly not, and fifteen years ago they would have set fire to the theatre'.

This exchange summarizes the critical response to the play very well. Both men see its production as part of a desirable process of modernization and liberalization in Ireland, with Linehan describing the play's detractors as 'very conservative', and Byrne noting with approval that it couldn't have been produced five years earlier. His somewhat flippant reference to Ernest Blythe going 'ballistic in his grave' is intended to show how much the theatre had changed under Mason – and, by inference, to show that Ireland itself has changed. Their critical response is very positive, with both men, like Emer O'Kelly, describing the play as essential viewing. Yet Byrne's comments in particular suggest that the play's treatment of homosexuality was in some ways challenging, and he appears to struggle to find an appropriate way to talk about it. Nevertheless, even if Byrne appears himself to have been somewhat outraged by the play's content and language, he is careful to give it his endorsement – albeit stating that audiences should see it not for its themes but for its theatricality. This is rather like Emer O'Kelly's presentation of the play as important not simply because it deals with homosexuality, but also because it allows Irish audiences to come to terms with discrimination against Travellers. As Gerry McCloskey might put it, the treatment of homosexuality in and for itself 'does not, as it were, enter into it' in Irish criticism at this time.

The production, as directed by Mason, was certainly one of the most impressive to appear on the Abbey's stage during the 1990s. A number of decisions appear to have been made that depart somewhat from Kushner's script, and it is possible that they might have been intended to make the play more accessible to Irish audiences.[6] In the play's eighth scene, for example, Prior shockingly recounts a story of how a ship filled with Irish immigrants sank off the coast of Nova Scotia:

> [The] crew took seventy women and kids in the ship's only longboat, this big open rowboat, and when the weather got too rough, and they thought the boat was overcrowded, the crew started lifting people up and hurling them into the sea ... The boat was leaky, see; seventy people; they arrived in Halifax with nine people on board.
>
> (Kushner, 1992: 28)

As well as being a metaphor for the death of so many members of the New York gay community from AIDS, the story had local immediacy in that it concerned Irish women and children, a factor that seemed to have been emphasized by Jonathan Arun, the actor playing Prior.

There is much else in the play to which an Irish audience must relate. The early moments make explicit that the play is not simply about AIDS or homosexuality (issues which in any case are far from irrelevant in Ireland), but also about the experience of being part of a minority in the US. This theme is established by the opening scene's emphasis on family and emigration. The woman being buried was part of a 'large and loving family' states the Rabbi:

> In her was – not a person but a whole kind of person – the ones who crossed the ocean, who brought with us to America the villages of Russia and Lithuania – and how we struggled, and how we fought, for the family, for the Jewish home, so that you would not grow up *here*.
>
> (Kushner, 1992: 2)

This emphasis on family and emigration must have resonated with the Abbey audience: the previous year had seen an election fought in Ireland on the issue of emigration and unemployment. And the notion that America was a 'land of opportunity' had plenty of currency in Ireland at this time, both from the appearance of such films as Ron Howard's *Far and Away* (1992), and from the participation of the Irish soccer team in the 1994 World Cup, which was held in the USA.

Another possible concession to Irish audiences' tastes was the representation of American politics. For instance, Joe's statement that Ronald Reagan has restored truth and the law to American society (15) was declaimed direct to the audience in an ironic tone – giving rise to loud and incredulous laughter from the audience, whose political sympathies would probably have been closer to those of Brendan McGahon's 'left-wing Dublin 4 trendies' than Roy Cohen's.

Also significant was Joe Vanek's decision to move beyond Kushner's suggested stage directions. In his introduction to *Millennium Approaches*, Kushner recommends that the play be performed with an emphasis on its theatricality:

> The plot benefits from a pared-down style of presentation, with minimal scenery and scene shifts done rapidly (no blackouts!) employing the cast as well as stage-hands – which makes for an actor-driven event, as this must be. The moments of magic . . . are to be fully realized, as bits of wonderful *Theatrical* illusion – which means it's OK if the wires show, and maybe it is good that they do, but the magic should at the same time be thoroughly amazing.
>
> (Kushner, 1992: vii)

The style of presentation designed by Vanek was certainly very 'pared down', but the action was performed in what seems to me to have been a style of cinematic naturalism. It may be that the decision by Mason and Vanek to represent the action more naturalistically than Kushner suggests was based on a desire to make the piece seem more recognizable to Irish audiences. There were blackouts between scenes, and set changes occurred at a slow pace, with music being used to maintain the audience's attention. The cast may have been involved in changing scenes, but this was not always made visible to the audience, so that it may have been difficult for them to attune themselves to Kushner's notion that the play is an 'actor-driven' event. The scenes involving Mr Lies were presented in a style that could (charitably) be termed magical realism: the character walked on and off stage rather than disappearing, and only a very subtle shift in lighting texture indicated that Harper was experiencing an illusion, or that the audience was experiencing 'moments of magic'.

This move towards a more naturalistic style of performance might be explained in relation to the play's politicized aesthetics. As was mentioned in Chapter 3, one of the reasons that Garry Hynes's *The Plough and the Stars* was so harshly attacked in 1991 was her use of Brechtian techniques in an Irish context. *Angels in America* can certainly be seen as a Brechtian play. As Art Borreca states, 'although the play owes a great deal to other theatrical traditions and genres – for example, the poetic realism of O'Neill and Williams; the avant-garde "theatre of images"; the Theatre of the Ridiculous; the realistic AIDS play – a Brechtian spirit resides at the center of the work' (245). Similarly, James Fisher remarks that 'Kushner's politics are based in a socialism inspired, in part, by Brecht's dramatic aesthetic, which created for Kushner a template for political drama' (2001: 57). It would be an exaggeration to suggest that Irish audiences were hostile to Epic Theatre – indeed, Mason had shown in a 1991 Gate production of *The Threepenny Opera* that he could direct a production of Brecht that would be popular with an Irish audience. Nevertheless, as is hinted at by Gay Byrne's reference to Kushner as a 'very left-wing Marxist', there may have been an extent to which Irish audiences were hostile to theatre that was perceived as being overtly politicized or experimental – and of course *Angels* is both of those things, often simultaneously. Mason's use of naturalism could thus be seen as an attempt to overcome any attempt at *Verfremdungseffekt* in Kushner's script: the Abbey production may have been attempting to make the unfamiliar seem familiar again.

In any case, there are many affinities between *Angels in America* and the Irish theatre embedded in the text, notably in Kushner's representation of the body. In its two parts, the play represents a call for openness, borrowing Gorbachev's doctrine of *perestroika* to demand a renewed engagement between the political and the social. The corruption of American political life is represented figuratively in the denial by Harper and Joe of Joe's sexuality, and by Roy Cohen's abuse of power. Kushner's presentation of that character highlights a growing disjunction between what words mean literally and what their social effects are. In one of the play's most famous scenes, Cohen tells his doctor that all labels:

> [T]ell you one thing and one thing only: where does an individual so identified fit in the food chain, in the pecking order? Not ideology or sexual taste, but something much simpler: clout . . . [W]*hat* I am is defined entirely by *who* I am. Roy Cohen is not a homosexual. Roy Cohen is a heterosexual man, Henry, who fucks around with guys.
>
> (Kushner, 1992: 31–2, emphasis in original)

The crisis of American society is thus represented as a crisis of meaning, of things appearing to be what they are not. The problem for American society is that personal/sexual identity is not expressed by openness about sexuality, but by the performance of roles that are determined by the availability of power: when Roy terms himself a 'heterosexual man', he is not referring to his sexuality, but to his social status. Kushner contrasts the deliberate dishonesty of Cohen with his own use of the theatrical, which presents the fantastic in order to reveal underlying truths. Just as Harper's delusions about Antarctica reveal the actual frigidity of her relationship with Joe, so do Kushner's representation of angels and ghosts represent a deeper truth about the corruption of the religious spirit in America, where 'lawyers are the high priests' (56) and angels 'incredibly powerful bureaucrats' (Kushner, 1994: 26). Kushner uses the theatrical – uses play, in fact – to critique America under Reagan, asking his audience to consider whether substantial differences exist between Harper's delusions, Prior's visions, Roy's public persona, and his actors' performance of these characters. By emphasizing the pretence involved in the theatrical, Kushner reveals the pretence of American political life, and uses the power of the theatrical to call for greater levels of openness in the social realm.

The need for such openness is made apparent by a politicized representation of the suffering body as an analogue for a corrupt state. The destruction of the New York gay community by AIDS acts both as a political fact and as a metaphor for the destruction of American political life. This is made explicit by Roy in *Millennium Approaches*, when he speaks of 'gastric juices churning . . . this is enzymes and acids, this is intestinal is what it is, bowel movement and blood-red meat – this stinks, this is *politics*, Joe, the game of being alive' (150). Kushner insists on representing the body in its least dignified forms, showing his characters shitting, bleeding, fucking, and, in the case of Roy, dying. This insistence on representing all aspects of the life of the body on stage might also be seen as a call for political openness. Similarly, Prior's quasi-religious transcendence of his illness is a way for Kushner to pay tribute to people who have died of AIDS, but it also acts as a form of redemption for American society in its entirety.

It might be argued that Irish audiences would have been attuned to such a politicization of the body. As we've seen already, such plays as Yeats's *Cathleen ni Houlihan* present the body of a woman as a figuration of the nation, with physical beauty and youth operating as a metaphor for the transformation that would be brought about by national independence. Such representations use the physical to represent a transcendent abstraction, making the body an object of national ambition, rather than an agent of sexual or social expression. As I discuss in more detail in the next chapter, this feature of Irish drama took on a renewed significance during the 1990s, thanks in large part to the works of Marina Carr, which attempt to use physical deformity, violence, or disease to represent the nation.

I am suggesting therefore that the direction and design of the production ought to have made the play seem more accessible to Irish audiences, and that there were clear affinities between Kushner's play and many of the classics of the Irish repertoire anyway. Yet audiences simply stayed away from *Angels in America*, so that, as one journalist put it, its 'anal sex scene . . . barely elicited an embarrassed cough from an audience which, a week into the run, only half-filled the theatre' (*Phoenix Magazine*, 1995: 18). To understand this situation fully, it is necessary to move from the play itself to a consideration of the presence of international drama in Irish theatre.

Imagining the international – iconoclasm and outsideness

Mason was certainly thinking about America when he programmed *Angels*. Speaking to *Variety* magazine some months after *Angels* premiered in Dublin, he stated that it is 'clear that the model for the 16-year-old Irish playwright is not Brian Friel or Tom Murphy or even Frank McGuinness – it is Quentin Tarantino. That's both worrying and enlightening at the same time. So this year, I said, let's look at American culture, through American theater' (quoted by Fricker, 1995: 55). The 1995 programme Mason delivered illustrates his desire to examine the impact of American culture on Irish life. Opening the year with Friel's *Philadelphia Here I Come!*, the theatre presented Arthur Miller's *The Crucible* in March and *Angels in America* in June. The first two of those productions were critically and commercially successful, while *Angels* was not.

The categorization of something as 'international' is often more complex than might be supposed. For instance, as discussed in the last chapter, much of the controversy generated by the career of Martin McDonagh has been fuelled by problems of definition, about whether he is Irish (and therefore laughing with us) or English (and therefore laughing at us). Three problems exist here. First, as a collaborative medium, theatre frequently draws on personnel from many different countries and cultures – so the decision to describe such works in national terms is often likely to omit or occlude some important contribution. Secondly, the increasing mobility of peoples makes our understanding of national identity more complicated. Is Martin McDonagh a cosmopolitan writer, identifying only with the global city of London? Is he a member of the so-called Irish diaspora? And do any of these terms help us to understand his plays and their meaning for audiences? And the third problem relates to how the international functions within a national culture. What I would suggest, then, is that the 'international', like all forms of outsideness, is frequently condemned to a kind of creative double bind: it asserts power in a way that ultimately reasserts its marginal status. The international, that is, is presented as having an iconoclastic power that can be used to reinvigorate and renew a national culture. But, because it is characterized as coming from a non-national space, the international will also always be understood as inherently different. We can see therefore that the tendency is for national cultures to assimilate from 'the international' whatever is useful, and to position the remainder as perpetually outside the national space. This is evident in most national theatrical traditions in the West, and can be illustrated by a brief consideration of how the development of modern Irish drama can be seen in an international context.

Histories of the modern Irish stage are dominated by considerations of Irish playwriting, which is often presented as a linear narrative that stretches from Synge to Friel, and on to Marina Carr and others.[7] That approach is entirely valid, but I would suggest that to emphasize dramatic writing risks overlooking many other aspects of Irish theatre. One issue that has received insufficient consideration to date is the fact that many Irish theatre companies were established *not* to produce new Irish plays, but to challenge a perceived Irish insularity by producing work from abroad, or by importing other cultures' ideas about theatre to Irish settings.

Indeed, the development of new Irish writing has never occurred in isolation from international trends. The defining moment of the early Irish dramatic movement – *The Playboy* controversy of 1907 – occurred at much the same time as Hibernicized versions on the Abbey stage of Molière's *The Doctor in Spite of Himself* (1906), Maeterlinck's *Interior* (1907), Sudermann's *Teja* and Molière's *The Miser* (both 1908), Goldoni's *Mirandolina* (1910), and Hauptman's *Hannele* and Strindberg's *There are Crimes and Crimes* and *The Stronger* (1913).[8] It might be assumed that the revolutionary period of Irish history (1916–22) would have stimulated a greater level of interest in exclusively Irish work. Yet from 1918 to 1928, the Abbey stage and resources were frequently given over to the Dublin Drama League, which produced plays that, in almost every case, were written by contemporary authors from abroad, such as Eugene O'Neill, Jean Cocteau, Pirandello, and d'Annunzio. As Christopher Fitz-Simon points out, 'the fact that these authors attracted good attendances proves that there was a desire in Dublin . . . to experience the breeze blowing across the seas from America and from the European mainland' (1983: 184; also see Clarke and Ferrar, 1979).

A desire to experience the 'breeze blowing' from America and Europe motivated the Dublin Drama League and led ultimately to the foundation in 1928 of the Gate Theatre, which was to provide Ireland with what Fitz-Simon calls 'a kaleidoscopic cross-section of modern European and American drama, at a time when Ireland floated in cultural isolation in mid-Atlantic' (1994: 13). While the Gate's programming eventually became as predictable and conservative as the Abbey's (being dominated by lavish productions of Wilde and Shakespeare), it was in this theatre that Irish audiences first encountered the work of such writers as David Mamet, Tom Stoppard, Neil LaBute, and many others.

The Abbey was founded at the beginning of the 20th century to challenge theatrical norms; the Gate, 24 years later, was founded to provide an alternative to the Abbey's mainly Irish ethos. A similar impetus was evident in the 1950s, not only with the establishment of the Dublin Theatre Festival (discussed briefly in Chapter 1), but also with the opening of the Pike Theatre, the small company that premiered work by Brendan Behan and Samuel Beckett. Alan Simpson describes his theatre's establishment in 1953 as an attempt to provide an alternative to the drama that was then dominating the Irish stage. 'We wanted [the Pike] to be a revolutionary force of small means which, by its ingenuity, would stir up the theatrical lethargy of post-war Ireland', he writes, explaining that the purpose of the Pike was to present plays that 'for one reason or another, would not otherwise be seen in Dublin' (1962: 1–2). Simpson was bankrupted after his trial for indecency following the Pike's production of Tennessee Williams's *The Rose Tattoo* in 1957, an event that shows precisely the extent to which non-Irish work was perceived to threaten existing social norms (see Simpson, 1962; Whelan and Swift, 2002).

Contemporary Irish interest in work from abroad follows the tradition evident in the foundation of the Gate and the Pike. Its roots are in the late 1960s and early 1970s, with the foundation of the Focus Theatre in Dublin and Druid Theatre in Galway. The Focus was one of the first theatres in Ireland to introduce ideas about performance from abroad, with its founder, the American director Deirdre O'Connell, establishing Ireland's first Stanislavski Studio in 1963. Druid, founded in

1975, is now known principally for its commitment to the development of new work by such writers as Martin McDonagh, Tom Murphy, and others; but it also showed how Irish theatre companies could benefit from producing work from abroad, particularly in their early years. In a 1997 *Irish Times* interview, Garry Hynes stated that the range of Irish drama means that it is possible for her to focus on Irish dramatists without being artistically limited. Her interviewer, Eileen Battersby, remarks that 'her commitment to Irish drama has long been recognised' but, as Hynes admits, 'that wasn't always so. We did Ionesco and Edward Albee [because] it took a while to grow up and look at Irish writing' (Battersby, 1997: 13). Hence, the majority of Druid's earliest productions were by writers who are not Irish. During its first year in existence, it presented Fernando Arrabal's *Orison* and Williams's *The Glass Menagerie*; subsequent years saw productions of Edward Albee, Alan Ayckbourn, Tom Stoppard, and many other international playwrights. Indeed, almost half of Druid's earliest productions were of work from abroad. This figure fell during the 1980s as the company's interest in new writing grew, until in the 1990s it ceased altogether, the 1992 version of Polish dramatist Teresa Lubkiewicz's *Werewolves* being its last production (as of 2008) of a new international play.[9]

This model – of using international work before 'growing up' to focus on new Irish plays – is evident in the development of many other Irish companies. Rough Magic, for example, was founded in 1984 with a remit to produce new work from abroad. During the first five years of the company's life, it produced 14 international plays, 11 of which were Irish premieres.[10] The importance of Rough Magic was that it brought new work to Irish audiences very quickly, so that such plays as Caryl Churchill's *Top Girls* (1982) and *Serious Money* (1987), and Wallace Shawn's *Aunt Dan and Lemon* (1985) were seen in Ireland within two years of their world premieres. Rough Magic's artistic director Lynne Parker outlines the importance of international work to the company's development. 'Irish theatre, when we started off, was quite inward looking', she says. 'There was the posh stuff being done at the Gate, and there were the Irish classics being done at the Abbey . . . We felt very strongly that we were of a generation whose main influences were British and American television and American film as well, and that we were definitely being influenced by other cultures' (quoted by Chambers *et al.*, 2001: 394). Rough Magic can thus be seen as another company established because of its founders' perception that Irish theatre needed to connect with the global influences on Irish life. Like Druid, Rough Magic moved quickly from producing foreign plays to commissioning new Irish writing, so that after their Irish premiere of Timberlake Wertenbaker's *Our Country's Good* in 1989, it produced no further international work until 2000, when it brought Richard Greenberg's *Three Days of Rain* to the Project Arts Centre. In the intervening 11 years, the company had instead nurtured several young Irish writers, including Gina Moxley, Pom Boyd, and Declan Hughes.

This pattern is also evident in Irish theatre practice. For instance, three companies were established during the 1990s to explore non-Irish approaches to performance – and all of them gradually began to devise new works, often in an Irish idiom. Barabbas was formed in 1993 to explore the 'Theatre of Clown'. With productions such as an adaptation of Lennox Robinson's *Whiteheaded Boy* (1997) and John Banville's *God's Gift* (2000), it introduced Irish audiences to international methodologies and performance styles, such as corporeal mime and Lecoq. Also influenced by Lecoq is Blue Raincoat, which was founded in Sligo in 1991. One of the few Irish theatre companies to have its own dedicated performance space (the Factory in Sligo, which was opened by Marcel Marceau in 1993), Blue Raincoat is a full-time ensemble that produces work influenced by theories of movement and performance from Japan, America, and continental Europe, such as Corporeal Mime, Viewpoints, and Suzuki method. While it continues to produce works by European writers like Ionesco and Stratiev, it has also gone on to produce new Irish plays, many of them written by the company's co-founder, Malcolm Hamilton. Finally, the Corn Exchange has since 1995 set about the production of *Commedia dell'Arte* pieces. Again, we see a movement from the international to the local in their development. The company produced adaptations such as *Lolita* (2001) and international plays like *Mud* by María Irene Fornés in 2003. In 2004, however, it devised *Dublin By Lamplight* (by Michael West and the company), a satirical treatment of the foundation of the Abbey Theatre, which it followed with *Everyday* (2006), a production charting one day in the life of a transformed Dublin.

Irish writers have also been quick to point out the importance of international work. Tom Murphy says that as a young writer he felt that 'anything Irish is a pain in the arse', and instead sought out the work of Lorca and Tennessee Williams (quoted by Grene, 2002: 94). Similarly, Brian Friel has written of the significance of his time at the Tyrone Guthrie Theatre in Minneapolis in the 1960s, explaining that his visit to America 'gave me a sense of liberation – remember, this was my first parole from inbred, claustrophobic Ireland – and that sense of liberation conferred on me a valuable self-confidence and a necessary perspective' (quoted by Coult, 2003: 29). Younger writers such as Mark O'Rowe and

Conor McPherson resist attempts to relate their work to that of the canonical Irish dramatists, Synge and O'Casey, instead citing Mamet, Pinter, and Arthur Miller as their influences. And, although Marina Carr acknowledges being influenced by Synge, she appears most indebted to Tennessee Williams.[11]

What this means is that the international has been seen within Irish theatre as a means to an end, and rarely as an end in itself. As Bakhtin reminds us,

> In the realm of culture, outsideness is a most powerful factor in understanding. It is only in the eyes of another culture that foreign culture reveals itself fully and profoundly . . . A meaning only reveals its depths once it has encountered and come into contact with another, foreign meaning: they engage in a kind of dialogue which surmounts the closedness and one-sidedness of these particular meanings, these cultures. We raise new questions for a foreign culture, ones that it did not raise for itself; we seek answers to our own questions in it; and the foreign culture responds to us by revealing to us its new aspects and new semantic depths.
>
> (Bakhtin, 1986: 7)

The point, therefore, is that the 'international' can be used to regenerate the national culture: the nation assimilates whatever it requires from the 'international' but the remainder is perpetually marked out as foreign. This is particularly – but by no means exclusively – true of Ireland, where international work has always been produced from the periphery of Irish society and theatre, as a means of challenging a dominant ideology or practice. Many of its producers have begun their careers on the margins of Irish life: Edwards and MacLíammóir as gay men in Catholic Ireland, Druid as a regional company headed by a woman, Rough Magic as an urbanized, cosmopolitan company headed by a woman from Northern Ireland. This reveals the importance within Ireland of international work: it has motivated and inspired the development of a great deal of Irish drama. The peripheral and iconoclastic status of that work is also important: the international functions within Ireland as a cultural category that is used to critique mainstream Irish values. I think therefore that this helps us to understand the reception of *Angels in America* in Dublin. The play may have been seen as (in Mason's words) 'not about us' but it introduced the Abbey audience and its creative personnel to a set of signifiers and practices that would soon find their way into mainstream Irish theatre – as I discuss in the next section.

Queering the national stage: Patrick Mason at the Abbey, 1994–99

During a 1999 interview to mark the end of his tenure as the Abbey's artistic director, Patrick Mason claimed that he had originally been considered for the position in the mid-1980s, but that his candidacy had been rejected with a 'racist and sexist' objection from a member of the Abbey's Board of Directors. 'I was referred to as a "Brit queer"', Mason said. 'Isn't that interesting! I wasn't called a "queer Brit"!' (quoted by Jackson 1999: 16). When he finally did take charge of the Abbey, the Board's primary concern was not with Mason's sexuality, or his place of birth (as it happens, he is an Irish citizen), but with the theatre's operating deficit of £600,000 (approximately €762,000).

Mason's credentials for the post were strong. Since his inaugural Abbey production in 1976 (Thornton Wilder's *Our Town*), he has occupied a prominent place in Irish theatre, directing the premieres of many of the major works in the modern repertoire, including Tom Mac Intyre's *The Great Hunger* (1983), Murphy's *The Gigli Concert* (1983), McGuinness's *Observe the Sons of Ulster Marching Towards the Somme* (1985), and, as discussed in Chapter 2, *Dancing at Lughnasa*. His collaborations with McIntyre and Tom Hickey in plays like *The Great Hunger* had shown that he was capable of pushing Irish drama into exciting new areas, but his direction of *Lughnasa* showed that he could achieve commercial and critical success both at home and abroad. These and other factors made him the outstanding candidate to replace Garry Hynes when the theatre's Board decided not to renew her contract in 1993.

Although there were problems at the outset of his tenure, when his decision to present neglected plays from the Irish canon resulted in financial losses, Mason's artistic directorship is notable for many reasons. As Robert Welch points out, 'after Mason's appointment there followed a period of stability in the management of the theatre which was in marked contrast with what had gone before' (1999: 212). As we've seen in the discussion of Ben Barnes's tenure at the theatre (in Chapter 4), Mason's time in charge was also in marked contrast with much of what would follow. This stability brought the theatre out of deficit, and improved the Abbey's status in the wider theatrical community, both nationally and internationally.

Perhaps the most memorable of Mason's achievements during this period was his celebrated 1994 revival of McGuinness's *Observe the Sons of Ulster*, a play that had taken on renewed relevance following the first

IRA ceasefire and the beginnings of the Peace Process. Placing more emphasis on the relationship between Piper and Craig than had been evident in the original production, the revival was regarded as a triumph in Ireland and abroad, having a major influence on the restoration of the national theatre's credibility as a cultural and political force in the 1990s.

Mason's productions of McGuinness, together with that of *Angels*, need to be seen in relation to his use of the national stage to express and articulate homosexual voices. Throughout his six years as artistic director at the Abbey, Mason produced major plays that allowed for an exploration of the place of homosexuality in Irish life and culture. As stated, he directed *Observe the Sons of Ulster* in 1994, and *Angels in America* in 1995. In 1996, Mason did something that no Abbey artistic director had done before: he produced Oscar Wilde's *A Woman of No Importance* on the theatre's main stage. Wilde's *The Importance of Being Earnest* followed in 1997. He also directed Thomas Kilroy's *The Secret Fall of Constance Wilde* (1997), a play that makes explicit the relationship between Wilde's theatre and his sexuality. His final production as Abbey artistic director – *Dolly West's Kitchen* (1999), again by McGuinness – was also an attempt to consider the importance of sexuality and nation in an Irish setting. With the exception of *Angels*, all of these productions were theatrically and financially successful, and *Observe the Sons of Ulster*, *Constance Wilde*, and *Dolly West* all toured internationally.

Because it is the culmination of a process that involved *Angels in America*, *Dolly West's Kitchen* is worth considering in a little detail. The play is set in McGuinness's hometown of Buncrana, County Donegal, a space that is both 'in and out' of the nation: politically, it is part of the Republic of Ireland, but geographically it is located within the natural hinterland of Derry City in Northern Ireland. McGuinness therefore sets his play in a space between the two Irelands. Taking place in 1942, the play considers the military neutrality of the Irish Free State, contrasting it with the participation of Northern Ireland and Great Britain in the Second World War. Being close to, but separate from, a state that is at war increases the isolation of McGuinness's characters – a family called the Wests. Yet, within this bordered space, McGuinness uses the image of the kitchen to create a space in which identities may be reconfigured.

The use of the kitchen as a symbol of the nation is extremely important – because that image would have been seen in 1999 as utterly exhausted. That sense of weariness can be seen in the contrast between two articles published during the following year in Eamonn Jordan's *Theatre Stuff*: the first by Thomas Kilroy (born in 1934) and the second by Declan Hughes (born in 1963). Kilroy, whose first play, *The Death and Resurrection of Mr Roche*, premiered in 1968, describes himself as coming from a generation of writers whose work he defines as 'a mixture of traditional material and formal inventiveness' (2003: 3) – people like Friel, Murphy, Hugh Leonard, and others who emerged in the 1960s. As a writer and a founder member of Rough Magic, Declan Hughes was one of the dominant voices of the younger generation of writers who emerged after 1990. There are many differences between both generations, and between Kilroy and Hughes – but both share a frustration with received images of Irishness. Kilroy notes with approval that, when Tom Murphy decided in 1959 to write his first play, he declared that 'one thing is fucking sure, it's not going to be set in a kitchen' (5). Similarly, Hughes complains that, 40 years on, Irish writers 'persist in defining ourselves by the ethnic, the pastoral (and that qualified form, the tragic pastoral). Even if we do it in an iconoclastic way, the iconography remains powerfully the same: half door, pint bottle, sacred heart' (2000: 12). Interestingly, Hughes is particularly scathing about 'the country kitchen' and its ubiquity on the Irish stage (11).

McGuinness's use of the kitchen could have been seen as clichéd, but in fact he's attempting to use that familiar image to establish a depoliticized space in which all are welcome. At the heart of the kitchen is a table, from which, according to McGuinness's stage directions, 'nothing should detract' (McGuinness, 1999: iv). Setting a play about war in the feminized space of the kitchen is a bold gesture on McGuinness's part; one that allows him to include his characters' potentially conflicting identities (including gender, nation, and sexuality) under one all-encompassing identifier: family. The play does not elide differences, but rather establishes a space in which those differences may be included in a collective. As in his earlier work *Someone Who'll Watch Over Me* (1992), McGuinness presents Irish, American, and English people on stage. He also presents a variety of age-groups, giving us young, middle-aged, and elderly women, as well as many forms of sexual identity: homosexual, heterosexual, bisexual, and (perhaps) celibate. Finally, he explores a variety of different familial relations, showing that traditional conceptions of the nuclear family are only one way for people to band together. Indeed, he shows that paternity itself may be performed in his characterization of the relationship between Dolly's sister Esther and her husband Ned, who may (or may not) be the biological father of the baby who appears in the play's final scenes.

Personal identities may be chosen – but that doesn't mean that they should be treated frivolously. This can be seen in an exchange between Justin (an Irish soldier whose bigotry against others seems an attempt to disguise his sexuality) and Marco, an openly gay American GI who has 'crossed the border' from his base in Derry into Donegal. Justin asks Marco whether he knows 'what the Nazis do to men like you', to which Marco bluntly replies, 'why the fuck do you think I'm fighting them?' (33). Similarly, the eponymous heroine Dolly declares to her English lover Alec that 'you love your country and I do mine, as I love you, but if you and your Allies invade Ireland, I will be the first to put a bullet through your brain' (66). Sexuality and national identity are worth fighting for and, for some, may seem worth killing for too.

Although these identifiers define people, they do not limit them. Indeed, the play establishes homosexuality as offering the potential for the renewal of other forms of identity. The use of camp by Justin shows that all of the other forms of identity in the play can be seen as performance, allowing McGuinness to develop a sustained metaphor about passing through borders: the border in this play is not something that keeps people within boundaries, but instead is something that one travels through, often by means of disguise. This is established from an early point in the play when the move from Northern Ireland to the Free State becomes a joke. 'You've crossed the border', states Justin. 'Hasn't everyone?' Marco replies (29). Allegiance to a uniform or a national symbol is therefore shown to be valuable and appropriate at particular times. The crucial point for McGuinness is that, in the space of Dolly West's kitchen, people will remove their uniforms and find different ways of relating to each other. Homosexual identity is therefore presented as offering a model that can apply to all citizens of the nation: Dolly West's kitchen becomes a nationalized space that has been regenerated through the inclusion of homosexual identities.

This inclusion, I would suggest, makes *Dolly West* an important metaphor for what Mason tried to do at the Abbey, the stage of which was for him a symbolic space that allowed audiences to imagine new ways of being Irish.

Mason also used his status as director of the Abbey to campaign against prejudice. For instance, he became involved in an American controversy about the decision to refuse a gay pride organization permission to march in a St Patrick's Day parade. According to reports in the American media, a protestor 'read a message from Patrick Mason, artistic director of Dublin's famed Abbey Theatre, saying that to allow Irish people who are gay to join the St. Patrick's Day Parade would be fitting on the centennial of famed Irish playwright Oscar Wilde's trial for homosexual offenses' (see Associated Press, 1995: A04). Mason thus used the cultural capital of the Abbey to intervene in an Irish-American debate – an interesting reversal of the cultural flow between the two countries.

It is important to place Mason's achievement in an historical and cultural context. Treatments of homosexuality had provoked controversy in the past in Ireland, with Thomas Kilroy's *The Death and Resurrection of Mr Roche* and Friel's *The Gentle Island* (both of which feature explicit treatments of homosexuality) encountering hostile responses at the 1968 and 1971 Dublin Theatre Festivals respectively. McGuinness's *Innocence* also received much criticism in its 1986 Gate Theatre premiere (which was also directed by Mason), though this may have had as much to do with its perceived anti-clericalism as its treatment of sexuality.

From the early 1980s onwards, however, there was an increase in the profile of gay theatre in Ireland. Ireland's first gay and lesbian theatre company, Muted Cupid, was founded in 1984 in order to challenge what its members thought of as a glut of plays focusing on the impact of AIDS on the gay community. As founder member Frank Thackaberry (1991) explains, there was a perception that Irish theatre productions about homosexuality were excessively focused on 'the idea of Gay-As-Victim, be it from AIDS, queer-bashing or persecution'. Muted Cupid was established to 'explore a wider range of lesbian and gay issues . . . nearer to the issues of day-to-day living than the issues of life and death' (27). A major example of how such plays became more prominent from the mid-1980s onwards was Wet Paint Theatre Company's devised work *Tangles*, a *Commedia*-inspired piece for young people that premiered at Dublin's Project Arts Centre in 1990 before touring to Scotland and the RNT in 1992. *Tangles* certainly deals with the issues of homophobia and prejudice – but again it does so by focusing on the day-to-day realities of life for gay and lesbian people in Ireland (see Grant, 1997).

One of the most popular plays of 1996, the year after *Angels* appeared at the Abbey, was Gerard Stembridge's *The Gay Detective*, a thriller about a gay Irish policeman who is given the responsibility of investigating the murder of a TD. Like *Angels in America*, *The Gay Detective* is explicit in its treatment of homosexuality – though unlike *Angels*, it is rather conservative in form, a fact that may partially explain its popularity. Another major difference between the two plays was that Stembridge included local references that Irish audiences would have been likely to find engaging. This is evident in the opening of the second act, in

which the play's hero describes how the case he's investigating has provoked huge media attention:

> Nothing else was talked about on 'Liveline' for a week. Dr Anthony
> Clare popping up on the 'Gay Byrne Show' to enlighten us all about the
> mind-set of the closet homosexual in public life. TDs from Louth and
> Limerick West calling for the reintroduction of the death penalty . . .
> Then within a fortnight, Fintan O'Toole published a book telling us
> what it all meant.
>
> (Stembridge, 1996: 41)

That set of references would be largely incomprehensible to an international audience, but in Ireland they would probably have been seen as
a witty statement about how current events are discussed by the Irish
media.[12] This passage is an interesting example of how Irish attitudes
towards representations of homosexuality on stage were rapidly changing. Indeed, the joke about a TD from Louth calling for the reintroduc-
tion of the death penalty is an obvious sneer at Brendan McGahon,
whose views on *Angels* are discussed above: Stembridge presupposes that
his audience will find views such as McGahon's inherently ridiculous.
He also appears to assume that they will understand the many cultural
references he makes. The plot seems to echo real events: focusing on a
closeted gay TD, the play may have been inspired partially by a 1994
scandal involving Emmet Stagg, a Junior Minister and TD for Kildare
North, who had been arrested in a part of Dublin's Phoenix Park which
is known to be frequented by male prostitutes.[13] There are no explicit
references to that event in Stembridge's play, but it seems reasonable to
assume that it would have framed the response to it in some ways: the
issue of political hypocrisy in relation to sexuality was certainly topical
in the mid-1990s. So, although the audience for the Project Arts Centre
would differ in some respects from that at the Abbey, it is interesting to
note that Irish audiences were perfectly willing to see plays that deal
explicitly with gay themes – once the 'otherness' of homosexuality was
contained within a familiar, Irish setting.

But an alteration in attitudes was also becoming more evident in the
mainstream Dublin theatre. In 1989, both *The Death and Resurrection of
Mr Roche* (directed by Ben Barnes) and *The Gentle Island* (directed by
Frank McGuinness) were revived at the Abbey, without negative commentary. As Lance Pettitt (1989) points out, 'two plays on at the Abbey
is not enough to counter ignorance or increase popular understanding'
of the challenges faced by gay people in Ireland; and he is critical of

reviewers' 'cursory references' to homosexuality in coverage of the plays. Nevertheless, the idea implicit in the Abbey's productions of these plays was that homosexuality is part of the national story and deserves inclusion on the national stage. The silence of reviewers in response to this proposition cannot, as Pettitt shows, be taken as evidence that homosexuality was being accepted. But we should similarly avoid the assumption that silence must be seen as evidence of hostility: we could argue instead that the Abbey was using its social and cultural capital to introduce issues into Irish discourse that the mainstream media were as yet unwilling to write about openly.

Irish views on homosexuality – or, to be more accurate, expression of those views in public – had generally been changing since the mid-1980s, when Senator David Norris and the Campaign for Homosexual Law Reform successfully took the Irish government to the European Court of Human Rights to demand the decriminalization of homosexuality. This goal was finally achieved in 1993, when the Irish government passed the Sexual Offences Act. While that legislation was perceived by some as an unenthusiastic response by the government to its obligation to abide by the ruling of Norris vs. Ireland, the Equal Status Act of 2000 was more positive in its attitude to Ireland's gay community. Legislating against prejudice is not the same thing as encouraging acceptance but, even so, legislative change in relation to sexuality during the 1990s indicates the beginnings of a transformation in Irish attitudes towards sexuality. It is noteworthy in this context that this change was made possible by Irish campaigners' ability to appeal to European institutions, which is one example of how Ireland's increased openness to other cultures has aided its liberalization.

This transformation is also evident in the changing representations of gay characters in popular Irish culture during the 1990s. Irish television and cinema audiences had responded positively to the growing presence of gay characters in television programming, first in British soap operas, then in such Hollywood movies as Jonathan Demme's *Philadelphia* (1993), and then finally on the Irish television channel RTE, which screened Irish television's first on-screen gay kiss in the soap opera *Fair City* only three months before the Abbey premiered *Angels in America* – another example of how change is first brought about by cultural products from abroad, and then (once they have been accepted) by cultural works produced from within Ireland itself. We also see this in Irish cinema: Neil Jordan's *The Crying Game* (1992) deals with the issue of homosexuality, yet this didn't prevent the film from being one of the most successful in Ireland's cinematic history (see Rockett and Rockett, 2003).

I do not wish to suggest for one moment that all of the cultural representations of homosexuality referred to above should be seen as positive. Indeed, many of them present homosexuality as inherently other, placing it under a heterosexual microscope in a way that risks reinforcing prejudices – or at the very least attempting to present heterosexuality as a norm from which homosexuality deviates. My purpose in mentioning this material, however, is to point out that *Angels in America* appeared during a period in which there was an alteration in representations of homosexuality within Irish culture – almost none of which provoked outright hostility, and many of which were popular. So Mason's time at the Abbey coincides with a period within Irish life when cultural representations of gay and lesbian people were in flux. We can see that Mason used his position as artistic director of the Abbey to respond to – and indeed to lead – Irish responses to that fluidity.

So I'd argue that Mason's presentation of homosexuality on the national stage was not in any way a new development; rather, he was making use of a strategy that had been used by the Abbey's founders, who used what we might call 'otherness' to regenerate Irish identity at the turn of the 20th century. In a similar fashion, Mason in the 1990s used the inherent 'otherness' of plays on homosexual themes to regenerate the national theatre. That achievement deserves attention in its own right, but in the context of the broader argument I am developing, it also shows how intra-societal dialogue can function effectively within a national context. Irish audiences proved largely amenable to 'otherness' when the outsider figure was presented as coming from the margins of the national culture – while the sexuality of Oscar Wilde, or the characters in *Observe the Sons of Ulster* and *Dolly West* may be marginalized, the Irish identity of all was firmly asserted. Could this mean that *Angels in America* failed not because of its treatment of homosexuality – but because it wasn't Irish?

From the international to the global: tourism, celebrity culture, and the 'authentic'

Shortly after the Dublin premiere of *Angels*, an amusing report appeared in the *Sunday Independent*, describing how a group of 20 American pilgrims (who had been visiting Knock, a Catholic shrine in the west of Ireland) spontaneously decided to stop off at the Abbey to see Kushner's play while *en route* to Dublin Airport – either because of the 'lure of a trip to the national theatre' or because of the 'the patriotic sound of the production', states the reporter. When they were told by the theatre's staff about the play's themes, the pilgrims 'had an instant vote and unanimously decided to risk it'. Regrettably, however, 'the language and sex scenes were too much . . . At the interval, 17 of them couldn't take any more and walked out'. The report concludes with a quotation from Mason, who is described (ironically?) as the play's 'triumphant director'. 'At least we kept three', he said (1995: 3).

Like *Phoenix Magazine's* report about the absence of any 'embarrassed coughing' during the 'anal sex scene' in the play, this story shows how sections of the Irish media appeared to take pleasure in the failure of *Angels in America*. The tone is one of condescension, as if all involved in the Abbey's production should have known that Kushner's play was never going to succeed in Ireland. The media's reporting on the play's failure to attract an audience would most likely have undermined any positive impression created by reviews: an individual is unlikely to want to attend a play that no-one else is willing to see. This situation contrasts interestingly with the audience's response to Garry Hynes's *The Plough and the Stars* four years earlier. That production received negative reviews, but received good houses towards the end of its run due to positive word-of-mouth and ongoing media debates about its merits. *Angels* four years later received excellent reviews, but its audience dwindled away as the media continued to report on the theatre's woes. The lesson for Irish theatre producers was that reviews in and of themselves will do little to market a play: what is more important is positive advance publicity and, where possible, effective management of any story that develops during a play's run. As I discuss in more detail below, we see a shift towards this form of marketing of non-Irish plays from the mid-1990s onwards.

More importantly, this report shows the dangers inherent in reducing any nation's culture to one set of characteristics: both *Angels in America* itself and the pilgrims' walkout from it can be seen as examples of American culture at work. And a corollary of that is 'the international' can also mean different things in different contexts. The *Sunday Independent* report reminds us of the importance to theatres of 'international' tourists, who travel to a 'national' theatre in order to encounter the culture of the country they are visiting. It could be argued that one of the reasons that *Angels* failed commercially is simply that it was produced in June, at the height of the Irish holiday season – and therefore was inappropriate to the needs and interests of the theatres' primary audience at that time: tourists.

I have suggested above that there is a long-standing tradition in Ireland of companies using the 'international' as a force for renewal, but we seem to be dealing here with the Abbey's failure to capitalize on the 'international' as a market. As Susan Bennett reminds us, 'regimes of cultural commodification suggest how repertoires must be structured to recognize shifting audience constituencies – that is, what is likely to sell best in peak tourist season and what might fare better placed in the shoulder seasons' (2005: 425). This means that the Abbey seems to have made the mistake of putting on an international play for Irish audiences at a time when they should have been putting on an Irish play for international audiences.

The relationship between tourism and theatre is attracting increasing levels of scholarly attention, but it has been a part of the Abbey's ethos for decades: even in 1924, Lennox Robinson complained that 'the patrons of the theatre consisted almost entirely of visitors to the city' (cited in Hogan and Burnham, 1992: 188). We need to tread carefully, however: it is widely assumed that tourism plays an important role in the life of the Abbey Theatre, but no-one has ever published a quantitative study of the impact of tourist audiences on the construction of the theatre's repertoire.

In the absence of a detailed analysis of the Abbey's summer audiences, we must make inferences from other data. That approach has its limitations, but the available evidence suggests rather strongly that classic Irish plays will tend to do well at the Abbey during the tourist season, whereas works that are new (or not self-evidently 'Irish') will tend to be less well received. If we accept this inference as accurate, we can make another one: that tourist visitors to the Abbey *do not* go to have their expectations challenged, but instead to confirm a predetermined notion of what an Irish play should be like.[14]

These suggestions seem accurate when we consider the summer productions that took place during Mason's time at the Abbey – 16 in all between 1994 and 1999. Ten of the 16 are standard Irish classics. There were three revivals of plays by Brian Friel: *Philadelphia, Here I Come!* in 1995, *Translations* in 1996, and *Dancing at Lughnasa* in 1999. There were two plays by Shaw (*The Doctor's Dilemma* in 1994 and *St Joan* in 1998), two by Wilde (as discussed above), and one each by Synge (*The Well of the Saints* in 1995), O'Casey (*Juno and the Paycock* in 1997), and Boucicault (*The Colleen Bawn* in 1998). There were also three revivals of productions that had built up a reputation during the theatre's more difficult winter and spring seasons, such as *Observe the Sons of Ulster* (opened in Autumn 1994 and revived for summer 1995), Tom Murphy's *The Wake* (opening in January 1998, and revived in the summer of 1999), and Bernard Farrell's *Kevin's Bed* (opening in April 1998 and revived in the summer of 1999). One of the 16 plays was an adaptation of Patrick Kavanagh's *Tarry Flynn* by Conall Morrison, which premiered in May 1997: strictly speaking, this was a new play, though it draws on a popular Irish novel (originally published in 1948) by a prominent Irish writer, and would therefore have been well known (at least by reputation) to most prospective audience members.[15] That leaves us with two others plays, both of them Irish premieres: Hugh Leonard's *Chamber Music* in 1994 and *Angels in America* in 1995. Interestingly, both were commercially unsuccessful.

Indeed, between 1990 and 2005, the only new play to achieve success during the tourist season at the Abbey was Gerard Stembridge's comedy *That Was Then* (2002), a light-hearted production about Anglo-Irish relations which received a marketing boost from the success of Stembridge's movie *About Adam*, which had been released during the previous year. Every other new play that appeared on the theatre's main-stage in the summertime during the period covered by this book was either commercially or critically unsuccessful, in some cases disastrously so: notable summertime flops include Niall Williams's *The Murphy Initiative* (August 1991), Brian Friel's *Wonderful Tennessee* (June 1993), Jim Nolan's *Blackwater Angel* (May 2001), and Vincent Woods's *A Cry from Heaven* (June 2005) – and of course *Angels in America*. So put simply, every Irish classic staged at the Abbey during the summer has done well (critically and commercially), but almost every play premiered during the summer has done badly. This suggests strongly that the success of the Abbey's repertoire is determined by the need to programme conservatively during the summer months, when the theatre's tourist audience is at its height.

Does this mean that Mason should simply have programmed *Angels in America* for a different time of the year, perhaps as the Abbey's offering for the 1995 Dublin Theatre Festival? Maybe. After all, most companies in Dublin schedule their productions of international, experimental, and new work at times other than summer; the Abbey's decision to stage *Angels* in June is, considered in this context, surprising. Many regular Dublin theatregoers would have been holidaying at this time; the majority of Dublin's university lecturers and students were occupied with exams; and the average 16-year-old, whom Mason described as part of his target audience for the play in his *Variety* interview, would have been taking the state-run Junior Certificate examination at the time. The Abbey had therefore presented the play during a period when many people who might have been inclined to attend it were unable to do so – while many of those who might have wished to attend the Abbey would probably have hoped to see a recognizable Irish classic. So one possible explanation for the commercial failure of *Angels* is that, perhaps ironically, the theatre had failed to take account of the needs of international visitors to Dublin during 1995.

But there is more than just scheduling at stake here. Mason's interest in American culture was not unprecedented in the Irish theatre: there were many successful mainstream productions of American plays during the 1990s. Garry Hynes had overseen the presentation of a 1992 production of *The Iceman Cometh* at the Abbey, and the Gate produced a popular 'American Festival' in 1998, comprising *Long Day's Journey into Night* and *A Streetcar Named Desire* (featuring Frances McDormand as Blanche). O'Toole's assertion (mentioned earlier) that *Angels in America* 'went the way of practically every well staged international classic on the Dublin stage in the last few years' is therefore not entirely accurate.

However, the Abbey's *Angels in America* lacks something that most of those other productions had: an international celebrity in one of the leading roles. We've seen already how international success was used to brand Irish plays – how *Lughnasa* was better received in Ireland when it had been successful abroad, for instance. There is a similar representation of the international in the use by theatre producers of celebrity casting, where plays from other countries are no longer defined as *foreign*, but are instead marketed by using the aura of the international celebrity.

Throughout the 1990s, there was a gradually increasing fashion on the Anglophone stage for the casting of international celebrities in plays that might otherwise have struggled to find an audience – something that has been part of theatre marketing throughout its history, but which began to intensify greatly from the mid-1990s onwards (see Luckhurst and Moody 2005). This saw the intensification of celebrity-driven casting, which has since dominated the Anglophone stage, notably in London. A variety of well-known Hollywood actors such as Nicole Kidman, Kevin Spacey, Kathleen Turner, Liam Neeson, Gwyneth Paltrow, and Madonna have starred in plays on the British stage. Similarly, writers who had become well known in other media, such as Irvine Welsh, Ben Elton, and Jeffrey Archer, have had plays produced on the strength of their reputations in those other fields, and not necessarily because of their plays being of high quality. Writers have also achieved success by writing plays *about* celebrities. Terry Johnson's *Cleo, Camping, Emmanuelle and Dick* (1998) presented audiences with a fictional biography of Barbara Windsor, Sid James, and Kenneth Williams. Similarly, *The Play What I Wrote* (2001) by Sean Foley and Hamish McColl is not only about Morecambe and Wise, but also starred a different celebrity on each night of its original London run. As Martina

Lipton shows, celebrity has also been a factor in the renewal of British pantomime, with symbiotic relationships developing between pantomime and television (see Lipton, 2007). It is clear, therefore, that celebrity, in all of its forms, has become an important aspect of London theatre; and that impact is becoming more evident elsewhere.

The appearance of celebrities in theatres usually benefits audiences – but it is also beneficial to the celebrity himself or herself. Appearing in a stage play can boost the credibility of a star, whose ability to cope with live performance can be used to 'prove' that the person can 'really' act (this was an interesting feature of the casting of *Harry Potter* star Daniel Radcliffe in a 2007 revival of Peter Schafer's *Equus* in London). Stage performance can also boost the aura of the star. As Sean Redmond points out, 'contemporary fame speaks and is spoken about through the language of intimacy' (2006: 36). Referring to the appearance of Tom Cruise at a London movie premiere, Redmond writes that 'the "special" opportunity through which fans were able to meet and talk in person to . . . Cruise at the premiere of *The War of the Worlds* works actually to heighten his auratic quality and to increase the desire for his onscreen image' (37).

The casting of international celebrities in theatre can be seen as offering similarly 'special' opportunities to engage intimately with the star. As stated already, we need to see these events in relation to the use of branding to allow audiences to engage with what Walter Benjamin terms the 'aura' of a mass-mediated theatrical product. The live body of the actor (which would previously have been seen only on cinema or television screens) will be received by the audience as an example of the 'the presence of the original' which, for Benjamin was 'the prerequisite to the concept of authenticity' so that 'the original preserved all its authority' (1992: 223). I suggested in Chapter 3 that the processes of branding remove the site of authenticity and authority – the production's 'aura' – from the live performance and make it conceptual: the authenticity of a cultural product is now grounded in the perceived authenticity of its cultural sources. Celebrity casting operates in almost exactly the opposite way, using the liveness of the celebrity to emphasize authenticity. But what is important is that audiences consume the experience of the live encounter with the celebrity, which they perceive as valuable because of its authenticity and its liveness.

This development has certainly not been universally well received: the use of celebrity casting in London's West End has received a great deal of commentary in Britain, and seems to provoke both anxiety and resentment – some critics have complained about the possibility that

British actors might be losing out to actors from overseas, while Michael Billington has expressed concern that the West End's preference for American culture is leading Britain into becoming culturally as well as politically subservient to the United States (see also Christalis, 2002). No such concerns seem to have occupied Irish critics, however. So from 1997 onwards, a growing number of celebrities – most of them relatively obscure Hollywood actors, and some Irish actors who had achieved success abroad – appeared in Irish theatres, usually in non-Irish works. Almost without exception, those productions were extremely successful.

There are many significant examples of the use of international celebrity to market non-Irish plays between 1990 and 2005. The success of *The Iceman Cometh* at the Abbey in 1992 was strongly determined by the appearance of Brian Dennehy in the cast. As mentioned above, the Gate Theatre used the presence of one celebrity – Frances McDormand – to brand two plays together as an 'American Festival'. In 2001 alone, three international plays that might otherwise have struggled to find an audience gained a high profile by casting internationally famous actors. Tyne Daly appeared in a Hibernicized version of *Mother Courage* at the Olympia, Ian Holm and Ian Hart featured in the Gate's revival of Pinter's *The Homecoming*, and Jason Patric starred in Neil LaBute's *Bash* at the same venue. During the same year, Glenne Headley was cast in Geraldine Aron's *My Brilliant Divorce* for Druid (strictly speaking, this should be seen as an Irish rather than an international play), while John Hurt played the title role in Beckett's *Krapp's Last Tape* at the Gate.

An important element of the marketing for these productions was that many played only for a limited run: they were, in other words, *Evented*. Ethan Hawke's appearance for a reading of Shepard's *The Late Henry Moss* at the Peacock in 2002 was, to use the old marketing cliché, 'for one night only'. Similarly, Anne Nelson's play about the 11 September attacks on the United States, *The Guys*, played for only four nights in Dublin's Peacock in August 2002. Tickets went on sale for those four performances on the Sunday before the run began, and had sold out within 30 minutes of the box office opening: many ticket holders had camped out since before six in the morning to be sure of getting seats.[16] During July of that year, Michael Healy's *The Drawer Boy* played for only one week in the Galway Arts Festival before transferring to the Peacock for a three-week run that sold out before the production had even opened: not because anyone knew who Healy was, and certainly not because of any Irish interest in Canadian drama, but because *Frasier's* John Mahoney was one of the production's lead actors. A feature of the marketing strategy in these cases is the deliberate creation of a sense that tickets for these plays are in demand, and the hiring of celebrity actors is an intrinsic part of this process. Audiences have one chance, and once chance only, to share a space with actors such as Hawke, Robbins, and Sarandon – transforming the experience from theatrical enjoyment to a once-in-a-lifetime experience.

It might be assumed that, if celebrity casting encourages the growth of new audiences, it might ultimately benefit the development of Irish theatre. Apparently not. Ben Barnes describes the limited value of having a celebrity in a production by comparing the success of the Abbey's 2000 production of *Medea* with its relatively unsuccessful *Iphigenia at Aulis*[17] the following year:

> The quality of the ensemble work [in *Iphigenia*] was glittering, the use of the Abbey stage was breathtaking, the design and lighting were boldly theatrical and the fierce intelligence, integrity and commitment of Katie Mitchell's direction, in my view confirmed why she was regarded as one of the great European directors. The production and choice of the show also challenged pre-conceived notions about what the Abbey should be doing and how it should be doing it. The production never broke fifty percent attendance. *Medea* on the other hand, also had an iconoclastic production but with a star actor [Fiona Shaw] in the leading role was turning people away at matinees and went on to a successful run in London and will open next year [2002] in New York.
>
> (quoted in Chambers *et al.*, 2001: 8)

A third Abbey production of a Greek Tragedy directed by a woman, Lorraine Pintal in 2004 – Seamus Heaney's version of *Antigone, The Burial at Thebes* – was even less successful than *Medea* and *Iphigenia*, achieving an average seat occupancy of approximately 36 per cent (according to McKeon, 2004b). It appears, therefore, that the priority for those who saw Fiona Shaw in *Medea* was her presence on stage; had they valued the play more, they might have returned for a production of *Iphigenia* regarded by many as superior to *Medea*, or to Heaney's *Antigone*.

It is unlikely that the Abbey would have produced *Iphigenia* without the success of *Medea*. And the appearance of such actors as Ethan Hawke, John Hurt, Ian Holm, and Fiona Shaw on the Irish stage should be regarded as positive, not only for the audiences before whom such talented people perform, but also for the young actors with whom they share the stage. But does the increased presence of these plays in the Irish repertoire mean that Irish audiences have developed an interest in work from abroad? Or were these plays successful because their foreign qualities were obscured by the involvement of a celebrity?

It would appear that the only thing promoted by the inclusion of a celebrity in a play's cast is celebrity itself. Of the audience at a 2001 Dublin production of *Mother Courage*, how many were interested in Brecht, and how many had come to see Tyne Daly, formerly the star of *Cagney and Lacey*, in the lead role? Did people queue for hours outside the Abbey on a rainy Sunday morning to buy tickets for *The Guys* because of a sense of affinity with the victims of the September 11 attacks on the World Trade Centre? Or was the casting of Susan Sarandon and Tim Robbins the decisive factor?

It is important, therefore, to see the 'failure' of *Angels* in the context of two ways of thinking about 'the international'. The staging of the play in June, it seems to me, was a mistake, arising from a misapprehension of the audience's interests at that time of the year. In part, that mistake arises because that audience is comprised of a large proportion of tourists who have clearly defined expectations about what a trip to any country's national theatre ought to entail. And I am also arguing that *Angels in America* was less successful than other international plays – like *The Iceman Cometh* or *The Guys* – because the theatre did not use celebrity casting to market it. Central to both of these suggestions is the idea that audiences have a desire to attend productions that – for whatever reason – they perceive as offering an *authentic* experience. *Angels* did not offer international tourists an experience that they could see as 'authentically' Irish; nor did it offer Irish audiences an opportunity to experience the liveness of an international celebrity.

Conclusions

It is undoubtedly the case that homophobia was a factor in the reception of *Angels in America* in Dublin. Undoubtedly, a lack of interest in work from abroad also had an impact. Perhaps, too, the play failed to gain an audience because of inappropriate programming, poor marketing, and its treatment of homosexuality. The obvious question to emerge from this discussion is this: why does the 'failure' of *Angels* in Dublin matter?

It matters firstly because the reception of the production may be invoked to support certain arguments that, although widely believed, are not borne out by the evidence. It is easy to point to the play as evidence of Irish homophobia, conservatism, and insularity, but its reception is influenced by causes that are considerably more complicated than that. Irish theatre, far from being insular, has historically been dependent upon work from abroad, and Irish theatre practitioners have repeatedly invoked the category of the 'international' as a means of countering a dominant Irish discourse. There is, therefore, a clear parallel between the staging of international work and the subsequent development of new Irish writing. Likewise, we see that the experience of 'Americanization' is experienced in multiple ways within national cultures – as witnessed by Irish audiences' indifference to an American play, enthusiasm for Hollywood celebrities, and their cynicism about certain elements of American politics. The evidence in relation to *Angels* and subsequent plays starring American celebrities suggests that audiences are interested in 'American' culture when it is mass-mediated and familiar; they are not necessarily prepared to invest the intellectual energy in engaging with elements of American culture that are different to what they are used to seeing at home. I'd suggest, therefore, that the notion that globalization and Americanization are interconnected is an oversimplification of a complex situation: certainly much global culture emerges from the United States, but it is not necessarily the case that such mass-mediated products do anything to further understanding of – or genuine engagement with – American culture as it is evident in plays like Kushner's.

Moving from the international to the national, I would also suggest that Patrick Mason's achievement at the Abbey needs to be seen in social and cultural terms: the 'failure' of *Angels* in 1995 can only be viewed as such if taken in isolation from everything else that he did at the theatre. The production of *Angels* ought to be seen as an important stage in the process of bringing homosexual voices firmly into the national theatre, a task that has had an obvious impact on society broadly. We therefore see in Mason's time at the Abbey an example of how theatre – especially national theatre – can lead a society.

The case of *Angels in America* in Dublin also has some interesting consequences for scholars, since it shows the challenges involved in using certain kinds of evidence for theatre research. In general, most theatre scholarship makes use of some of the sources or techniques I've mentioned in this chapter: interviews with practitioners, commentary by journalists, textual analysis, box office figures, theatre reviews, and comparative analyses of similar plays. I hope that I have shown the limitations of each of those approaches. If, as I have been arguing, one of the consequences of global theatre is that audiences' reactions to plays will be reflexive, we must also become more aware of how theatre production is influenced by a considerable variety of factors, many of which work against each other. As theatre research itself becomes more globalized, academics and critics will be required to adopt considerably more sophisticated methodologies than those currently regarded as normal. At the very least, the exclusive use of newspaper reviews as evidence of popular opinion should be rejected as methodologically unsound. But box office figures can obscure matters too: the fact that not many people went to a play doesn't mean that the play had no impact on its society.

I've also attempted to trace a number of different exchanges, all of them occurring within a national framework. I see Patrick Mason's inclusion of homosexual themes and voices on the stage of the Abbey as an example of intra-societal exchange – of a hitherto marginalized voice being used to renew and regenerate the dominant culture. Likewise, I would present the international, as it functions with national theatres, as having a similarly regenerative potential, offering us new frameworks in which to explore national preoccupations. Both forms of exchange show how an engagement with difference stimulates the development of the self. Gadamer (1989) puts it well when he writes that 'self-understanding always comes through understanding something other than the self, and includes the unity and integrity of the other' (83). Through genuinely engaging with material outside of itself, national theatre comes to understand its own practices and methodologies better; through genuinely engaging with a culture outside of (or peripheral to) itself, a nation can broaden and deepen its attitudes towards ethics and citizenship (an issue I return to in the final chapter).

I would contrast international and intra-societal exchanges with the kinds of transactions that occur when the theatrical experience becomes commodified by the use of a globalized brand – the 'Irish' national brand that is sold to tourist visitors to the national theatre, the 'international star' brand that is sold to people who attend plays that use celebrity casting. The point about these exchanges is that audiences pay to get exactly what they expect: the tourist who goes to the Abbey expects an Irish classic, and the tourist who sees Kevin Spacey in the West End expects to see the 'original' – the live version of a body that has been 'consumed' in mass-mediated products in the past. Hence, if international and intra-societal dialogue broadens our sense of who we are, globalized exchanges tend instead merely to confirm our expectations, and therefore to narrow our horizons. A major question that arises from this observation is this: if globalization means that theatre audiences want to have their expectations confirmed, how is this affecting the composition of new plays? Does globalization deepen or restrict the theatrical imagination?

Part IV Imagining Globalization

7
Globalizing Gender and Dramatic Form

It is possible to trace a pattern in this book involving representations of the body, particularly through dance. In 1990, *Dancing at Lughnasa* presented audiences with the sight of five women dancing, in a scene that was received nationally and internationally as celebratory. The following year, Declan Hughes concluded *Digging for Fire* with one of his characters dancing alone to New Order's 'True Faith' (1991: 75). In 1994, *Riverdance* achieved international success by combining traditional Irish dancing with Broadway-style showmanship. And in 1999, *Stones In His Pockets* criticized the representations of Irishness within mass-mediated forms of entertainment such as *Riverdance*, but included a dance scene that audiences received in much the same way that they had viewed *Lughnasa* and *Riverdance*. Marie Jones's use of the joke in *Stones In His Pockets* that if 'the Irish know one thing, it's how to dance' (41) could stand as an overarching statement of the status of Irish theatre during the 1990s.

We've also seen, however, that Irish attitudes to physicality are more complex than might at first seem to be the case. I suggested in Chapter 2 that the dance scene in *Lughnasa* should be understood *not* as an expression of euphoric release, but rather as an outburst of frustration: the Mundy sisters resort to dance because they are denied access to other forms of expression. I've also considered how the Dublin production of *Angels in America* presented Irish audiences with the sexualized body as an analogue for the nation itself, a trope that has been frequently used in Irish plays. So, in Irish theatre since the early 1990s, there is a tension between the imaginative spaces generated in theatres, and the most intimate physical space of all – the human body.

The issue of gender complicates that tension. There is a clear contrast between the verbal freedom of male characters – from Gerry in *Lughnasa*, to Conn in *The Shaughraun*, to Roy in *Angels in America*, to Charlie and

Jake in *Stones In His Pockets* – with the non-verbal physicality of women characters, particularly the dancing Mundy sisters in *Lughnasa*. The message conveyed by Irish drama since 1990 might be that men talk, but women dance.

This gendering of speech and movement can be illustrated further by a brief comparison of two Irish productions from 2003: Mannix Flynn's monologue *James X* and Fabulous Beast's dance theatre production, *Giselle*.

Michael Keegan-Dolan's *Giselle* (2003) is set in an imagined version of the Irish midlands, although at no time in the play is there any reference to a real Irish place. 'The town where it's set is called Ballyfeeney', states Keegan-Dolan, 'but there's probably a Ballyfeeney in Texas' – that is, the play is intended to be seen as being about 'humans in situations of suffering or struggle, and national identity has to be secondary to that' (Dublin Theatre Festival, 2007). As in the original ballet, the production comprises a series of movements in which the unspeaking Giselle is brutalized by the men in her life, particularly her brother Hilario. That brutalization is presented in terms of the restriction of her movement: she is literally tied up throughout the play. The action concludes with a wordless performance of a dance, in which the spirit of Giselle rises from the dead to confront the men responsible for her death. Speech has given way entirely to movement, restriction to fluidity.

The play thus involves a movement away from speech and towards physical expression. The first scenes include naturalistic narrative, with characters relating directly to the audience and each other using conventional modes of stage speech, such as monologue and dialogue. There is a strong association between the violence of the men and their use of language, which is generally crude and delivered in harsh tones. Crucially, the redemption of Giselle in the final scene is presented entirely through dance; the rejection of the controlling narratives of the male characters is signalled by the expressiveness and freedom of her movement. *Giselle* is therefore a celebration of the body, using dance as a mode of escapism from physical violence. The brutalization of the body of Giselle throughout the action means that the redemptive dance at the end of the play cannot be mistaken as anything other than an expression of power, rage, and – surprisingly – of beauty. But what is important is that the redemption comes from a rejection of speech, and it is presented symbolically through the body of a woman.

James X is a very different kind of theatre, written and performed by Mannix Flynn. Like *Giselle*, it also involves a movement away from a controlling narrative – in this case, the Irish state's legal file on a man who was brutalized and sexually abused in a series of institutions run by the Catholic Church. But whereas *Giselle* represents a movement away from speech towards visual expression, *James X* instead uses monologue as a way of reclaiming agency.

That monologue is performed directly to the audience by Flynn, who sets his play in the lobby of a courtroom, where the title character is about to give evidence to a state enquiry into institutional abuse. Flynn's character presents a re-imagined version of his upbringing, telling a story that is highly theatrical, frequently humorous, and – as we learn at the conclusion of the play – for the most part an invention. As he continues to narrate the story, we slowly learn that his monologue is not an expression of the truth, but a shield from it – it is the story that his character has devised over the years to control his sense of guilt and shame for the abuse he suffered. Similarly, the theatricality of Flynn's performance is not an aid in communicating the facts of what happened to him, but is instead an attempt to persuade the audience that his invented version of events is true.

The final moments of the play involve a rejection both of performance and of the state's ability to define James's life. Holding up the state's file, which describes in clinical legal detail James's repeated imprisonment, James delivers a short monologue which is entirely factual, presented directly to the audience without adornment of any kind. What he communicates is a genuinely disturbing series of events, describing how the young James was institutionalized successively, raped by priests who were supposed to be caring for him, raped by a fellow prisoner in the jail to which he was sent at the age of 15, and – after his requests for assistance were ignored by the Irish authorities – eventually taken to a hospital for the criminally insane. Finally confronting the truth about himself, James decides not to participate in the court hearing. 'This is not my shame anymore', he says, and, directly facing the audience, he tells us, 'It is yours'. Holding up the file about his past, he describes it as the property of 'the state, the church, their servants and agents, and you the citizens' (73). He flings it to the ground and leaves the auditorium, walking out amongst the audience. The impact of this gesture arises from its intimacy – from the tension between Flynn's story about an abused body, and the presence of the live body of the performer which is used to deliver this story to the audience. It is precisely because this play is *not* a series of written words, but is instead a physical performance, that it has such power.

Flynn's play can thus be seen as a rejection of certain forms of narrative: of the performances of witnesses and lawyers in court-cases, of the dehumanization of people in the state's legal files, and perhaps even of the theatre itself. His performance for much of the play is in fact an attempt to prepare us for the revelation of what really happened to him. The contrast between his theatricality at the start of the play and his honesty at the conclusion allows the audience to face and, one hopes, to accept its actual responsibilities within Irish society. Audiences may be comforted by Flynn's performance: its humour, its anecdotal quality, its use of idiom – all traits that conform to Irish audiences' expectations about characters on the Irish stage. By revealing these to be theatrical gestures, Flynn forces the audience to confront its own complacency.

The reception of both *Giselle* and *James X* was very positive, with both plays being seen as evidence of Irish society's increased willingness to come to terms with the sexual and physical abuse of so many of its citizens, both in domestic and institutional settings. Both productions can be seen as an attempt to account honestly for the existence of such abuse, which is shown to have been produced not by individuals but by entire communities – whose members either ignore, tolerate, contribute to, or directly enact such abuse. The productions are also significant in offering to Irish audiences an opportunity to move forward, since both respond to the brutalization of Irish bodies through embodiment: *Giselle* by using dance, and *James X* through the physical presentation of Flynn's script in the theatre.

The problem with both plays is their presentation of communication in relation to gender. A comparison of the two shows that in both cases there is a movement away from verbal performance towards an unadorned expression of a truth, but whereas the male character's response to violence is represented through speech, the female's is represented through dance. I would generally resist the tendency to see monologue as a literary medium – Flynn's play (and many of the plays I discuss below) show that monologue is entirely dependent for its success on the physical presence of a performer. However, what is significant is that both *Giselle* and *James X* seem to follow the gendered pattern identified above: James speaks to assert his power, but Giselle dances.

This presentation of gender is not new. As I've mentioned already, the use of the female body as a symbol of the nation was one of the dominant tropes of the Irish Revival and, although the great moments of narrative invention in Irish theatre are usually inspired by women, they are almost always enacted by male characters (as is perhaps best illustrated by the relationship between Pegeen and Christy in Synge's *Playboy*, or between Cecily/Gwendolyn and Algernon/Jack in Wilde's *Importance of*

Being Earnest). We therefore see within the history of Irish drama a strong identification of storytelling with masculinity. There are of course exceptions, such as Tom Murphy's *Bailegangaire,* which presents us with an irrepressible female storyteller, or his *Alice Trilogy* (2005), which features a powerful presentation of a female character's capacity for self-reflection, invention, and redemption through speech. But, in general, it appears that one of the traits most frequently presented in Irish drama is a tendency for male characters to *narrate*: for the qualities of authenticity and meaning to be mediated through the speech of a male subject. That tendency to see speech and movement in gendered terms helps us to understand the international reception of *Lughnasa.* Critics and audiences appear to have been excessively inclined to read Michael as an onstage representative of Friel himself, to see the play as being directly autobiographical in an uncomplicated sense, to take Michael's version of events as 'the truth', despite the discrepancies between his narrative and the Mundys' actions. Likewise, the dance scene was often misinterpreted as an example of liberation because the female body was being misread due to its similarity to existing tropes. Because Ireland was liberating itself during the 1990s from decades of gloom and repression, it was tempting for audiences to see the Mundys' dance as a symbolic performance of that sense of national relief – to assume that, once again, the bodies of women were being used to perform the fate of the nation.

The relationship between masculinity and speech is not in itself negative; what *is* negative, however, is that such identification tends to be denied to female characters. This happens at a time in our culture when the female body is constantly subjected to commodification and transformation into various kinds of symbol. As Nicholas Mirzoeff explains, 'this current moment of 'globalization' is especially enacted on, through and by the female body . . . Globalization in the West is culturally figured as feminine' (2002: 16–7). There are numerous examples of this phenomenon, from the commodification of women's bodies in advertising, to the impact of pornography on the development of the World Wide Web. There is also the relationship between the construction of femininity and the reporting of violence in the mass media, with images of women and children acting as a form of emotional shorthand in reports on military atrocity. As I've argued above, the globalization of theatre internationally has led to the development of drama that aims to be accessible to international audiences through the diminution of language in favour of visual spectacle: dance, and movement generally, acts as a form of non-verbal communication that is understood across linguistic boundaries.

A key element of this abrogation of language is the recycling of globalized images from the mass media for productions that tour internationally. Hence, I would suggest, stereotypical presentations of female images from the mass media are increasingly being used in global theatre productions. One obvious example of this is the symbolic use of the figure of the woman who has experienced sexual assault in the Yugoslav civil wars. In those wars, women were sexually assaulted not just as individuals, but as symbols of the nation under attack – that is, their bodies were not just violated, but translated into an abstract image of something that they were not. Countless writers have further translated those women's bodies into another symbol, using them as a symbol for suffering and injustice. That 'translation' can be used to analyse the way that Westerners develop their own sense of self through interaction with the victims of the rape camps, as can be seen in such plays as *The Body of Woman as a Battlefield in the Bosnian War* by Matei Visniec (2000). It also appears in settings that can seem crass or manipulative: Eve Ensler's *The Vagina Monologues* (1996), for instance, uses real testimony from a victim of the Yugoslav rape camps as a filler between comedic sketches about orgasms and the difficultly of speaking frankly about sex. In any case, we are seeing the development – or perhaps more accurately, the renewal – of a visual language about gender, with the figure of the abject female *other* acquiring new potency as it becomes more globalized.

I suggested in the last chapter that globalization causes audiences to expect that theatre will confirm their expectations. It is for this reason, I argue, that we see an increase in the number of Irish plays that reproduce the apparently old-fashioned gendered tropes, whereby masculinity and eloquence, and femininity and embodiment, are strongly associated with each other. As we will see, many Irish writers show that they have been influenced by globalization, in that their plays reproduce the tropes that will make their work seem globally familiar. However, they also adopt strategies that allow them to react against, analyse, and re-imagine those tropes. I want in this chapter to explore how those tropes present themselves within theatre. Should we see productions like *James X* and *Giselle* as cynical attempts to 'cash in' on clichéd images of Irishness? Or are they instead questioning audiences' willingness to consume such images uncritically? Is it possible to exploit globalization while also analysing it? And can writers be positively and negatively influenced by globalization – simultaneously?

Performing embodiment: Marina Carr

In the last chapter, I suggested that one of the features of *Angels in America* is that it represents the deterioration of a society in and through the destruction and renewal of the human body. Marina Carr, whose works repeatedly dramatize the problems caused by presenting the nation in gendered terms, has also used this strategy. Her first major play was *Low in the Dark* (1989), an absurdist treatment of gender and fertility that can be read as a commentary on the Irish debate about women's access to abortion, and as a challenge to traditional representations of women on the Irish stage. That play hasn't been revived professionally in Ireland since its premiere, but it could speak easily to contemporary concerns about the impact of pornography on the presentation of women in the mass media. Much of its humour – and much of its depth – arises from its exploration of how societies can define women's identities in relation to visibility, a theme made most explicit by Carr's presentation of a character called Curtains.

That theme also dominates her series of five plays set in the Irish midlands, produced in almost every case at the Abbey Theatre between 1994 and 2002.[1] These works are notable for their highly stylized language and their violence, and in particular for a bleak representation of women's lives. Thus, they release a great deal of suppressed female energy, but that energy always leads to destruction and violence which, more than anyone else, usually affects the female character at the centre of Carr's plays. In *The Mai* (1994), the title character commits suicide after her husband leaves her. The protagonist of *Portia Coughlan* (1996) also kills herself, in fulfilment of a suicide pact with her twin brother Gabriel. In *By the Bog of Cats* (1998), Hester Swayne commits suicide, but first murders her daughter Josie (I return to this play below). *On Raftery's Hill* (2000), arguably Carr's most brutal play, portrays a family suffering from horrendous abuse by their father, and includes a shocking scene of incestuous rape. Finally, in *Ariel* (2002), a midlands politician kills his daughter for political advancement before himself being killed by his wife – who is in turn killed by their other daughter.

If considered exclusively in terms of plot, these plays might seem melodramatic but, as Carr's use of absurdism in her earlier work shows, she is a writer with a strong sense of the power of metaphor: she does not represent reality, but exaggerates it to underline and make unavoidable the actual conditions under which people live. An essential aspect of this style of writing is her use of legend. *The Mai* is grounded in Irish myth, *By the Bog of Cats* closely resembles *Medea*, and *Ariel* draws heavily from *Iphigenia at Aulis, Electra,* and *Faust.* Carr's treatment of the physical aspects of women's lives cannot easily be resolved within the framework available to her: most of the female protagonists in her five 'midlands' plays are subjected to acts of extreme violence, often self-inflicted. In this respect, they have much in common with the great heroines of world literature, from Medea to Emma Bovary to Hedda Gabler to Anna Karenina.

This makes the plays a powerfully politicized rejection of existing Irish stage conventions. That process culminates in *Ariel,* Carr's most explicitly political work, which represents public corruption in Ireland during the 1980s and 1990s through the presentation of a TD who murders his daughter as part of a supernatural pact. Carr emphasizes throughout the play that Fermoy's killing of one female is consistent with his sense that self-expression can be achieved through control over a feminized body. He compares himself to Napoleon, who 'talked about hees battlefields like they were women' (Carr, 2002: 42), and he associates political power with sexual prowess: 'I've more women than votes linin up for me. Beauhiful young women, bodies a bronze, minds a gold, sophisticahed, beauhiful women, teeth like delph, high bellied, tauh as fish on a line' (49). Carr thus represents political corruption in Ireland as analogous to sexual exploitation: if the nation is female, then violence against women and political corruption become entangled.

How, then, should writers come to terms with such presentations of gender? The answer to that question is presented most powerfully in *By the Bog of Cats* – arguably, Carr's masterpiece. Hester Swayne occupies a number of roles that set her apart from a society that rejects her, even as she transcends her surroundings. On one level, she is a heroic figure, a contemporary Medea; on another, she is a social outcast – in Ireland, she would be referred to as a settled Traveller, a person isolated from mainstream Irish life because of her ethnicity, and from the Traveller community because she has become settled. The energy of Carr's play arises from her ability to show how Hester's identity is conditioned by social, literary, and cultural roles: she cannot be other than she is, and she can do nothing to prevent her death because her environment makes it impossible for her to be *herself.*

As well as being restricted to these roles, Hester's life is determined by powers that she fails to understand, and over which she has little control. In the play's first scene, she learns from the Ghost Fancier that she will die before nightfall, and that nothing she does can change that. And as her character develops, Carr relates Hester to a series of other literary heroines: she is not just linked to Medea, but (by her name) to the heroine of Nathaniel Hawthorne's *The Scarlet Letter* (1850), and (by her appearance in a ruined wedding dress) to Miss Havisham in Dickens's *Great Expectations*. Through her association with a man called Carthage Kilbride, she also reminds us of Virgil's Dido, and thus of Shakespeare's Cleopatra. It is worth reminding ourselves, of course, that men created all of those characters. The play therefore evokes some of the great female figures of Western literature – but it shows how writers have restricted women characters to a tiny number of possible roles. If they are not the vengeful harridan, they must be the timid wife, a choice that Carr dramatizes in the play's pivotal scene: a wedding feast where we see not one but four females, all dressed in white (Hester, Josie, Caroline, and Mrs K).

Carr's play takes those presentations of women, and works them through to their logical conclusion. In doing so, she uses the gendered symbolism of nation as woman – but turns that representation against itself. The audience's engagement with Hester arises from their admiration of her rejection of the roles that others attempt to force upon her. She refuses, for example, to be bound by legal conventions and contracts which are 'bits of paper, writin', [it] means nothin', can aisy be unsigned' (1998: 29). She also refused to be used, to be treated like an object. 'You cut your teeth on me, Carthage Kilbride', she says. 'Gnawed and sucked till all that's left is auld bone you think to fling on the dunghill, now you've no more use for me. If you think I'm goin' to let you walk over me like that, ya don't know me at all' (34). Hester draws attention to the way her society uses law, literature, religious ceremony, morality, and language to limit women. Her death is tragic because it is the only option available to her: she literally cannot continue to exist in such an environment.

Victor Merriman and others have criticized Carr for her presentation of figures like Hester, arguing that because she represents women from disadvantaged socio-economic groups being controlled by fate, she is implying that real Irish people from similar social groups are not in control of their own lives. This denial of agency to impoverished Irish women may suggest to theatre audiences that nothing can be done to improve poverty, Merriman suggests (1999). There is probably some merit in this reading, though it probably takes Carr's plays a little too literally, while also failing to place faith in audiences' ability to think critically about what they are seeing. I'd draw instead on an article by Lib Taylor, who acknowledges that Carr's plays may confirm 'the unhomely woman as hysteric', but reminds us that the 'unhomely may become a site whose very indeterminacy fuels the production of alternative identities' (2003: 189–90). When we are confronted with a figure like Hester – and as we experience the emotional impact of her death – we should feel compelled to imagine how the situation being dramatized arose in the first place, and thus are being forced to imagine alternative identities.

It would be wrong to see Carr's play as directly or explicitly tackling issues related to globalization. Rather, I think the significance of her work for contemporary audiences is that she analyses the consequences of presenting gender in limited and limiting ways – when, as Mirzoeff (2002) states, globalization is doing precisely the same thing. Her plays can therefore be seen as offering a form of resistance to the tendency within our culture to commodify the unspeaking female body.

To move this discussion towards a consideration of the monologue, I will conclude this section by discussing Tara Maria Lovett's *The Call*, an Irish play that manages to give its central female character the opportunity to verbalize her experiences in great detail, while also allowing her full expression of her physicality.

Premiered in Dublin in 2002 in the cavernous basement of a centuries old building in the grounds of Dublin Castle, *The Call* intriguingly takes place *inside* the body of its protagonist. As audiences enter the performance space, they realize that they have entered a human body: the room pulses with red lighting as they take their seats around a ribcage, with a pile of stones at its centre representing a human heart. The owner of this body, Maddie, emerges and, prompted by a mysterious 'voice' (played by a male actor, who appears on stage), she describes her upbringing and the development of her sense of sexuality and spirituality. Taking us from her childhood to young adulthood in a series of vignettes, Maddie explains how she has struggled to understand herself and her relationships with a number of different men, all of whom are performed by a second male actor.

The paralysis being dramatized is not so much one of the heart as the mouth: the audience does not witness the development of Maddie's sexuality, but her ability to articulate it to herself. Sexuality and desire are the play's main subjects, but they are never spoken about directly, instead represented in code, analogy, and silence. The play begins with the romantic declarations of Scarlett and Rhett in *Gone With The Wind* and, in a disturbing scene, with a man who sexually abuses Maddie when she is a child, promising to take her horse-riding, but first making her 'practise', sitting on his knee. As a teenager, Maddie observes her teacher's struggles to name the parts of the female body, displayed before her on a wallchart; and in adulthood, Maddie wrestles with various men: with the unspeaking insistence of a solider and the inarticulate banalities of a young male drug addict. The play's conclusion appears to be that Maddie's ability to express herself as a sexual person might be based in her spirituality. This suggestion comes from her dialogue with 'the voice', which, intriguingly, is the voice of a man.

Lovett combines many themes in *The Call* – sexuality, spirituality, and gender – and faces all of their contradictions and complexities. While it might have been tempting for her to tackle the issue of sexual suppression as a by-product of Catholic guilt, Lovett instead presents a character who is witty and likeable, desperate to protect herself, and in pain from her inability to express her desires. Importantly, although this play is based mainly in the monologue form, it is also extremely carnal. Its audience is seated in a human body, and their attention is constantly returned to the physical. The beating of a heart represented by two stones being thrust together, the movement of the actors – even the heat of the performance space – mean that the audience is made as aware of the body as of the spirit by this play. Lovett's use of the monologue in so physical a manner draws attention to synthesize the presentation of the body and the voice on the Irish stage – which she achieves symbolically by having her female protagonist's 'soul' performed by a male actor.

For this reason, *The Call* shows both the limitations and the strengths of the monologue form. On one level, it might be seen as an Irish response to the move from the physical to the conceptual: rather than embodying action, many of our dramatists instead narrate it. Yet Lovett shows that, by placing an actor before an audience, the liveness of the monologue can be used to reassert the importance of the physical, the bodily, the carnal. I want now to explore this feature of the Irish monologue during the 1990s, explaining how its existence – together with the changing treatment of the Irish body – can be seen in relation to globalization.

Monologue and community: McPherson, O'Rowe, Walsh

In early 2006, Irish newspapers reported on an unfortunate incident that occurred during a performance of Brian Friel's *Faith Healer* at the Gate Theatre in Dublin (see Keane, 2006 for one example). Ralph Fiennes, who was playing the lead role of Frank Hardy, had been building toward the conclusion of his performance when, suddenly, a mobile phone began to ring. The guilty patron (who was sitting in the front row) reportedly pretended that the phone was not hers. It continued to ring until, exasperated, Fiennes shouted at her to 'turn that fucking machine off'.

I wonder if we can see that outburst as Fiennes dropping out of character? The illusion at work in Friel's play is that the audience is being addressed directly by a personality – that there is no fourth wall separating performance and audience. This characteristic of the Irish monologue has been an interesting feature of its development, appearing most explicitly in Conor McPherson's 2002 play *Port Authority*, which, according to the stage directions, 'is set in the theatre' (2004: 132).

It also partially explains the popularity of the form: monologue can involve the creation of a rapport between actor and audience that is considerably more intimate than what ordinarily arises in most other forms of theatre. The audience at a monologue play is being addressed directly by an individual – who is free to tell us to 'fuck off' if we distract him, without necessarily undermining the integrity of the performance. I've written already of how audiences in a global environment seek out intimate experiences in the theatre, particularly with celebrity figures (like Fiennes). It is for this reason that monologue has become so popular internationally, and why it attracts actors like Fiennes and others.

Monologue has always been an important part of Anglophone drama, particularly in recent years. In English drama of the 1990s, Bryony Lavery's *Frozen* (1998) is a major example of a work that makes extensive use of monologue. It was also, of course, very popular when used by Alan Bennett in his series *Talking Heads* (1988); Mark Ravenhill's *Product* (2005) neatly uses the form to show the self-centredness of his protagonist, a film producer who sees global conflict only in terms of how much money can be made from dramatizing it. The form also appears occasionally in American drama, in such plays as Neil LaBute's *Bash* (1999) and Tony Kushner's *Homebody* (2001). However, its use became particularly common in Ireland from the late 1990s onwards, being strongly associated with a trio of young male authors who emerged in the middle of the decade: Conor McPherson, Mark O'Rowe, and Enda Walsh. In the following discussion, I concentrate on that trio, though I do refer in passing to some of the other major writers of the form.

The appearance of monologue in Irish drama from the mid-1990s onwards was certainly not unprecedented. Beckett used the form extensively, in such plays as *Happy Days* (1961), *Play* (1964), and *Not I* (1972). Friel's *Faith Healer* (1979) has also been very influential. And the form has been used periodically from the 1980s onwards, in such works as Frank McGuinness's *Bag Lady* (1985) and Dermot Bolger's *In High Germany* and *The Holy Ground* (both 1990). However, to speak of the Irish monologue as a distinctive style or genre is problematic, since the term encompasses a diversity of performance styles, modes of representation, and formal approaches. Irish monologues since the mid-1990s some-times involve direct testimony by an individual to an audience, as in McPherson's *St Nicholas* (1997) and O'Rowe's *Terminus* (2007). They sometimes involve the interplay and overlap of different stories from individuals sharing the same stage, as in Friel's *Molly Sweeney*, Enda Walsh's *Disco Pigs* (1996), O'Rowe's *Howie the Rookie* (1999), or Eugene O'Brien's *Eden* (2001). It also appeared at a time when there was a grow-ing number of successful 'one-man shows', in which one actor performs a variety of different roles, as in Donal O'Kelly's *Catalpa* (1996) and Mac Intyre's *The Gallant John Joe* (2001). Analyses of the form might also consider plays that make significant use of monologue within a natura-listic narrative, as in McPherson's *The Weir* (1997) and McDonagh's *The Pillowman*. Also important are theatrical adaptations of novels that were written in the first person, such as Alan Gilsenan's version of Banville's *The Book of Evidence* (2001). So, although the monologue may have dom-inated Irish drama from the mid-1990s, the variety of ways in which it was used makes categorization difficult.

It is possible, however, to isolate a number of features that are common to most Irish monologues, particularly those of McPherson, O'Rowe, and Walsh. Some of those features may arise because they conform to audi-ences' expectations about what Irish plays ought to involve: the presen-tation of gender, the poeticization of speech, and the use of storytelling, among other characteristics. However, monologue also provides writers with opportunities to resist and reflect upon globalization – and I will dis-cuss how many Irish writers have used the form to explore such phe-nomena as time-space compression, mobility, and individualization. By exploring these issues, I will make an argument that is similar to that just concluded about the plays of Marina Carr: theatre can achieve global success by using techniques and stereotypes that are internationally recognizable – but it can also use audiences' familiarity with those traits to engage in a critique of globalization itself.

The obvious place to begin this discussion is with gender. In Ireland, monologue is a form dominated by male writers; it frequently focuses on issues of male inadequacy, both sexual and social; and it tends to involve plotting that is resolved in outbursts of male violence. Writing about McPherson's *Port Authority* and O'Rowe's (naturalistic) *Made in China* (2001), Karen Fricker observes that 'the plays . . . don't embody women at all . . . Women however hover over both plays as idealized symbols and possessors of both virtue and agency, in contrast to the impotent, morally impaired males who actually inhabit the plays' (2002: 86). For Fricker, this represents a reinscription of the Revival's idealization of woman, with both plays reinforcing stereotypical, conservative images of gender.

While Fricker's critique of McPherson and O'Rowe cannot necessarily be applied to all Irish monologues, it is notable that very few examples of monologues written by Irish women exist. Marie Jones's *A Night in November* and Geraldine Aron's *My Brilliant Divorce* are among them; neither play has received serious critical attention, and Jones's features a male protagonist whose wife is represented in extremely unflattering terms. Similarly, there are relatively few examples of women characters in Irish monologues: O'Rowe's *Crestfall* has an entirely female cast, and two of the three characters in *Terminus* are women – but few similar examples exist. Looking further into the past, it is notable that Beckett's female speakers tend to construct themselves as objects rather than subjects: Winnie in *Happy Days* is more concerned with her physical appearance than inner knowledge, and of course Mouth in *Not I* is entirely alienated from her own sense of subjectivity. Only Friel's *Molly Sweeney*, which considers how the female subject can be controlled by masculine discourses, can be said to have successfully used monologue to represent issues of gender, because Molly directly tells the audience how she must be seen. As I mentioned in Chapter 2, this places her in interesting contrast with the Mundy sisters in *Lughnasa*.

The presentation of gender in the Irish monologue tends to result in an attempt to poeticize the language of male characters. The speech used by O'Rowe and Walsh in particular is a highly poeticized version of Irish urban idioms, which uses techniques such as rhythm, onomatopoeia, and literary allusion to produce dramatic effect. Walsh's *Disco Pigs* uses an extremely dense linguistic pattern, accurately representing a poeticized version of Cork idiom, while using wordplay to reveal underlying relationships between apparently disconnected elements of Irish life. Speaking of the victory of Irish athlete and Cork native Sonia O'Sullivan at the 1995 World Athletics Championship in Gothenburg, Pig says:

> Ya noel wen Sonia finally become chapion da wonder horse an gallop her way to *suckycess* bak in old Godden-berg, yeah? An Sonia stan on da winny po-dium wid da whirl medal, all a dangle from da pretty liddle neck as da *nationalist rant-hymn* blast da fuck oudda da sky an da green white an porridge all a flutter in da breeze. An all da Irish around da track an in da whirl, an anybody who ever fuck an Irish dey all have a liddle tear a boy in der eye when dey say, 'Dis is a great day for Our-land!'. Well Runt, dis is a bettur day!
>
> (Walsh, 1999: 182–3)[2]

This passage provides an excellent example of Walsh's desire to use monologue to create a poetics of inarticulacy. As he explains, 'I have this serious hang-up about being inarticulate. I went through years of speech therapy. I had a stammer. That has largely impacted on everything I have done: the sort of characters, the structure of my writing and the style of my writing. It is the poetry of being inarticulate' (quoted by Thornton and White, 2002: 20). This outlook is evident in the quotation above. The paragraph contains puns that reveal Pig's iconoclastic and anti-social view of his environment (shown in italics above): he shows his contempt for high achievement by rendering 'success' as 'suckycess', while his disdain for expressions of national pride is shown when he pronounces the words 'national anthem' as 'nationalist rant-hymn'. Also notable are the rhythmic features of this piece, with Walsh's use of the 'd' sound occurring at short intervals (shown above in bold), which have the effect of intensifying the speed of the speech, while emphasizing the manic quality of Pig's character. Also interesting is Pig's pronunciation of 'world' as 'whirl', a blurring of two meanings that highlights the chaotic quality of the environment in which Pig and Runt find themselves. Walsh's achievement in *Disco Pigs* is thus to provide an accurate representation of the slang, intonation, and pronunciation of certain modes of speech in urban Cork, while also presenting a form of language that may be subjected to the kind of close reading more commonly used for poetry.

Such linguistic density may seem anti-theatrical, but it could be argued that the purpose of such writing is to stimulate the audience's imagination. The stage directions for Donal O'Kelly's one man show *Catalpa* show how this may be achieved:

> The theatrical challenge is to flick images into the audience's heads, to stimulate their imaginations so that they will see the Catalpa at sea, they will see and hear and feel and smell the Atlantic swell, the whole blubber, the scorched Australian shore. The instruments used to do this are the text itself – the images described, the bits of dialogue, the words used, the sounds, with movement, gesture, energy, stillness, with music sometimes, with lighting and the use of a few selected props. But the main function of all of these is to kick-start the most important instrument of all: the audience's imagination.
>
> (O'Kelly, 1997: i)

Monologue thus *may* be used to stimulate the imaginations of the audience, using sound, gesture, movement, and other effects to achieve this aim. So, although the linguistic elements of the form may be subjected to close literary analysis, they may also be used to contribute to the kinetic effects of a performance.

The third way in which the Irish monologue conforms to international expectations about masculinity and Irishness is its use of storytelling. In *The Irish Storyteller*, George Zimmerman (2001) shows how a cross-linguistic tradition of storytelling exists within Irish literature. He states that the 19th-century Irish novel integrated the folk traditions of oracular storytelling, especially in *Castle Rackrent*. This feature of 19th-century Irish literature is also evident in drama: it may be observed in *The Shaughraun*, which features many examples of storytelling, particularly from Conn. This Irish tradition of storytelling has persisted into 20th-century Irish drama, in which there are many examples of the power of reported speech. For example, much of the action of *The Playboy of the Western World* – the 'murder' of Old Mahon and Christy's victory at the races – is reported in narrative accounts instead of being represented onstage; likewise, the Easter 1916 Rebellion is presented through reported speech in O'Casey's *The Plough and the Stars*. The Irish monologue thus capitalizes upon elements that are already present in Irish drama and rooted deeply in Irish culture.

One reason, then, for the prevalence of the monologue form during the late 1990s is that, at that time, it allowed writers to present figures who corresponded with international audiences' expectations about Irish masculinity, and hence about Irish plays. I do not wish to suggest that those writers were consciously or deliberately exploiting those expectations; rather, I am arguing that they made use of a vocabulary that was easily understood internationally – just as Carr's treatment of women made use of a different vocabulary at the same time. However, like Carr's dramas, these plays can be seen as explorations of issues that have become increasingly important as globalization has intensified.

This is most apparent in the monologue's inherent mobility. Conor McPherson amusingly explains how his early monologue *The Good Thief* (1994) was re-written specifically for a national tour around Ireland. The actor in the piece, Garrett Keough, had 'come up with a surefire money-maker' writes McPherson: a national tour. 'The Arts Council in Ireland gives rural venues money to pay for touring productions to come and visit', he explains. 'Once the venue decides they'd like you to perform, they give you a guaranteed payment, even if no audience turns up. So we went back into rehearsals and slimmed the whole thing [the script of *The Good Thief*] down . . . All we needed was a chair, and the tour began' (2000: 184). The show thus required little preparation and very few financial inputs. Keough's preparation during a visit to Monaghan was thus rather basic: he 'ate some steak and chips and then finally went for a snooze in the car' (184), writes McPherson. Similarly, McPherson writes about how he provided technical support for the tour. 'It turned out that I was going to be operating the lights for the show', he states. This, it seems, was a relatively straightforward task: 'They come up at the beginning and went down at the end' (184).

The inherent mobility of the monologue thus allowed emerging writers like McPherson to produce their own theatre without the need to incur any of the expenses generally associated with theatre, such as set design and costuming. So one of the reasons that monologue arises during a period of increased globalization is simply because it allows authors to write plays that can travel freely; all you need is an actor and an audience, and the play can begin. Monologue thus requires little investment from producers, but can reap large rewards from audiences.

Monologue also became popular during the Celtic Tiger period because audiences were better equipped to process the kinds of compressed bursts of information that appear in such plays. Globalization, as I argued in relation to *Dancing at Lughnasa*, involves an overwhelming sensation that the world is shrinking. Less frequently articulated, however, is the idea that geographical compression also involves a new awareness of time – we are now expected to be able to process more information in shorter periods. Hence, we find that the production and reception of culture has become dominated by speed. 'To avoid frustration', notes Bauman, 'one would do better to refrain from developing habits and attachments or entering into lasting commitments. The objects of desire are better enjoyed on the spot and then disposed of; markets see to it that they are made in such a way that both the gratification and the obsoleteness occur in an instant' (2001: 156). What he means in that statement is that the gap between consumption and desire has been reduced – an idea also developed by James Gleik, who suggests that we are witnessing the 'acceleration of just about everything' (116). Many aspects of human life, notes Gleik, have accelerated in recent years, from commerce to employment practices to the production and reception of culture. This acceleration has resulted in a situation whereby people are now expected to be able to 'multi-task' in many aspects of their lives – that is, they have become used to performing a number of simple tasks simultaneously, rather than devoting their attention to one specific complicated activity, as they might have done in the past.

David Harvey (1989) has argued that multi-tasking is a consequence of the spread of global capitalism, which, he states, has been 'characterized by continuous efforts to shorten turnover times, thereby speeding up social processes while reducing the time-horizons of meaningful decision-making' (229). This acceleration doesn't just affect the way that we work: it also has an impact on how we receive information. This alteration in the speed with which we consume entertainment is in many ways determined by a desire to control the way in which individuals receive culture. Arguably, the best example of this phenomenon is that contemporary television has developed strategies to determine how viewers use their remote controls. Robert Levine cites studies that show that the television no longer has viewers, but 'grazers': people who change channel up to 22 times in one minute, who 'approach the airwaves as a vast smorgasbord, all of which must be sampled, no matter how meager the helpings' (cited in Gleik, 2000: 183). Because of 'grazing', audiences form superficial views of the programming, which reduces their satisfaction levels. TV networks have responded by ensuring that the audiences will not be given any reason to hit the remote control button: Gleik mentions how a 'new forward-looking unit within the NBC' has been taking 'an electronic scalpel to the barely perceptible instants when a show fades to black and then re-materializes as a commercial. Over the course of a night, this can save the network as much as fifteen precious seconds, maybe even twenty'. As a result of such techniques, writes Gleik, 'the viewer, at every instant, is in a hurry' (175); they are also being bombarded with information that is intended to stimulate them to such an extent that they do not think of changing channel – not only are we being rushed, we are being subjected to a constant state of distraction.

The desire to quicken the pace of entertainment has also affected the recent development of theatre. The traditional three or five act structure of plays has generally been replaced by loosely structured series of short scenes that tend not to last longer than 15 minutes each. The risk of an audience becoming bored is minimized in many plays, with action taking place quickly enough to be perceived, but too quickly to be analysed, and by the frequently gratuitous use of shocking images such as explicit on-stage sex, as in the Abbey's *Barbaric Comedies*, or intensely cruel violence, as in McDonagh's *Lieutenant of Inishmore*. Audiences have generally responded positively to the attempt within new drama to provoke spontaneous emotional reactions rather than considered intellectual responses – since this is what they have become used to in almost every other visual medium, from cinema to television news reports. The increasing use of such qualities as speed and compression in drama should not be misunderstood as resulting in a decline in standards.

Michael Colgan admits that 'theatre is getting shorter'. 'I've had arguments with people who feel that our imaginations are in some way failing . . . But I disagree with that entirely. I think we have new imaginations, different imaginations' (quoted in Chambers *et al.*, 2001: 82). These 'different imaginations' are sometimes described derogatorily as evidence of cultural 'dumbing down' – but they could just as easily be used to explain developments such as the growing popularity of Beckett's work in Dublin throughout the 1990s. When, in 1991, the Gate Theatre staged its first Beckett Festival, it was praised as a daring, innovative initiative; ten years later, the decision to produce *Krapp's Last Tape* in September 2001 was regarded as conservative and rather dull programming. This may partly be because of the Gate's gradual introduction of Beckett to Dublin audiences, but it may also be due to Dublin audiences' development during the 1990s of cognitive abilities that render the level of compression in Beckett's plays far more manageable in 2001 than it had been in 1991.

This improved ability to process information is a significant explanation for the popularity of the monologue form. It uses chronological compression: it does not present events unfolding in place and time, but instead summarizes the essential elements of both to provide audiences with 'edited highlights' of the action. It also involves geographical compression, using the space of the theatrical stage to lay out before us multiple geographical locations and various public and domestic spaces. Most importantly, the success of the monologue play requires of its audience that they perform multiple simple tasks simultaneously. The meaning of the story is derived not from direct engagement with any character's interpretation of events, but in the critical evaluation of the contrasts and points of similarity between all of the characters, or between all of the elements of one narrator's story. An audience member at a monologue play must therefore receive information, process it, evaluate it, and compare it with information already received. This requires the ability to process an account of action that is chronologically, geographically, and linguistically compressed. These processes are not unique to the monologue form, but they appear more prominently there than in other kinds of writing.

This reminds us of the importance of audience at a monologue play – which shows how the form can be used to resist the processes of individualization, which are associated with globalization. A significant feature of the form in Ireland is that the audience will rarely share the background of the characters on stage. Many Irish monologues are written in poeticized versions of urban working-class idioms (as in *Howie the*

Rookie, Disco Pigs, and McPherson's *The Good Thief*), and feature characters on the social margins, who are generally shown to be involved in
activities deemed in some way anti-social, such as drug-use or gangster-
ism. There is certainly a class divide between the middle-class audiences
before whom most of these plays were premiered and the mostly working-
class characters that populate the stage.

Other forms of isolation can be presented, however. Marie Jones's *A
Night In November* presents a middle-class Unionist from Belfast whose
support for the Republic's football team in the 1994 World Cup makes
him an outsider in his own community in Northern Ireland, while his
religion and politics make him an outsider in the rest of the island.
Similarly, in Michael West's *Foley* (2001), the eponymous character
describes himself as isolated from society, notwithstanding his affluence
and respectability. In a passage that reveals much about the isolated status of characters in Irish monologues, Foley states that, 'I used to associate solitude with self-improvement and self-knowledge; it was linked
in my mind with the idea of travel, of bravely setting off into the
unknown, defiant and independent. Solitude, like travel, was a choice
you made to affirm your identity' (2001: 1).

There are many reasons for this social marginalization, but such characters often perform in monologue because they cannot credibly be
represented in naturalistic encounters with others. Many of Howie's
statements in *Howie the Rookie* arise from his awareness of the difference
between his public persona and his private thoughts. This creates a
moving contrast between the actions he participates in and his private
commentary upon them, as, for instance, when he states that 'I'm a bit
put off' from beating up the Rookie – showing his sense of ambivalence
about the violence he's participating in (O'Rowe, 1999: 21). Monologue
thus acts as a symbol of the isolation of the characters onstage: they are
'talking to themselves' because no-one else is listening to them.

It seems significant that such a large number of narratives about isolated individuals appeared when individualization was becoming a
powerful force throughout the West. This is evident in economic terms
in the way in which individuals with access to money or credit were
encouraged to put self-interest ahead of what might be termed communal values, with economic policies being determined by the promotion
of self-interest in the hope of a 'trickledown effect' to those who are less
well off. It was also evident culturally, with the increased influence of
cultural products that need to be consumed individually rather than
communally, such as the internet, video games, digital television, and
so on. The growth of individualization as a response to such processes

was occurring internationally, particularly in the West, in the same period. While few of the monologues written in Irish drama address such issues directly or explicitly, it is notable that narratives about isolation, marginalization, and the impossibility of communication appeared when such experiences were becoming common in Irish society.

This leads us to consider again the impact of monologue upon the audience. While in simple terms, the audience is witnessing the unfolding of a narrative, the performance of a monologue cannot be considered similar to the recitation of a text, or a reading by an author of a work of fiction. The significance of the monologue is not that it presents events in a linear self-contained fashion, but rather that it represents an interpretation of those events, delivered in a subjective, sometimes self-deceiving, and often confusing manner. In Irish monologues – especially those that feature more than one character – part of the role of the audience is to piece together the strands of information, judging the credibility of the narration, and attempting to understand the gap between the deeds being described onstage and their mode of transmission. Being part of an audience at the performance of a monologue thus becomes a *communal* enterprise, in which meanings are created in the interplay between performers and audiences. Monologue disrupts the notion that stage representation should be regarded as discrete, reliable, and self-contained.

Conclusion

In this chapter, I've suggested that globalization has affected the development of one kind of theatrical form – in this case, monologue – and that it also explains why the work of Marina Carr has taken on particular urgency. To describe those developments in terms of the academic language of 'hegemony' and 'resistance' is to overlook their complexity. The popularity of the monologue form may arise because global audiences want their plays to correspond to stereotypes about the Irish. And that popularity may *also* arise because monologue allows audiences to exercise their ability to process information differently: to multi-task cognitively. And finally, monologue may be popular because the intimacy between actor and audience reasserts community when, thanks to globalization, audiences are experiencing excessive levels of individualization. This suggests that globalization is changing the way that audiences see plays and, more importantly, it alters too the way that writers compose their works. And what is interesting is that some of the processes associated with globalization (cognitive multi-tasking, for instance) allow us to enjoy plays that in turn help us to analyse critically the impact on our lives of other processes associated with globalization (such as individualization).

A major issue to emerge from this discussion is the extent to which technology affects the production and reception of theatre. It seems likely that, as Lev Manovich puts it, the 'gradual computerization of culture will eventually transform all of it' (2001: 6). There is an interesting conceptual parallel between globalization and digitization: both involve the transformation of the physical into the virtual. As a result, both have become interlinked, often to a point of being indistinguishable – as, for instance, in the development of social networking over the internet. The pervasiveness and power of digitization is thought to have had profound affects on all aspects of life: Lyotard's notion that ours is a 'computerized society' (1984: 3) seems increasingly accurate.

Indeed, we might argue that it is now possible to borrow from digital media the terminology that we need to understand recent developments in theatre. The audience that is bombarded with compressed information, which it then must sift through and analyse, is acting in a way that is analogous to a computer processor. The use of multiple scenes in drama can be compared to the use of multiple-interface technology. A play in which actors perform several parts simultaneously (as in *Stones In His Pockets*) could be thought of as proceeding in accordance with database logic. To make such comparisons might imply that computers have transformed theatre, but, although some level of 'transcoding' cannot be ruled out, there is another explanation for the fact that plays and computers seem to be working in similar ways.

There are many apparent analogies between theatrical perception and the alteration discussed above in cultural practices and new media. The person who is paid to perform several work tasks simultaneously is multi-tasking; a person who watches a play in which several scenes are being performed simultaneously is engaged in a comparable activity; and a computer that produces several different windows simultaneously is performing in a similar way. To assume a causal relationship between capitalism, creativity, and computerization is problematic. It may be the case that an audience member's familiarity with Microsoft Windows will, for instance, make the third act of Frank McGuinness's *Observe the Sons of Ulster Marching Towards the Somme* – which contains several interlinking scenes – easier to follow. In both cases, the viewer is confronted with a frame that contains multiple smaller frames that must be viewed consecutively and, at times, simultaneously. But that does not mean that McGuinness's play caused Microsoft to become popular. Before computers existed, it was necessary for them to be imagined as possible: plays such as *Observe the Sons of Ulster* were necessary imaginings of the potential of compression, out of which the development of digital media became possible. To attribute the power of influence to computers, capital, or art is to attribute power. This means that Manovich's notion of transcoding or Lyotard's of the computerized society should be treated with caution.

Also important is the question of utility. What is the function of technology in a globalizing society? In *Imagined Communities*, Benedict Anderson posits a relationship between artwork and social structure, describing the 19th-century novel as a vehicle for nationalism (1991). It might be possible to develop this idea to suggest that, in this postmodern and supposedly post-national era, the computer and digital media have similarly become the vehicle of globalization. Just as the novel was a space for a community to imagine itself as a nation, so too is the idea that geography has been eradicated imagined through the use of the computer, digital television, the internet, and mobile telecommunications. Globalization allows us to conceive of the world an imagined community in which the world is interconnected, where distance has been eliminated, where borders no longer exist, where nations have disappeared, and where identity, race, and class are invisible. Obviously, such claims have little basis in reality: like the nation imagined by 19th-century novelists, the globalized world could be understood as a useful fiction (or, as I suggested earlier, as a meme that is competing well), and the computer might be the primary vehicle for its transmission. Although the transformation of society referred to by Lyotard and others is interconnected with the development of information technology, the reverse statement is also true: computerization is driven by a much broader reconfiguration of creativity, space, consumption, and, most importantly, of cognition.

As my analysis of the monologue form suggests, those transformations can inspire theatre practitioners to develop new ways of writing. However, the discussion of Carr's work shows how digital technology is being used to imagine roles for men and women that are restrictive and damaging; theatre can in that case (and in others) act to imagine alternative identities – and, through engaging with its audience, to reassert the value of community at a time of individualization. I want now to move towards a conclusion of this book by considering further the issues of community, audience, and authorial responsibility.

8
Branding Identity: Irish Theatre in 2005

One of the major features of the current period of globalization is that it has involved massive movements of people around the planet. I've touched on some examples already of how this affects theatre, discussing the way in which playwrights develop work for global production, and considering how tourism affects the construction of the repertoires of national theatres. Another significant feature of global mobility is the growth of multiculturalism, which has been intensified by emigration, tourism, and the increased movement of refugees and asylum seekers internationally. How has that growth affected the development of theatre?

To an extent, that question is redundant: there are varieties of studies on multiculturalism and interculturalism in theatre, many of which have already been cited in this book.[1] I do not wish to repeat those arguments, but instead to consider how globalization can simultaneously inspire and inhibit genuine multiculturalism, both in society generally and in theatre particularly. We're used to hearing that globalization results in homogenization, in a flattening of difference between cultures; I've shown already how it also tends to lead to the production of nationalized 'brands', which present identities in ways that will be regarded globally as 'familiar' to audiences. Without wishing to oversimplify matters, my aim in this chapter is to show that the production of those homogenized brands works against the development of multiculturalism. I want to argue that the production through theatre and other media of an essentialized Irish 'brand' has occurred during a period in which Irish identity is rapidly changing, due to the growth of multiculturalism in the country. This means that representations of Irishness have narrowed as Irish identity has expanded, creating a tension between Irishness as it is presented to the world (through culture and by agencies like the IDA whose 'Irish mind' campaign was discussed in Chapter 3) and Irishness as it is experienced and expressed within the country itself.

As I've repeatedly stated in this book, globalization causes interrelated processes that can ultimately conflict with each other. It leads on the one hand to the production of essentialized versions of identity, while on the other it creates social conditions that require us to imagine forms of identity that are not limited in relation to race, ethnicity, religion, gender, or other factors. I've shown already how Irishness as a theatrical brand affects the representations of gender, and want now to broaden that investigation to consider the relationship between branding and racialization. I explore that issue by discussing two plays that appeared in 2005: Brian Friel's *The Home Place* and Elizabeth Kuti's *The Sugar Wife*. In different ways, these plays contextualize and historicize the 'branding' of identity which, I will suggest, draws on practices which in the past were related to imperialism, slavery, and other methods of commodifying individuals for economic gain.

'No Place Like Home': Brian Friel's *The Home Place* and Ireland's Citizenship Referendum

Ostensibly, Brian Friel's *The Home Place* seems like a return to the tone and themes of *Translations*, with a touch of Chekhov's *Cherry Orchard* evident too. It is set in the summer of 1878, three years after the election of Parnell, and a year before famine returned to Ireland – a catastrophe that would prompt a massive increase in evictions, which in turn provoked the beginning of the Land War between tenants and landlords (the struggle which, incidentally, is the subject of the film being made in Marie Jones's *Stones In His Pockets*). By setting the action during the summer, a year before a series of historical events occurs, Friel places *The Home Place* in the tradition of plays like *Translations* and *Lughnasa* (and many of his other works), with the relative peace of the setting acting in counterpoint to audiences' awareness of what would follow.

At the centre of the play are the father and son pair of Christopher and David, the last members of an Anglo-Irish family who have lived in Donegal for generations, though they still regard Warwickshire as their 'home place'. Both adopt a benevolent attitude towards the people living nearby; indeed, both are in love with the same local woman, Margaret O'Donnell. The men seem generally to be respected by their community, though Friel also emphasizes that their position was acquired through an act of violent dispossession centuries before. Rather unsubtly, he gives the family the surname 'Gore', and tellingly states towards the end of the play that one of the oldest trees on their estate was planted on 14 February 1779 – which is the day when Captain Cook, another English 'planter', was killed by the people of a Pacific island. The Gores thus seem unable to escape the legacies of colonialism: it is part of their cultural memory, is marked on their landscape, is indelibly a part of their sense of self.

The crisis of the play occurs when Christopher's brother Richard arrives in Donegal, seeking to measure the skulls of the local people in an attempt to explain the moral behaviour of the Irish by reference to their physical traits: 'if we could break into that vault', he states, referring to racial identity, 'we wouldn't just control an empire. We would rule the entire universe' (Friel, 2005: 36) – which means that he is suggesting that Britain can move from controlling land to controlling identity. That intended shift from the territorial to the conceptual prompts a group of local men to intervene. One is Johnny McLoone, 'a very large man in his sixties' (14), who (interestingly) happens to have the same surname as Friel's mother. The other is Con Doherty, who shares his forename with the hero of Boucicault's *Shaughraun*, though he is a very a different kind of vagabond, accompanying an escaped prisoner who has nothing in common with Robert Ffoliot. In an echo of O'Casey, Friel describes these men as 'shadowy' gunmen (57) who seem at one with the land: they 'melt' (11) and 'merge' (13) back into the thicket, according to the stage directions.

Like many of Friel's plays, *The Home Place* considers the relationship between identity and place, raising questions about whether a 'visitor' to Ireland – even one whose family has lived in the country for generations – is entitled to identify himself as genuinely Irish. For Christopher, that entitlement will be withdrawn because of a changing political situation, rendering his own feelings on the subject largely irrelevant. Indeed, all of the play's characters attempt (and sometimes achieve) self-realization through abandoning place rather than identifying with it. David believes that his love for Margaret can only be realized if they leave Ireland for somewhere else: Glasgow, Kenya – it doesn't seem to matter to him (25–6). Christopher himself will conclude the play by expressing a pitifully naïve wish to live in 'Africa, South America, India – anywhere where roles aren't imposed upon us – where we'll be free of history and heritage and the awful burden of this [*house*]' (65). And Richard's status as an anthropologist is dependent upon his ability to construct Ireland as a colonial outpost: to affirm the importance of his own home (England), he must leave it in search of a culture that he can present as marginal.

This emphasis on the abandonment of place is stated most explicitly in the play's final line, which is delivered by Margaret: 'in a short time Father will come up here for me', she says (75), giving up the independence and assertiveness that she has displayed throughout the play – thus revealing an interesting relationship between place, power, and gender. Indeed, Friel's recurrent use of such words as 'trespass' (14, 39, 55, 62) and his decision to call Christopher a 'lodger' (26) place the issue of territory firmly at the centre of the play.

The Home Place also considers the extent to which both science and literature may define and determine identity. Richard's visit to Ireland arises from a desire to explore what Christopher refers to as his 'ridiculous theories' (21) about the relationship between physical characteristics and behaviour – his attempt, that is, to map the conceptual, to see identity not as a process (as I defined it when discussing *Translations* in Chapter 2), but as an essence. His pseudo-scientific approach to the Irish is contrasted with the works of the great Irish poet Thomas Moore, who was born in 1779 (the year that Captain Cook died) and whose songs 'Oft in the Stilly Night' and 'The Young May Moon' feature in the play. Moore has the 'true measure' of the Irish, states Margaret's father Clement, whose references to the 'easy sentiment' of Moore's work appear to echo the famous manifesto for the Irish Literary Theatre mentioned earlier (Richard's description of Clement as a 'buffoon' might also be a reminder of Yeats's objection to plays like *The Shaughraun* in the same passage) (42). Clement's suggestion is that Moore 'divines us [Irish] accurately' (42), that he is our 'national poet' (41). This implies that it is art, not science, that best captures and expresses the essential traits of a nation. Importantly, art represents those traits in a way that allows room for diversity: whereas Richard's science aims to record *differences* between groups of people, Clement's art allows for harmony, for the combination of related parts to form a coherent whole.

The play has obvious resonances with contentious issues in Ireland in 2004–5, since it considers the issue of how a person becomes entitled to see himself as Irish at a time when many people were debating the relationship between citizenship, residence, and national identity. In part, that debate arose from many of the developments I've already discussed: the old identifiers of land, religion, language, and nationalism had become more irrelevant in a country that was more urbanized, more secular, multi-linguistic, and supposedly post-nationalist. But that debate was also influenced by Ireland's changing demography (mentioned already in relation to *Dancing at Lughnasa*), which saw Ireland transformed from a country of emigration to one of immigration. This change occurred rapidly. In 1996, 6 per cent of the population of Ireland had been born outside of the country – and the majority of that group were from places nearby, particularly the UK. By 2006, over 10 per cent of the people living in Ireland had been born abroad, and the population was somewhat more multi-ethnic than it had been six years earlier. In 1996, there had been just under 5000 people living in Ireland who were born in Africa; by 2002, that number had increased to over 26,000, and by 2006 had risen to 35,000. In the same period, the number of people originally from Asia grew from 8000 in 1996 to 28,000 in 2002, and to 46,000 in 2006. There was also a significant increase in immigrants from other European countries (other than the UK), rising to 190,000 by 2006. In global terms, these figures are tiny, almost trivial. What is significant, however, is the rate of transformation, which was extraordinarily rapid.

This gave rise to increasing levels of discussion about Irishness – as a national identity, a form of citizenship, a commodity. The debate became particularly heated in 2004, when the Irish government held a referendum to redefine Irish citizenship. In the first chapter of this book, I suggested that the 1998 Good Friday Agreement was an example of how Irish identity was becoming more conceptual than territorial: to be Irish is to exercise an entitlement to be Irish, which is granted through birth on the island. In 2004, the Irish government decided it needed to alter one element of the Agreement, in order to reassert the importance of territoriality as a way of defining (or, strictly speaking, of limiting) the entitlement of immigrants to Irish citizenship. Before 2004, an immigrant to the country automatically became entitled to citizenship if his or her child was born on the island of Ireland. The Irish Minister for Justice Michael McDowell claimed that this right to citizenship through birth should be seen as a 'loophole' in the Irish law, which was being exploited by women who 'travel to Ireland for the birth even where the journey is left so late as to put the mothers or their unborn babies at risk', claimed McDowell. He presented this as an 'abuse of Irish Citizenship' and a threat to the 'stability of the maternity services' in Ireland.[2] The debate around the Citizenship Referendum was extremely heated, drawing accusations of racism and political opportunism against the government, while feeding into broader debates about the transformation of Irish identity since the early 1990s.

Friel's play is relevant to that debate, as well as to the broader issues of identity and citizenship occasioned by the expansion of Ireland's population. Just as the 'Irishness' of Christopher is withdrawn in response to political forces in Friel's play, so would the Irish government withdraw the right to 'Irishness' from immigrants whose children were born in the country after June 2004. And it is notable that Friel shows how race and gender can be deliberately blurred for political gain during a period when anxieties were being expressed in the Irish media about the reproductive lives of immigrant women; that theme is also relevant to the issues discussed in the last chapter in relation to Marina Carr. Friel makes clear in the play – mainly through his presentation of Richard – that the construction of race (and other forms of identity) is directly related to the exercise of power. He places into stark contrast the pseudo-scientific measurements carried out by Richard with his subjects' need for food and money: Richard offers them a photograph in payment, calling it 'your personal trophy' (49), but is told by one of his subjects that 'it's money I need sir' (51). Richard's desire to find ways of measuring Irishness – to ask, as many academics do, what it means to be Irish – is therefore shown to be utterly irrelevant when compared with the need to correct the imbalance between privilege and destitution. This made the play highly pertinent in an Ireland debating its moral duties in relation to the developing world.

It has always been difficult to establish authorial intention in Friel's work, so it would be unwise to see *The Home Place* as a deliberate attempt to intervene in these debates. The script published by Gallery Press features an extract from *Studies in Irish Craniology* by A.C. Haddon, the inclusion of which could be seen as an attempt to assert the historical accuracy of the presentation of Richard (though Friel provides no direct commentary to suggest that was his intention). He gave no interviews about the play prior to its opening and he provides few clues about his own views on the events he's describing, aside from some personalized but ambiguous references in the text: as stated above, one of Friel's characters shares a surname with his mother, while another is a schoolteacher who organizes a choir, like his father.

My interest, however, is not so much with Friel's intentions, as with Irish audiences' reflexive responses to his play. *The Home Place* was produced at Dublin's Gate Theatre in 2005, seven months after the Citizenship Referendum. During that period, many other dramatists were using strategies similar to Friel's to explore issues of race and citizenship more explicitly. Like *The Home Place*, Donal O'Kelly's *The Cambria* used 19th-century Ireland to explore the present, using Frederick Douglass's visit to Ireland after his escape from slavery as a way of forcing a reconsideration of how the country treats more recent arrivals who, like Douglass, seek asylum in Ireland from oppression and state-sanctioned violence. The English playwright Sheelagh Stevenson produced *Enlightenment* (2005) at the Peacock in Dublin, using the story of a young English backpacker who disappears in Thailand to consider how the wealth of the West is related to the impoverishment of the developing world. Although that play was set in England, it was assumed that its concerns would be equally relevant to Ireland: both countries were presented as interchangeable spaces in the West, something that reveals much about the transformation of Irish identity and politics since the early 1980s, again showing a shift from the postcolonial to the global in perspective. And, as we'll see below, Elizabeth Kuti's *The Sugar Wife* (2005) places issues of race and Irishness in a historical context that draws disturbing parallels between globalization and imperialism. So *The Home Place* appeared during a period when Irish audiences and Irish playwrights were engaged in serious debates about the need to find new ways of thinking about the relationship between place and identity, when Ireland was (quite literally) trying to find its place in the world, struggling to come to terms with the way that the old markers of identity – poverty, race, religion – were being reformulated at a dizzying speed.

This gives rise to one of the problems with Friel's play. If one analyses the script, it seems generally appropriate to adopt a postcolonial perspective to it: the play considers Anglo-Irish relations, race, the use of scientific discourse for the exercise of power, the use of gender to represent the nation, and so on – all staple themes in postcolonial criticism. Yet to view *The Home Place* through that postcolonial lens – to see Ireland as a victim rather than a subject of global inequalities – is deeply problematic. Unlike such countries as the UK or the USA, Ireland claims an affinity (albeit a contested one) with cultures in postcolonial countries. Yet economic growth, political integration into the European Union, and economic integration into the American-led world economy have brought Ireland firmly into the West. Ireland now has a substantial community of immigrants from other countries, many of whom are part of the developing world, and its economy is based on practices that contribute to global inequalities. It is also true that Irish society has itself become more unequal: according to the UN, the gap between rich and poor in Ireland is one of the widest in the world, second only to that in the United States (see United Nations Development Programme, 2004). As we've seen, the economic practices used by Irish theatre are similar to those employed in most other countries in the West. But unlike most of those countries, the history of Irish literature, theatre, and its criticism are grounded on the notion that Ireland is a victim rather than a perpetrator of global inequality. To put it simplistically,

The Home Place reads like an example of the theatre of the oppressed, but it was produced in a country that has become one of the oppressors. How can we come to terms with that apparent contradiction?

This problem becomes more evident when we attempt to understand the play's production. *The Home Place* opened on 1 February 2005 at Dublin's Gate Theatre for an eight-week run, prior to a transfer to London's West End, where it played for just under three months (opening on 25 May and closing on 13 August). The show's producer, Michael Colgan, stated at that time that he saw *The Home Place* as having a major role in the branding of the Gate Theatre as a producer of an internationally prestigious theatre product. 'You tour for different reasons', Colgan told Peter Crawley: 'for money . . . for prestige . . . and for the morale of the actors' (2005: 12). But, for him, the most important reason for bringing *The Home Place* to the West End was to attract international talent to his theatre. 'I don't have to explain the Gate Theatre to Ralph Fiennes because he's already seen the work' in London, states Colgan, referring to the Gate's production of Friel's *Faith Healer*, which opened in Dublin in 2006 before a successful Broadway run. So part of Colgan's producing philosophy in staging *The Home Place* was to build the reputation of his theatre, to use one Friel play to help him to produce another.

I do not want to suggest that the Gate's international productions – or the casting of Ralph Fiennes as Frank Hardy – should be criticized; on the contrary, Colgan has done much to raise the international profile of Irish theatre, and to attract international talent to Irish stages. Rather, I wish to draw attention to the way that *The Home Place* can be seen as part of the Gate's management of their increasing globalized brand. Colgan assembled an impressive group of well-known international figures to add to the prestige of his production: Tom Courtenay played the lead role, while Adrian Noble directed. As a result, the Irish run was perceived in some quarters as a rehearsal for a West End transfer – grumblings which were intensified when a number of Irish critics were denied tickets for the production's opening night, while many of the leading British newspaper reviewers were present.[3] This exposed the Gate to the accusation that it was more concerned with favourable advance publicity for the West End run than with generating debate within Ireland about the play's themes.

So in the Gate's production – with its emphasis on branding, international touring, celebrity casting, and the performance of Irishness abroad – we can see an interesting contrast. Friel's play may allow Irish audiences to consider how globalization has transformed the demography of Ireland, but the Gate's production wholeheartedly embraces global-ization. The impact on local audiences of that globalized approach is worth lingering on. The Gate did little to promote discussion of the play in the Irish media, and produced it in Dublin for a much shorter run than they had in London. The success of the production in the West End is poor compensation for any Irish theatregoers who couldn't get tickets to the play, or for the Irish newspaper readers who lost the opportunity to read critics' reflections on its significance. This shows how the ten-sions between local and global significantly affect our understanding of what Irish theatre is, and for whom it is being produced. *The Home Place* has resonances for domestic Irish audiences that are immediate and urgent, yet despite the intense local demand for tickets, its Irish run was considerably shorter than its sojourn in the West End. This is ironic, given the history of colonial relations between Ireland and England, not to mention the themes of the play.

The case of *The Home Place* is an excellent illustration of the clash between identity and brand. The success of Irish theatre internationally has been predicated on a 'branding' of Irish identity as representing a nar-row set of characteristics. At a time of increased multiculturalism, we might have expected Irish theatre to seek to redefine, expand, and trans-gress the boundaries that mark out Irish citizenship – for theatre practi-tioners to show that Irishness need not be tied to religion (whether Catholic or Protestant), ethnicity, or other essentialized markers of iden-tity. The problem, however, is that the international success of Irish plays appears largely determined by their use of familiar Irish stereotypes. Globalization has brought multiculturalism to Ireland, but the globaliza-tion of Irish theatre has, regrettably, meant that the most successful Irish plays are those that present Irishness in narrow and indeed restricted ways. To consider the consequences of this, I will explore the relationship between the Irish 'brand' and the racialization of Irish identity.

Branding and race

I want now to draw on my analysis of the Irish brand in Chapters 3 and 4, using it to sketch a genealogy of the Irish 'brand'. I've shown already how Irishness has always been constructed for audiences who are pre-supposed to be from places other than Ireland. I now want to relate that commodified 'otherness' to the process of racialization.

As mentioned already, the economics of the Irish stage and publish-ing industries are such that Irish writing has always been conditioned by the need to be accessible to audiences both at home and abroad; at first in Britain, subsequently in North America, and at present in a glob-alized marketplace. As stated in Chapter 4, a play must be meaningful to an Irish audience if it is to be successful there – but to be successful abroad, its central 'Irish' narrative must also be framed or mediated in some way. I outlined in relation to *The Shaughraun* how such mediation functioned in the 19th-century.

We've also seen that 'outsideness' operates importantly within Ireland. As has been discussed in relation to *Angels in America*, an engagement with otherness may also stimulate the development of the self. Accordingly, the dramatists of the Irish Revival recalibrated Boucicault's presentation of otherness as a way of constructing an emergent national identity. Otherness thus became a key feature of Irish drama of the Irish Revival, with a 'stranger in the house' motif (a reference to Yeats's *Cathleen ni Houlihan*) being the most common example of this phenomenon. Nicholas Grene describes how it generally presents itself:

> A room within a house, a family within a room, stand in for nation-ality, for ordinary, familiar life; into the room there enters a stranger, and the incursion of that extrinsic, extraordinary figure alters, poten-tially transforms the scene.
>
> (Grene, 1999: 52)

This motif, states Grene, has its basis in the plays of Synge, Yeats, and Gregory – though it was perhaps borrowed from the later work of Ibsen. But what is at work in those plays is a notion of using the other as a way of defining the self, of showing that the transformative power of the 'stranger in the house' might alter the environment into which that stranger arrives. This kind of transformation makes for good drama, but its purpose within the context of the Irish Revival was to imagine the possibility of a transformed Ireland – one that could become independ-ent of colonial rule.

Interestingly, despite the fact that Ireland achieved partial independ-ence from Britain over 80 years ago, this motif has persisted into con-temporary Irish drama. As Grene notes,

> On the whole, Irish drama has continued to look to social margins for its setting, whether the western country districts or the working-class inner city. It is thus typically other people that a largely middle-class urban audience watches in an Irish play, other people who speak differently – more colloquially, more comically, more poetically.
>
> (Grene, 1999: 264)

While it makes sense for a colonized culture to deploy ideas of otherness to counter the dominant ideology, it is surprising that Irish drama continues to use this strategy. In some cases, it may be used positively. As we've seen, many of the plays of Frank McGuinness turn on the dramatic consequences of the appearance of an outsider into a claustrophobic social setting, which has allowed McGuinness to present gay sexuality as offering the potential to restore social justice, or to renew national identities. However, we've also encountered the argument that the presentation of rural Ireland as a 'benighted dystopia' might obscure real social injustice. Merriman argues that the people presented in much recent Irish drama should be understood as 'gross caricatures with no purchase on the experience of today's audiences':

> Their appeal to the new consumer Irish consensus lies in their appearance as ludicrous Manichean opposites – the colonized simian reborn. In each belly laugh which greets the preposterous malevolence of its actions there is a huge cathartic roar of relief that this is all past – 'we' have left it all behind.
>
> (Merriman, 1999: 313)

I've explained in previous chapters why I disagree with Merriman's arguments about Carr and McDonagh, but his consideration of the presentation of Ireland as a dystopia shows how otherness in Irish drama may be deployed both positively and negatively, and how the trope is open to supportive and hostile readings. At the turn of the 20th century, otherness was used as a way of imagining an independent Ireland. At the turn of the 21st century, otherness was a means by which Irish audiences could evade their responsibilities, according to Merriman. It might therefore be argued that the problems Irish dramatists have in dealing with those forms of otherness that actually exist in contemporary Irish society – in terms of gender, religion, sexuality, ethnicity, etc – arise not from a lack of awareness of the other, but from excessive familiarity with otherness. How can we represent genuine *difference* if our theatrical vocabulary sees Irishness as itself genuinely different? This leaves Irish theatre ill equipped to speak about and understand racial difference. Accordingly, the first step in unravelling Irish attitudes to race is to unravel the racialization of Irishness itself.

Two categories are inherently involved in racialization: domination and essentialization. Accordingly, racialization can be seen as a *process* whereby a people are represented and controlled by the application of essentialist categories. Racialization always involves *becoming* a race, and is subject to variation, conditionality, and other factors. Theodore Allen (1994) argues that the racialization of the Irish can be traced to the 18th century (27–52, 112–4); Luke Gibbons locates it a century earlier, drawing attention to the 'widespread equation of the "mere Irish" with the native Americans in the seventeenth century [which] served as a pretext for wholesale confiscations and plantations [in Ireland] . . . ' (2004: n.p.). This process excluded Irish 'Catholics from citizenship and political life [and] rendered them, in Edmund Burke's phrase, *foreigners in their native land*. There was no need to go abroad to experience the "multiple identities" of the diaspora valorised in postcolonial theory: the uncanny experience of being a *stranger to oneself* was already a feature of life back home' (Gibbons, 2004: n.p.). Gibbons's comment can be used as a way of thinking about the predicament of Christopher in *The Home Place*, but I am quoting it because it positions the racialization of Irishness in the context not only of colonialism, but also of transatlantic exchange. As we'll see below in the discussion of *The Sugar Wife*, this perspective is extremely important.

Although the racialization of Irishness has been written about in terms of the United States and Britain, it also had an effect on the construction of identity within Ireland itself. Declan Kiberd, borrowing from Said's *Orientalism*, suggests that this was especially true during the 19th century, when Ireland found itself being represented as England's 'unconscious'. 'Victorian imperialists attributed to the Irish all the emotions and impulses which a harsh mercantile code had led them to suppress in themselves', he suggests. 'If John Bull was industrious and reliable, Paddy was held to be indolent and contrary; if the former was mature and rational, the latter must be unstable and emotional; if the English were adults and manly, the Irish must be childish and feminine' (1995: 30–1). If the Irish were a spiritual people, they redeemed something of the materialism of Empire; if childlike and innocent, they redeemed the disillusioned maturity of Britain. This process worked reciprocally: in return for their spirituality and innocence, the Irish benefited from British business acumen and were permitted to join in the Imperialist enterprise. This racialization was not fixed: an Irish person could be presented as stupid and feckless, or 'charming and threatening by turns', as Kiberd puts it (29), but was always in an essentially inferior relationship to the English, defined perpetually not as a self, but as the *opposite* to the English self.

Race played an important role in this relationship. In another study that is relevant to *The Home Place*, Liz Curtis describes the work of a Victorian physician who invented the 'index of nigrescence', a 'formula to identify the racial components of a given people. He concluded that the Irish were darker than the people of . . . England, and were closer to the aborigines of the British Isles, who in turn had traces of "negro" ancestry in their appearances', she explains (1984: 55). Yet, as Dyer shows, 'in other circumstances, the Irish could be seen as white' (1997: 53). Whiteness was seen as a permeable barrier that the Irish could cross, not necessarily to a position of equality but to one of acceptance. Although they reach different conclusions, both Roy Foster (1993) and L.P. Curtis (1996) have illustrated, through the analysis of Victorian caricature, how the representation of the Irish passed through different, progressively less positive levels. Curtis identifies four broad categories of representation for the Irish. The first and 'least unflattering' is the 'tall and muscular image of the Northern Irish Protestant, especially the loyalist Ulsterman or Orangeman, whose high facial angle and handsome features made him resemble, however faintly, a respectable or honest Englishman'. The second category was a 'reasonably good-looking rustic male of the small farmer or laborer variety, whom we will call Pat . . . [a] droll and politically innocent peasant, who delivered Irish bulls with feckless abandon'. Third, Curtis states, was the image of the 'prognathous and somewhat hairy or unshaven plebeian Irishman, better known as Paddy . . . [whose] elements of humanity were few . . . [when compared with] the fourth basic type, simian Paddy, who longed to use physical force to free his country from British rule' (xxi–xxii).

Such representations were often related to whiteness. In Victorian Britain, whiteness was not just racialized but also moralized, used as a way of defining those characteristics considered most admirable within that society. Purity, chastity, and morality were all related to colour; so too was imperialism, with the British Empire praised because the sun never set upon it. The corollary of this was that blackness, or the absence of light, became an acceptable way of describing that which was abnormal or unfamiliar. Hence, Dickens could express his fears about the industrialization of England in the famous opening paragraph of his 1853 novels *Bleak House* with 'fog everywhere', and pieces of soot that are like snowflakes 'gone into mourning for the death of the sun' (1985: 1). This moralization meant that, not only was whiteness figured as a *choice* for the Irish, who could move with some freedom (compared to other colonized subjects) through four categories of identification; it also meant that whiteness was the (morally) *right* choice, meaning that to be English was to be good, and to be good was to be English. This in turn implied that to be Irish was in itself inherently negative. Whiteness was thus a form of legitimization for the Irish, which could be granted or withheld by means of British representation.

In America, the racialization of the Irish worked similarly, though not as an instrument of colonial control. While immigration from Ireland to America had been strong before the American Revolution, it was not until after the unsuccessful 1798 rebellion that anti-Irish sentiment in the United States grew, sometimes as a result of the arrival of large numbers of Irish revolutionaries, who provoked hostility from a public suspicious of the new arrivals' republicanism and Catholicism. Throughout the early 19th century, the numbers of Irish immigrants to America grew steadily, in most cases because of the various famines that culminated in the 1845–48 Great Famine in Ireland. As Luke Gibbons (2003) shows in his analysis of Irish characters in American gothic, the Irish were represented throughout the early 19th century as a potentially destabilizing influence on American society, and this was often rendered by the use of light and dark imagery.[4] Socially, a similar development was underway, so that it soon became the case that 'to be called an "Irishman" [came] to be nearly as great an insult as to be called a "nigger"' – according to David Roediger, anyway (1999: 133). He explains how Irish difference was quickly racialized. 'A variety of writers, particularly ethnologists, praised Anglo-Saxon virtues as the bedrock of liberty and derided the "Celtic race"', he states. 'Some suggested that the Irish were part of a separate caste or a "dark" race, possibly originally African. Racial comparisons of Irish and Blacks were not infrequently flattering to the latter group' (133). As in Victorian Britain, whiteness was conferred upon the Irish, who 'became white', as Ignatiev puts it, through necessity:

> To the extent that color consciousness existed among newly arrived immigrants from Ireland, it was one among several ways they had of identifying themselves. To become white they had to learn to subordinate county, religious, or national animosities, not to mention any natural sympathies they may have felt for their fellow creatures, to a new solidarity based on color – a bond which, it must be remembered, was contradicted by their experience in Ireland.
>
> (Ignatiev, 1996: 96)

This does not mean that the Irish became racialized through their entry to the United States. Rather, they were given the opportunity to give up a racialized version of Irishness for the emptiness of whiteness. This is

an example of how social class can stimulate racism: Irishness was associated with poverty, wealth with whiteness. As Wallerstein notes,

> [Racialization] provides a legitimation to the hierarchical reality of
> capitalism that does not offend the formal equality before the law
> which is one of its avowed political premises . . . Ethnicization, or
> peoplehood, resolves one of the basic contradictions of historical
> capitalism – its simultaneous thrust for theoretical equality and prac-
> tical inequality – and it does so by utilizing the mentalities of the
> world's working classes.
>
> (Wallerstein, 1991: 192)

Both in Britain and in the United States, the racialization of the Irish
was a means of control – in the former case, the system of control was
colonialism; in the latter, it was class. Whiteness was granted to the Irish
like parole to well-behaved prisoners: the Irish had freedom, but the
condition of that freedom was the perpetual reminder that it could be
revoked. In this respect, Boucicault's *The Octoroon* (1859) – about an
apparently white subject who runs the risk of losing freedom by having
racialization attributed to her on the basis of an invisible but essential
attribute – operates as a metaphor for the status of the Irish in 19th-
century America. Like Boucicault's Zoë, they lived under perpetual
threat of banishment to the slaves' quarters. This may go some way
towards explaining (without justifying) the prevalence of 19th-century
Irish-American racism.

The consciousness of oppression produces race. When that consciousness is framed within a colonial context, it also produces nationalism. The growth of Irish nationalism in the 19th century did not
involve the rejection of a racialized construction of identity. Rather, it
concerned the recasting of that identity into a form that mimicked the
nationalism of the colonizer. Bhabha explains how colonial identity is
formed as a result of imitation or metonymy. 'Mimicry is like camou-
flage, not a harmonization of repression of difference, but a form of
resemblance, that differs from or defends presence by displaying it in
part, metonymically', he states. 'Its threat . . . comes from the prodi-
gious and strategic production of conflictual, fantastic, discriminatory
"identity effects" in the play of a power that is elusive because it hides
no essence, no "itself"' (1994: 90). Emergent nationalism is usually a
derivative of the colonial project that it sets out to resist. Far from being
a rejection of racialization, nationalism *embraces* it, but rejects the negative connotations attached to it. This means that in the emergent state,

identity is presented as a preordained given, or in Ireland that, as Seamus Deane puts it, 'Irish freedom declined into the freedom to be Irish in predestined ways' (1990: 13).

This freedom to express a predetermined identity is a feature of post-colonialism generally, but was intensified in the case of Ireland by the partition of the country in 1922 into a 'Free State' of 26 counties, comprised almost entirely of Catholics and/or nationalists, and the six-county Northern Ireland, approximately two-thirds of which was composed of Unionists and/or Protestants. The partitioned state deviates from other modern states in one crucial way: its construction of race. As Goldberg writes:

> The modern state . . . fashions differentiated internal spaces, once conceived deeply in relatedly racial and gendered terms. These differentiated spaces are made possible most clearly through policies and laws . . . These various features of the state, fractured and at odds with each other though they often may be, are held together loosely by a logic of the state at odds with itself . . . This internal fracturing of the state is a product in part of the tension between the state's instrumentality, its serving interests defined external to itself, and the inherent logic of state formation, bureaucracy, and exercise.
>
> (Goldberg, 2002: 8)

The partitioned state arises when a nation at odds with itself is split into two parts, Goldberg's 'internal fracturing' being externalized in the formation of states within national spaces, such as Ireland/Northern Ireland, Palestine/Israel, and India/Pakistan. The ideology of postcolonial partition is inherently linked with racialization, since it is grounded in the conviction that a state should be ethnically homogenous. As Joe Cleary puts it, 'the idea of state division . . . always involves matters of national identity . . . Partition, in short, entails a reorganisation of political space that invariably triggers complex reconstructions of national identity within and across the borders of the states involved'. Cleary points to the need to 'recognize that the principle that subtends partition as a political policy . . . is, philosophically speaking, impeccably and even dogmatically ethnic nationalist' (2000: 20–1).

The effect of partition in Ireland was that the two new Irish states – each with contesting notions of its own legitimacy, and hostility towards each other – were constructed upon essentialist ethnic lines. In the Free State, this meant that Irish identity involved the reconfiguration of those qualities marked as negative by British colonialism into positive national traits: rural backwardness became rustic authenticity, superstitious religion became pious Catholicism, the almost dead language of Gaelic became the first official language of the newborn state. The difficulty with this is, as Cullingford suggests, that 'the price of insight into one injustice (in this case the injustice of British rule in Ireland) may be blindness to a variety of others'. The others of Irish society to whom Cullingford refers are 'numerous, and they are both real and fictive. Ireland is accustomed to being stigmatized as the feminized object of English discourse, but in women, gays, abused children, travellers and the working class it has produced its own internal Others' (6–7). A similar process occurred in Northern Ireland, a self-proclaimed 'Protestant state for a Protestant people', with the minority Catholic population effectively denied citizenship through gerrymandered electoral districts and discrimination in relation to housing and education. Irish independence might have led to an end of the racialization of Irishness, but the partition of the country along essentialist lines had the effect of instead cementing racialization firmly in place.

With the outbreak of the Northern Irish Troubles in 1969, racialization became reactivated. The awareness that the Northern conflict's apparent intractability lay in the essentialized characteristics of the opposing sides – their 'diamond absolutes' as Heaney put it – led to a backlash against racialization itself, regarded now not as a sign of oppression or resistance, but of backwardness. To construct one's identity in ethnic terms leads to the kind of 'tribal' conflict that, for many, Northern Ireland seemed to be. Race thus became a deeply negative signifier within Irish discourse.

One way of understanding that phenomenon is with reference to the concept of race treachery, the term used in the United States to describe the need to produce people who 'openly break the rules of whiteness and disrupt the institutions that propagate white privilege: the criminal justice system, schools, employment networks. The existence of the white race depends on the willingness of those assigned to it to place their racial interests above class, gender, or any other interests they hold' states David W. Stowe (1994: 75). Whereas in the United States, race treachery involves the racialization of whiteness as a means of combating discrimination, in Ireland the momentum is towards the reconstruction of Irishness as an empty signifier. It could thus be argued that contemporary Irish society is again constructing identity as a process of 'becoming white', but for the first time within its own borders at – ironically and worryingly – a period when for the first time in its history Ireland is also becoming a multiracial society. This explains why in Irish drama the model of the benighted dystopia has become so current: Irish audiences are enabled to reject the racialized construction of themselves as prone to violence, religious superstition, incontinence, fecklessness, and unreliability. Instead, a positive representation of Irishness is now considered one that presents Irishness as indistinguishable from any other place or identity in the globalized West. This explains why Ireland's new-found wealth has not resulted in solidarity with postcolonial subjects: to be racialized is to be part of a past that Ireland likes to think it has left behind.

This is most notably the case in the recurrent identification of Ireland to the so-called Third World, a rhetorical device very common in the 1980s, but still current at present.[5] As a result of political corruption, poor infrastructure, and economic dependency on Europe, added to high unemployment, during the 1980s, Irish commentators frequently referred disparagingly to Ireland as a 'Third World' country. This comparison was hyperbolic, the purpose of the exaggeration being – with occasionally racist undertones – to indicate the severity of Ireland's situation by suggesting that it might be possible to compare it with somewhere in the developing world. Irish commentators' invocation of the Third World – especially of Africa – as a sign of Ireland's dreadful state was not a form of identification, solidarity, or empathy. On the contrary, the exaggeration worked on the basis that Ireland ought, such commentators appeared to feel, to have *nothing* in common with these countries but that, as a (white) European nation, it was degrading that the comparison was even possible.

A similar comparison is that between the Irish and African-Americans, which appears most famously in Roddy Doyle's *The Commitments* (1988).

> – The Irish are the niggers of Europe, lads
> They nearly gasped: it was so true
> – An' Dubliners are the niggers of Ireland. The culchies have fuckin' everythin'. An' the northside Dubliners are the niggers o' Dublin. – say it loud. I'm black and I'm proud.
>
> (Doyle, 1998: 8)

This ahistorical and (to my mind) self-indulgent statement is cited with depressing frequency as if were sociologically accurate, despite the fact that the Irish have never been subjected to organized discrimination in Europe, and that Irish 'culchies' – people from rural Ireland – are generally marginalized within Irish discourse. In fact, as Elizabeth Butler

Cullingford rightly points out, those who refer to this passage frequently do so in a simplistic and unfounded misreading of the novel in its entirety:

> The analogy between the Irish and the African-Americans is well meaning but inappropriate: it reinscribes both ethnicities within the suspect rubrics of 'timeless' primitivism, emotionalism, and rhythm . . . Moreover, in light of the dismal history of Irish-American hostility to African-Americans . . . the analogy is historically misleading.
>
> (Cullingford, 2001: 159)

To identify with the other can be a powerful gesture. But in Ireland's case, it may also be a deeply racist expression of self-loathing, with the degradation of the Irish self-expressed through the inescapability of racialization: things are bad, the implication goes, because 'we' are like 'them'.

The relationship between Irish identity and race is thus shown to be deeply entangled. Race is sometimes imposed upon the Irish as a form of degradation; at other times, it is invoked with pride by the Irish as a form of self-expression. At all times, racialization is presented as a moral choice. And in every instance, it is evident that the consciousness of race in the Irish subject is always heavily invested in national, and self, identity. The consequences for the development of Irish theatre that arise from this require careful consideration.

Irish theatre as an 'irresistible market': Elizabeth Kuti's *The Sugar Wife*

Shortly after Friel's play premiered at the Gate, Rough Magic produced a new work in Dublin that answered many of the questions raised by *The Home Place*, and which resolved many of the tensions referred to in the last section. The play was the English dramatist Elizabeth Kuti's *The Sugar Wife* (2005), an historical drama with contemporary resonances. Kuti's play draws parallels between the Dublin of 1850 and the Ireland of today, which implies that her aim with *The Sugar Wife* is to challenge much of the received wisdom about Ireland's past while emphasizing the country's responsibilities in the present as one of the wealthiest nations in the globalizing world.

The play is set in post-famine Dublin and focuses on Samuel and Hannah Tewkley, a Quaker couple who run a successful coffee shop in Dublin's South Great George's Street, while also importing sugar, tea, and coffee to Ireland – a business that is obviously modelled on the real Irish company of Bewleys, whose chain of coffee shops was an essential element of Dublin life throughout the 20th century, and whose name continues to be used to brand tea and coffee.

As the play opens, the Tewkleys are hosting a visit to Dublin by Sarah Worth, a freed African-American slave, and her companion Alfred Darby, a young Englishman who has turned his back on his family of British industrialists, choosing instead to support abolitionism: he seems in many respects a masculine version of Shaw's Major Barbara. The play also features a fifth character, an impoverished young woman called Martha Ryan, who is visited regularly in her tenement in Dublin's Liberties (one of the city's poorest locations) by Hannah.

As in Kuti's earlier play *Treehouses*, *The Sugar Wife* adopts an unconventional approach to time, using deliberately anachronistic language and a relatively complex chronology. She intercuts a naturalistic linear plot with two other forms of representation, both of them set after the main action of the play has concluded: an abolitionist speech delivered in five parts by Sarah, and interior monologues from Hannah and Samuel as they pray silently at a midweek meeting in the Quaker meeting house in Dublin (a place still located one block away from the Project Arts Centre, where the play was first staged). The purpose of Sarah's speech is to address the audience directly, turning them from a passive group of spectators into 'a crowd that has come to hear Sarah', as it states in the stage directions (Kuti, 2005: 35). And because the audience is allowed access to the private thoughts of Hannah and Samuel, the auditorium itself becomes a Quaker meeting house, notably at the play's conclusion when Hannah directly addresses the audience, asking for their blessing for her unborn child, which she hopes will be a 'promise of light . . . at the end of a long winter's darkness' (85).

The use of these modes of direct address – as well as the fact that the play ends with a sense of hope for a future that has since become our past – prevents the audience from seeing *The Sugar Wife* as a closed historical narrative. The spectators of the play also have a role to play within the action, which should encourage them to think about the play's relevance to their own preoccupations. *The Sugar Wife* also engages with ideas that are extremely current. Kuti's consideration of the relationship between the post-famine Irish and African-American slaves appears to show a familiarity with works by such writers as Ignatiev, Allen, and Roediger. And it could be seen as a response to those critics, since she shows how social class and identity operated within Ireland itself, while also reminding us that the people who actually got to leave Ireland were often much luckier than those who were forced to stay behind. Likewise, her references to Orientalism appear grounded in a reading of Said, notably in her consideration of how Chinese clothing and art were used to market the Tewkleys/Bewleys brand. She focuses on the way that slavery contributed to the economies of countries on the Atlantic rim, and shows how it was intimately connected to the production of luxury goods such as tobacco, sugar, chocolate, and caffeine – and therefore Kuti seems to be responding to Paul Gilroy's *Black Atlantic,* as well as many of his shorter articles. Finally, her creation of the character of Sarah Worth seems to display an awareness of the visit to Ireland by Frederick Douglass in 1845, and of his subsequent writings on the poverty that he encountered there (which are echoed by Sarah's earliest lines of dialogue).

The play's main theme, I would suggest, is the construction of pleasure: how it is experienced, commodified, sold, reproduced, and aestheticized. Kuti's argument appears to be that our economic system is organized in such a way that, as one character states, 'nothing gets done without desire' – a 19th-century doctrine that has lasting historical consequences. Central to this argument is Kuti's exploration of the relationship between art and violence, with her characters being constructed as commodities in a world where meaning arises not from the interplay of signifiers, but the exchange of tokens. This can be seen in many ways in the play: in Kuti's consideration of marriage, business, slavery, impoverishment, emigration, and so on.

As the play opens, Hannah (the titular Sugar Wife) is visiting Martha, an impoverished and syphilitic young woman. Hannah engages in such charitable acts, her husband Samuel suggests, because she has 'acquired a taste for atrocities' (30), and he asks with some bemusement (and condescension) why they must 'forever talk of syphilis at the dinner table'. Hannah 'has a fondness for syphilitics', he says. 'She collects them, any she can get her hands on' (19). Samuel's use of the language of appetite and sensual gratification implies that, for Hannah, charity is not a matter of religious duty, but a response to some form of compulsion.

To a certain extent, Samuel's observations prove accurate. Hannah explains her desire to undertake such activities by claiming that 'I want to be of use' (7) and that 'I must do my work in the world too'. 'I have to', she states, 'otherwise I – what am I? What am I? I have nothing' (13). The charitable actions Hannah will – and will not – perform therefore reveal more about her needs than Martha's. For instance, she presents Martha with a pair of white linen stockings – an entirely impractical gift since, as Martha says, 'nothing stays white around' a tenement in

Dublin's Liberties (6). The whiteness is 'a sign', explains Hannah, 'that in the blood of the Lamb we are washed clean' (6). Later in the play, she brings Martha an alphabet book, which she intends to use to teach her how to read, thereby expressing her belief that 'the word is the seed by which we change the world' (10). This is another well-intentioned but entirely impractical gift – as an opium-addicted prostitute dying of syphilis and malnourishment, Martha has more immediate problems than her illiteracy.

This gives rise to an obvious question: 'why can't you just help me out like I've been asking you, Mrs Tewkley?' asks Martha. Hannah appears unwilling to accept Martha's own view of what is right for her, refusing to give her money to travel to the United States, where she might begin a new life. Martha is merely an object upon whom Hannah may enact dramas of transformation: the washing clean of sin, the flowering of a seed. She is therefore enabled to feel 'of use' through Martha: by helping her, she believes that although '[w]e can't change everything all at once . . . we will go forward together. In hope' (7). The relationship between the two women thus involves a set of transactions, with Hannah appearing to gain far more than the woman she's attempting to help. Martha seems alert to this: she flatters and attempts to manipulate Hannah at first, before becoming frustrated and abusive when she realizes that her requests will go unanswered.

The play reminds us that the exchange of money within any relationship determines people's sense of relative power. We see this in the play's treatment of marriage; we see it in Hannah's dealings with Martha; and Martha herself shows an awareness of it when she refuses to accept money from Sarah – because she's black. 'Taking money from a hottentot, Jesus', she says. 'We collect money for the likes of you on a plate in the church' (42). Martha's sense of identity is, like Hannah's, asserted through charity: despite her own poverty, she is still allowed a sense of individualism by providing money for Catholic missions in Africa. This places Kuti's play firmly in the context of the debate about the racialization of Irishness present in the works of Roediger and Ignatiev.

The relationship between Alfred and Sarah involves similar examples of financial transactions being used to assert identity. 'The Abolition movement has kept us shod and fed and sheltered for several years now', states Sarah (24), explaining that when Alfred's 'pockets ran dry' they 'started on the lecture circuit' (25). So although Alfred has 'no money, no profession' due to his estrangement from his family, he lives comfortably because Sarah is – by her own description – the 'goose that lays the golden eggs' (24).

It is important to consider in this context the reasons for Alfred's decision to purchase Sarah. 'I saw her', he tells Samuel, 'literally on the auction-block . . . half-naked, and a mass of scars. . . . A truly pitiful sight. Her price was three hundred dollars because the trader couldn't convince bidders she was strong enough to bear children . . . And the trader said "done" and that was it. She was mine. And from that moment on, my life was transformed. The scales fell from my eyes' (29). Just as Martha allows Hannah to feel 'useful', Sarah provides Alfred with a meaning to his own life: she is his 'road to Damascus' and his 'muse' (29, 32). And just as Martha is happy to play a role for Hannah, Sarah shows that she can manipulate Alfred too:

> First time I saw him, I knew he was rich. He was at the back of the crowd, but he was edging forward, and I knew he was hungry for something. I knew he wanted to bid and that if I looked at him right, he would do it . . . I saw how he couldn't take his eyes off me, how he drunk me up . . . I saw him as he was: he knew that I saw his darkness and his pain and the heavy burden on his back; and I told him bid, and through me he could put that burden down; bid and I would pour all my honey into him; bid and I would heal him. . . . And sure enough, he raised his hand to bid.
>
> (Kuti, 2005: 76–7)

Again, we see the language of appetite and gratification being employed: Sarah recognizes that Alfred was 'hungry', and watches how he had 'drunk' her up. She uses words to describe Alfred that are far more appropriate to describe slaves themselves: she refers to his 'blackness', his 'pain', and 'the heavy burden on his back', all of which she promises to alleviate. What Sarah has recognized, therefore, is that Alfred is 'in love with suffering' (74) and that her freedom can be achieved by successfully performing a role: she will play the victim, and in doing so recognizes his own abjection. Like Martha, she is aware that her suffering is a commodity; the difference between the two women is that Sarah successfully exploits that commodity while Martha does not. The play seems to suggest, therefore, that the reason that Sarah lives while Martha dies is because Sarah is a more convincing actor – and perhaps because Alfred's love for Sarah's suffering is stronger than Hannah's appetite for Martha's pain.

Significantly, Alfred's objectification of Sarah is continued beyond the slave auction: he carries with him a selection of photographs of her in various states of suffering: muzzled, bleeding, scarred, and wearing a collar – which, he confesses, were not taken while she was a slave, but were 'reconstructed by my imagination at a later date . . . to capture her mystery, to convey her vulnerability' (32). His arrival in Dublin appears to stimulate his imagination even more. 'There are quite as many injustices to be catalogued here as in the southern states of America', he suggests. 'Could be a whole new market', Samuel enthuses. 'The Wrongs of Woman!' (45). Far from being irritated by Samuel's flippancy, Alfred seems to take him literally. 'I was thinking more of the Wrongs of the Irish. But, as you say, the Woman Question also must not be ignored' (45). Alfred therefore photographs Martha as well, saying of her portrait that 'it's the disease that is most affecting in her appearance . . . [It] . . . gives her beauty its piquancy . . . those beings under the most unbearable pressure – of poverty, of circumstance, of misery – release the strongest scent of themselves' (46).

There is an interesting collision between politics and the imagination here, and between conscience and the marketplace. Alfred's photographs are an attempt to 'capture' Sarah's image, to present the truth about her slavery through a staged act – or, in the case of Martha, to reveal a truth about the 'beauty' of humanity while doing nothing to prevent the death of the human being in front of him. Alfred thus is presented as a self-confessed 'tourist' (29) who, like Hannah, has an appetite for atrocity: the wrongs of woman, the wrongs of the Irish – these are not causes affecting real people for him, but subjects to be captured in a photograph that will assert his genius as an artist before revealing other truths. Or, as Samuel puts it, they are markets to be exploited like any other. We learn much about Alfred when he justifies his actions by quoting St Paul's 'to the pure all things are pure' (44). This, of course, is taken from the letter to Titus in which St Paul explains how 'purity' is compatible with slavery: 'tell slaves to be submissive to their masters and to give satisfaction in every respect . . . to show complete and perfect fidelity' (Titus, 2: 9–10). Alfred may have freed Sarah from slavery but as his choice of quotation emphasizes, he continues to see her body as an object to be captured and possessed.

The relationship between Alfred and Sarah is further complicated by his admission that he controls the content of the speeches she delivers against slavery. 'Sarah is a great natural storyteller', he states, 'but her material can sometimes be unwieldy or – of erratic quality – I can sometimes be of use in guiding shaping, perhaps, exerting . . . artistic input' (30). As we see in Sarah's lecture, there is much evidence of Alfred having not so much guided or shaped Sarah's story as of having edited it. The natural rhythms that occur in Sarah's conversation with Hannah, quoted above, are reproduced in her speech: just as she reproduces the word 'bid' in her description of Alfred's purchase of her, we also hear her repeating such words as 'yes' (35), 'hard' (35, 50, 69), and 'sweet' (50) in her own speeches. It is also true to say that she displays what Alfred calls the gifts of a great 'natural' storyteller in conversation with Hannah. Nevertheless, the final lines of her speech involve the rejection of a weapon branded with a dove, which she 'hurls . . . from her' and watches it 'disappear into the hungry waves' (78). This is the brand of the Slatebeck Iron and Steel Company – which is owned by Alfred's father, whose brand is a 'little bird of the Yorkshire dales [that] has left its mark all round the world' (21). Sarah's story about the voyage of a slave ship from Africa to America certainly reveals much about her past, but it is also a parable of sorts for Alfred, a story revealing that 'the wrongs of [his father's] company will one day be atoned for in blood' (22).

Much of the play is therefore about theatre – about acting, performing, and the use of those skills for personal gain. It also shows what happens when individuals assert their identity not in terms of essential traits, but in terms of their relative value in a market. The division between social performance and imagination becomes blurred by these arrangements: Sarah and Martha must 'perform' in order to survive, and their bodies become commodities that are dressed up, represented, and otherwise objectified by Alfred and Hannah. As the two idealists in the play, those characters rail against the conditions of the 'real world': 'we have raped the world', states Hannah. 'For sugar and tea and tobacco and chocolate . . . and everything we have flows from that' (83). Yet it is difficult to see what they can do except to 'make the best of a broken world' (75). As Sarah states, 'my people will not thank you for . . . futile gestures. My people cannot drink your tears nor be fed by your anguish' (75). Why express guilt about wealth, Sarah asks: a penniless philanthropist can do no-one any good.

This does not mean that the play is advising us merely to accept the status quo – Kuti seems too much aware of her play's themes to gratify our desire for easy answers. The play's complexity is such that its meaning cannot be presented simplistically. I do want to make one suggestion, however, about Kuti's intentions. To do so involves briefly considering the play's reception when it was produced in Dublin in 2005.

A major context for *The Sugar Wife* was the announcement shortly before it opened that Bewleys was to close down its chain of coffee shops in Dublin. This decision was met with general dismay, and was presented by some commentators as evidence of the impact of globalization on

Irish life, with fears that a so-called 'Irish institution' would be replaced by a globalized chain of coffee-houses such as Starbucks. Kuti's play is on the one hand a lament for the passing of Bewleys – a place which she celebrates as somewhere for 'folk to meet and drink and talk and write' (51). However, she also shows that the closure of Bewleys is not simply an example of an Irish business succumbing to the pressures of globalization. Bewleys itself, she shows, was established in the context of a globalizing world economy, since its success was founded on the importation to the metropolis of luxury products from the colonies: from the West Indies, China, India, and from the southern states of the USA too. By evoking the foundation of Bewleys when the business was closing, Kuti reminds us of the parallels between colonialism and slavery on the one hand, and globalization on the other, suggesting that the economic system we have inherited is founded upon colonialism and slavery, or what one character in the play calls an 'edifice of skulls'. She also points out that globalization, like colonialism, is based upon the exploitation of what in the play Samuel terms 'irresistible markets' (48) – commodities like sugar and sex that aim to gratify the appetite without even satisfying it fully. Kuti takes something that her audience is familiar with – branding – and shows how it is indistinguishable from something we think has passed – racialization. By merging the two, she shows that the term 'globalization' can be used to refer to processes that have been discredited.

The play therefore asks us to consider what we have inherited; to show that an Irish institution like Bewleys arose from the importation of luxury goods from the west and imagery from the east – to show that the colony has always been present in the metropolis, that if Dublin is a 'village', it has always been 'global'. *The Sugar Wife* thus shows how hunger – in all of its forms – determines Irish behaviour, Irish values, and the country's relationship with the rest of the world. There is a clear demand that we see globalization not as something new, but instead as a continuation of a process that has dominated the history of Ireland, and the rest of the world too.

Kuti's notion of how we live an environment of 'irresistible markets' that transform people into commodities is extremely pertinent to contemporary world theatre, and to Ireland specifically. It shows, firstly, that the construction of identity and the branding of products for consumption are interrelated processes: to construct oneself as artist, victim, husband, wife, free, or enslaved is to position oneself within a chain of exchanges – we choose to define ourselves in relation to a world of commodities, because that is how we understand the concept of value. The relationship between pleasure and exploitation is an essential part of this argument: the inequality between rich and poor (whether globally or locally) arises not because of an arbitrary social arrangement, but from choices made by individuals, who are motivated by desire. The sugar in a cup of coffee in the 19th century is a stimulant for one person, but it is the reason that another person has been enslaved – a relationship that Kuti's play makes explicit, and which demands of its audience that we consider the consequences of our own desire for pleasure and stimulation. To consume in the cosmopolitan centre a product from the local periphery may give pleasure, but it also affects that locality.

This is a useful way of understanding the flows of labour and capital that are caused by globalization, but it is also a way of thinking about theatre – about, for instance, how the desire to 'brand' *The Home Place* for consumption in the West End altered the way that Friel's play was received in Ireland. We might also think about how the branding of an identity is to mark it as belonging not to the branded individual, but to the person who owns the sign – hence, the tendency within global culture to present narrow representations of national identity limits our sense of what it means to be Irish, or British, and so on. Kuti's play therefore represents an ethical response to globalization. It challenges our sense that identity can or should be homogeneous by giving us five characters who are all, in their own way, outsiders (as Quakers, as women, as poor, as English, and so on). It reminds us that performance, acting, rhetoric – art in general – can take the suffering of real people and turn it into one more commodity to be consumed, and reminds us in doing so that we can confuse the suffering of others with 'authenticity'. It situates globalization in an historical context, showing what is new about it, but showing how much of it has been present for centuries. And finally – and most importantly – it reminds us that we have choices: we cannot stop globalization from being part of our lives, but we can decide how we will make use of it.

Conclusions

Racialization is a process that involves two factors: domination and essentialization. The same is true of nationalized forms of branding. It is a process that reduces national identity to a set of characteristics that are irrelevant to the life within nations at present. As the analysis of Irish racialization shows, race is not an essence, but a process. The problem with both racialization and branding is therefore that they attempt to *essentialize* their subjects. The manner in which a people are – or are not – branded is related to the maintenance and redistribution of power. The solution lies not in reversing racialization or attempting de-racialization, but in making choices between global opportunities and local responsibilities. Within Ireland itself, there is a need to broaden representations of identity, to suggest that an Irish citizen need not be someone who is white, or Catholic, or rural. The question for theatre practitioners is whether they are willing to acknowledge that multicul-turalism has made Irishness seem in many ways unrecognizable – and if they choose to capture that unrecognizable quality in their plays, they cannot brand themselves as 'Irish' for global consumption. In short, Irish practitioners may be faced with a choice: they can represent their country as it is, or they can exploit international audiences' stereotypi-cal views of the country for economic gain.

Of course, this is not a new choice: Boucicault made it, the founders of the Abbey Theatre made it. My concern, however, is that the use of the word 'globalization' to refer to contemporary circumstances may hide the extent to which dramatists, producers, audiences, and per-formers can choose to act. Globalization, I have suggested, is not a process over which we have no control, but a set of phenomena to which we can and must react; identity is not a brand arbitrarily imposed upon us, but a process to which we contribute.

Conclusion: Our Global Theatre

I have sought in this book to chart the emergence of a globalized theatre network, which I have defined as a conceptual framework that enables theatrical productions to travel and be received internationally. Like other global networks, it is not formally organized and controlled by one central authority; rather it arises from a set of interlinking processes, many of which are directed from within nations. Despite its lack of centralization, this network can be described in terms of a number of core features and values.

First, the dominant value in the global theatre network is *mobility*. Put simply, this involves the ability to move easily around the world. One of the reasons that *Stones In His Pockets* was successful was that its small cast and low production values made it inexpensive to tour. But, of course, another form of theatrical mobility is the capacity to cross cultural and geographical barriers. Mobility in theatre – as in many other aspects of life – has therefore become a signifier of success, and thus has become desirable for writers, producers, and actors. This affects the production, reception, and classification of theatre.

Many different modes of reception occur on the global theatre network because of that mobility. Some plays are widely diffused because they deal with concerns that are seen by audiences as 'universal'. Others are successful because they are homogenized examples of what Rebellato calls 'McTheatre': productions that aim to gratify instantly but superficially. What I would suggest, however, is that the major determinant of a play's success on the global stage is its reflexivity: its ability to allow audiences to relate the play's meaning to personal and/or local contexts. In some cases, a play that stimulates a reflexive response will also focus on a universal theme: Friel's treatment of doomed romance in *Translations* has universal appeal, for example, but his treatment of language can be applied to many different local contexts. In other cases, one play will provoke overwhelmingly different responses that are based entirely on local preoccupations, as we saw in the contrasting reactions from audiences to McDonagh's plays in the Aran Islands and Leenane, and in Australia and Turkey.

One of the ways in which producers aid a reflexive response to their work is through branding. This involves applying the principles of the 'Experience Economy' to the theatre, so that what is being sold is not access to a play, but the right to participate in a staged experience, about which the consumer will have strongly predetermined expectations. This means that productions are expected to conform to values implied by their branding. Thus, to see a play that is branded as 'Irish' does not mean that we encounter a work that literally originated in Ireland itself. It means that we consume a work that accords with our predefined notions of Irishness. It is not important the work *be* Irish; it is important instead that as people consume it, they are aware that it *seems* Irish.

Because of this kind of branding, producers will increasingly package theatre productions – or clusters of productions – as 'Events'. The desirability of the 'Event' is that it provides an opportunity for audiences to experience something that is either literally unique ('for one night only!') or so scarce as to feel exceptional. Just as Gilmore and Pine (2007) advise business people that they should create the illusion that their services are 'authentic', theatre producers are seeking opportunities to differentiate their works from other cultural products by branding them as authentic events that confer meaning upon the consumer.

One obvious impact of the move towards branding and eventing is that audiences are being encouraged to purchase tickets to plays that conform in some way with their pre-existing ideas – about Irishness, about a celebrity in the cast, about the authenticity of the production, and so on. This has a number of consequences. The first is that reviewing and other forms of criticism will necessarily become devalued as producers invest more time, money, and energy into pre-publicity. It might be argued that attendance at a play *should* be the beginning of a process: we watch the work, leave the theatre, and digest what we have seen. But the move towards advance publicity means that audiences' appetites are whetted – 'if you come here, this is what you will get', they're told. The theatrical experience is therefore the culmination of that process, involving the satisfaction of an appetite. It is possible that the presentation of theatre as the successful realization of a previously formed desire will reduce audiences' willingness to reflect critically on what they are seeing. And it is likely that if audiences are only ever encouraged to fulfil their expectations when they visit the theatre, the form will lose some of its power to challenge a society's assumptions. As I showed in my discussion of *Angels in America*, some plays are important not because they are financially successful, but because they help to change the way that people think. That can only happen, however, when theatre producers are prepared to challenge their audiences' sense of what is normal and familiar. Branding tends to work against that possibility.

A problem arising from reflexivity and mobility is that local audiences are losing opportunities to generate meanings about their own localities. The fate of the villagers in *Stones In His Pockets* is also the fate of theatre audiences throughout the world: if productions are conceived with one eye on the mass market, then issues of specifically local importance can only be presented implicitly, if they are presented at all. I suggested in Chapter 8 that Friel's *The Home Place* could have been analysed in relation to the Irish Citizenship Referendum, but that analysis was only possible if audiences in Ireland interpreted the action reflexively. Any production that dealt explicitly with the issues of citizenship would risk being relevant only in Ireland – and being relevant only in 2004. Given that dramatists depend for their livelihood on international productions, translation, and the revival of their works by professional and amateur groups, it therefore seems increasingly foolish to be topical.

This, I would suggest, is where national theatres may find renewed relevance as globalization intensifies. I do not suggest that such theatres should aim to produce productions that are (to use that awful word) 'relevant' to the present. Rather, they should show leadership within their societies, as Garry Hynes did with her version of *The Plough and the Stars* and as Patrick Mason did throughout his time at the Abbey. National theatres are uniquely positioned to address audiences that can be conceived of in civic rather than essentially national terms. Such theatres may present plays that are not about an abstract conception of a nation, but which instead address the concerns – or challenge the assumptions – of people who happen to be living in the same place at the same time. This does not require such theatres to be insular. On the contrary, one way of regenerating a national culture is by importing work from abroad, as we've seen. Nor does it mean national theatres cannot be mobile, as the National Theatre of Scotland has already shown so effectively in their short history.

For this reason, national theatres (and indeed other institutions) need to be cautious about the rhetoric associated with the 'Creative Industries'. The flow of information between business and theatre moves in both directions, as I hope I have shown in this book. Theatre is used as corporate entertainment, and it is used to differentiate one nation from another in the global hunt for FDI. But, as words like 'creativity' and 'authenticity' become more fashionable within business discourse, it is likely that scholars like Gilmore and Pine will continue to turn to theatre for inspiration. These are not inherently negative developments. Nor are they new developments, as anyone with a passing familiarity with the Italian Renaissance (or, for that matter, the career of Shakespeare) can attest. So I am sceptical about the value of presenting art and commerce as mutually exclusive categories, mainly because that opposition may obscure the extent to which theatre producers are constructing theatre as a commodity, and using practices that are as applicable to the franchising of a chain of cafes as they are to touring an international play.

My discussion of Boucicault and Kuti aimed to place these issues in an historical context: if nothing is done without desire, theatre will naturally present itself as an irresistible market. It is essential that scholars of theatre are prepared to address the consequences of that development by engaging more fully with the language of commerce and trade.

Kuti's play *The Sugar Wife* spells out the challenges resulting from this. Identity and meaning no longer arise through the interplay of signifiers, as postmodernity claimed. Rather, thanks to globalization, identity and meaning are reconstructed as tokens in a chain of commodity exchanges. The commodification of national and other identities places them in a marketplace where values rise and fall. This will inevitably affect the way that people think about themselves. The construction of self has always been determined by a relationship with the other, as I've stated in previous chapters. But now self-expression also involves a sense of how identity is formed in terms of its relative value against other identities.

This leads to another important conclusion: people get the theatre they deserve. One of the problems with the rhetoric of globalization is that it tends to suggest that people have no control over global processes. Another problem is that the word 'globalization' is so all encompassing that it creates the illusion that if we 'resist globalization', we must forgo some of its benefits. As consumers, audiences have choices about what they see: if critics deplore celebrity casting, or 'Americanization', or the rise of 'McTheatre', they must see those developments as arising in response to audiences' desires. It could be suggested that the 'reward' audiences in Dublin got for not seeing *The Home Place* was that they got to see Ralph Fiennes in *Faith Healer* at the same theatre the following year: if a theatre acts globally abroad, it will act globally at home too. We need to be cautious about accepting the validity of such arguments, and we certainly need to evaluate far more critically the role of audiences in determining what is staged. While scholars must continue literally to *review* theatrical productions – to see them as historical events that have passed – we must also dedicate more attention to how producers provoke particular desires in audiences before plays are staged. One of the problems with the rhetoric of globalization is that it tends to render agency invisible.

A corollary of that is that theatre-makers need to be aware that the kind of work they produce helps us to imagine globalization. In other words, if we see globalization as a meme, theatre is one way in which it may be replicated. If digital technology allows globalization to become an 'imagined community', theatre can imagine other kinds of community. Doing so will involve an awareness that the liveness of theatre offers something that cannot itself be mass produced or digitized: if a theatre audience has two or more people in it, it is already beginning to work against the processes of individualization that are associated with globalization. Dramatists and practitioners have responded to globalization imaginatively, by devising (or revising) techniques that take account of audiences' ability to consume information more quickly because of time-space compression. They are showing an increased awareness of a globalized vocabulary that is both linguistic (as in the plays of McDonagh and the films of Tarantino), and visual (as in the figuring of globalization in relation to the bodies of women, referred to in my discussion of Carr). Rather than seeing globalization as something that writers must simplistically 'resist', we should instead be aware of how changing conceptions of space, time, and community are stimulating the development of valuable new ways of writing.

Certainly, writers themselves are benefiting from globalization. There are obvious economic rewards in being produced internationally, and celebrity is becoming a more important factor in the reception of some writers. This is clearly the case with Martin McDonagh, but also affects the reception of Friel, Carr, and others. Similarly, the branding of national identity will undoubtedly continue to be a factor in the reception of various authors. Just as Druid Theatre 'authenticates' its productions of McDonagh and Synge by touring to places like Leenane and the Aran Islands, so will writers continue to be authenticated by their national or ethnic identities. What does a writer owe his or her national audience in this context? Is it a problem that someone like Conor McPherson is successful as an Irish playwright, but will only premiere his plays in London? And if it is not a problem, what does that tell us about Ireland's status as a supposedly postcolonial country?[1]

The question of whether drama that originates either in or for London can be regarded as genuinely 'Irish' will no doubt continue to provoke discussion – but perhaps, as the global perspective becomes more visible, it is a debate that will no longer provoke anxiety. The grow-ing dominance of mobility means that Friel's notion (1999a: 86) that Irish dramatists are talking to themselves and being overheard abroad must be reformulated for a world in which both communications and culture have become deterritorialized. Issues like Ireland's former colo-nial relationship with Britain remain important, but the fact that insti-tutions around the world now share many of the dilemmas faced by Irish theatres must also be acknowledged.

That said, there are issues in this book that are particularly pertinent to Ireland itself. One such issue is the changing presentation of Northern Ireland in theatre, which I have characterized as evidence of a shift in the country's drama from the postcolonial to the global. This shift was evi-dent in the contrast between the 1991 and 2002 Abbey productions of *The Plough and the Stars*, the first of which packaged the play as a direct intervention into debates about the 'national question', while the sec-ond packaged the play as an historical monument. Another example is the production of Martin McDonagh's *The Lieutenant of Inishmore*: if the purpose of many Irish plays in the past was to explain the historical basis of the Troubles in a way that international audiences might 'overhear', McDonagh's play offers Irish terrorism as an empty signifier that audi-ences internationally can apply to their own lives and localities.[2]

I think there are difficulties in this shift from the postcolonial to the global (though I also think that it is difficult to sustain the notion that Ireland is postcolonial when it is also one of the wealthiest countries in the world). As I've already mentioned, I am not calling for a rebranding of the postcolonial franchise within Irish Studies. Any attempt to use globalization in an academic context needs to be based on an awareness that the academy is itself one of the most globalized institutions in the world, a fact reflected not only institutionally but also in the intellec-tual structures that accompany academic enquiry, such as the emphasis on writing for a so-called 'international readership' or the use of theo-retical terms as if they are universally applicable. The impact of global-ization on academic formation may lead to what Kirby, Gibbons, and Cronin (2002) have termed 'ideological franchising'. This involves the 'wholesale import of concepts and analyses from a powerful centre . . . and their application in a Procrustean fashion to the local society' (14). I do think that many of the issues I've debated in this book are relevant to other countries, other historical periods, and other literary genres. But I also think that we need to be cautious about the totalizing impulses that are inherent in globalization, and to avoid assuming that it is possible to study Irish theatre in the same way everywhere, or that it is possible to study other countries' theatre in the same way as I've approached Irish theatre.

Ireland, of course, is not unique in being stereotyped on the global stage. As demonstrated by my discussion of McDonagh and Friel, it is possible for a writer to do much to challenge the reception of Irishness abroad – but it is also possible for audiences to ignore or misunderstand that presentation. The problem, therefore, is not with what any writer's intentions may be, but with the absence of a criticism that can deconstruct the conditions that lead audiences to misread plays.

A good starting point for such a criticism in Ireland might involve a consideration of why there is so much interest in the reception of Irish work abroad. Because of economic growth, peace in Northern Ireland, and many other factors, Irishness in the Celtic Tiger era has become increasingly indeterminate, leading to attempts to reconcile, or at least accommodate, the many contradictory versions of Irish identity that are now available. Many Irish plays touch off the nerves made raw by the clash of these desires, blending versions of Irishness that expose their contradictions. The plays of McDonagh, for instance, give us the Irish male as an inexplicably violent rural caveman, while his public persona is the 'chic' cosmopolitan Anglo-Irishman, a combination that places him at the fault-line between Ireland's traditional past and its postmodern present. Irish responses to McDonagh's reception abroad must be viewed as a sign of anxiety about a lack of control over the discourse surrounding Irish identity: we have, as Marie Jones puts it, been dispossessed.

However, a crisis of identity doesn't justify insularity; and self-absorption should not be misunderstood as self-knowledge. The celebratory tone of reports about the success of Irish theatre abroad during the 1990s contrasts strikingly with the fact that, during that decade, Irish illiteracy rates were shown consistently to be among the highest in the West.[3] Any attempt to cheer the progress of Irish drama abroad thus seems an irresponsible distraction from the fact that the country is far from being the stereotypical 'land of saints and scholars'. It is similarly difficult to celebrate Irish drama unambiguously when most of its biggest successes abroad would not have occurred without British money, British expertise, and England-based critics. Again – where does this leave Ireland's sense of itself as postcolonial?

Money, of course, is a factor. Whether Irish writers are subverting stereotypes or not, they are benefiting enormously from the prevalence of those stereotypes. And so, too, are many other people currently resident in Ireland. The strength of the Irish economy is at least partially dependent on the global proliferation of myths about Irishness: the tourism that results from it accounts for a significant proportion of Irish GDP, and Irish-branded exports – including cultural exports – play a significant role in the Irish economy, as the IDA's 'Irish Mind' campaign shows. Perhaps it could be said that to begin to criticize Irish drama on serious terms would be to deconstruct the basis of Irish economic prosperity.

This, I would suggest, is where the category of nation again becomes relevant in a globalized theatre discourse. Such a criticism could begin to tackle the problems with branding theatre along essentialized lines – and could, more importantly, begin to explore what those misrepresentations might mean for people living in the branded cultures. Such a criticism should not be inward looking, but must instead be *rooted* – again not in terms of essentialized models of identity, but in relation to citizenship. It must therefore be positioned to address the theatre of other countries on a dialogic basis, rather than considering other countries' cultural output only insofar as it confirms 'our' sense of who 'we' think we are. To do so in Ireland would involve a focus on issues of local importance: literacy, inequality, the role in Irish life of intellectual and creative activity, the responsibilities of those involved in Irish culture as promoters and bene-ficiaries of globalization, and so on. But the function of this criticism would also be to mediate the relationship between local theatre audiences and globalized theatre productions. This doesn't involve telling audiences what to think – but it might involve showing audiences how theatre pro-ducers are making assumptions about what they think.

An Irish resident who watches plays like *Stones In His Pockets, Dancing at Lughnasa, The Plough and the Stars, The Shaughraun, by the bog of cats . . . , The Sugar Wife,* and *The Home Place* will respond to those plays in terms of cultural and social factors that will not necessarily exist in other times and places. Audiences elsewhere will have necessarily different responses. It is vital that we do not fall into the trap of authenticating one kind of response while deriding another – but it is equally vital that critics bring an awareness of how local preoccupations shape their understanding of globally diffused plays.

I will conclude therefore by saying that theatre studies and Irish Studies do not need a new paradigm, but a new framework. The risk is that, by popularizing globalization theory, we will merely be rebrand-ing the postcolonial theory, presenting 'new and improved' critical terms that will do little to elucidate the actual conditions under which theatre is made and received, not only in Ireland, but throughout the world. We must instead bring local knowledge into a global conversation, with an awareness of how plays mean different things, to different audiences, in different parts of the world.

Notes

1 Globalization and Irish Theatre

1. A version of *Stones In His Pockets* appeared in 1996, produced by Dubbeljoint Theatre. Jones substantially rewrote the play for its 1999 outing – though she subsequently became embroiled in a 2004 court case about royalties with the show's original director, Pam Brighton. For an analysis of the legal consequences of the case, see Zemer (2006). My comments on the production refer to the 1999 Lyric version, directed by Ian McElhinny.
2. The trope of the feminized male being dominated by an assertive woman is very common in Irish drama. We see it in Goldsmith's *She Stoops to Conquer* (1773), in which Marlow is 'trained' by Kate to be an acceptable husband. And it recurs in the presentation of men in modern Irish drama, from Wilde's Algernon and Jack, to Synge's Christy, to O'Casey's Captain Boyle, and onwards.
3. Episodes of *The Simpsons* that focus on Hollywood include 'Radioactive Man', Season 7, Episode 2; 'A Star is Burns', Season 6, Episode 18; and 'When You Dish Upon a Star', Season 10, Episode 5.
4. See Mark Phelan, 2008, for a detailed reading of *Stones*. I wish to thank Mark for allowing me to read this essay before it was published.
5. See MacBride and Roach, 1989; Barber, 1995; Flusty, 2004.
6. See *The Guardian* newspaper, 'Fastsellers: The Best Performing Paperbacks of 2001', http://books.guardian.co.uk/fastsellers2002/0,864901,00.html.
7. Dawkins points out that the idea of the meme has itself become a meme, so it seems superfluous to quote directly from his discussion of that issue, which is outlined in Dawkins, 2006: 189–201.
8. Most commentators agree that the Celtic Tiger period of rapid economic growth due to globalization began in 1993–94, and continued unabated until 2001. After the global economic downturn of 2001–02, the Irish economy became dominated by the property market – that is, by economic factors that were predominantly national rather than global. Strictly speaking, therefore, the Celtic Tiger period should be considered as lasting from 1993 to 2001. I begin slightly before, and conclude slightly after, this period to show the extent and pace of social and cultural change, while establishing the long-term consequences of the Celtic Tiger period.
9. All figures are adapted from the online databases of the Central Statistics Office Ireland, *www.cso.ie*.
10. This passage has been cut from published versions of the play (see Hughes, 1997). I wish to thank Declan Hughes for providing this information.
11. *The Lieutenant of Inishmore* opened at the Other Place in Stratford in April 2001. A new version of *Too Late For Logic* was produced at the Royal Lyceum in Edinburgh in August 2001. *Made in China* opened at the Schauspiel Theatre in Germany in January 2001.
12. Carr's *Woman and Scarecrow* and Murphy's *Alice Trilogy* opened at the Royal Court in 2006 and 2005 respectively. Walsh's *The Small Things* premiered in

London in 2005. McGuinness's *Speaking Like Magpies* was produced in Stratford in 2005, and *There Came a Gypsy Riding* at the Donmar Warehouse in 2007. O'Reilly's *Is This About Sex?* opened in Edinburgh in August 2007. Barry's *The Pride of Parnell Street* opened at the Tricycle in London in September 2007; in the same month, Jones's *Rock Doves* premiered in New York. All of McPherson's plays since 1997 (except for the short piece *Come on Over*, which appeared at the Gate in 2002) have premiered in London.

13. For a useful survey of research on globalization and literature, see Robinson, 2007; Adams, 2007.

2 Globalizing Irish Theatre: Brian Friel's *Dancing at Lughnasa*, 1990/1999

1. *Dancing at Lughnasa* may be said to have inspired *Riverdance* in two ways. The presentation of the play's dance scene as a moment of euphoric release inspired the use of Irish traditional dance in *Riverdance*. The international success of the play also provided a model of how an Irish theatrical product might be received internationally. For commentary by Moya Doherty on the inspirational power of *Lughnasa*, see Stearns, 1996. I argue later in this chapter that *Riverdance* would in turn influence the reception of *Lughnasa*.

2. In the Republic of Ireland Census of 1981 (the year after *Translations* appeared), the number of residents who reported that they could speak Irish was 1,018,413 – roughly 32% of the population. See 'Irish speakers and non-Irish speakers aged 3 and over in each Province at each Census since 1926' on *www.cso.ie*.

3. The distance from Athlone to Glenties in Donegal (the town where Friel's aunts lived in 1936 and often seen as the 'real' Ballybeg) is just over 200 kilometres.

4. In the 1990 and 1999 Abbey productions directed by Patrick Mason, this element of the ceremony was made explicit by the blocking, with Chris sitting directly behind Gerry while this ritual was being enacted.

5. 'Marina Carr is a writer haunted by memories she could not possibly possess, but they seem determined to possess her'. Frank McGuinness, 1996: ix.

6. Annie M.P. Smithson (1873–1948) was an Irish novelist who presented Irish women as idealized figures in a series of best-selling romances.

7. The presentation of Agnes and Rose is partially autobiographical, as Thomas Kilroy (1999) explains.

8. The statistics listed in this chapter are adapted from the online databases of the Central Statistics Office Ireland.

9. Comments about the productions of *Dancing at Lughnasa* arise from my attendance at performances of the Abbey production in 1991, 1993, 1999, and 2000, and from a viewing of videotaped performances of the 1990 and 2000 productions at the Abbey Theatre Archive.

10. Christopher Murray ('Recording Tremors', 1997) and Fintan O'Toole ('Marking Times', 1997) both remark on the similarities between *The Glass Menagerie* and *Dancing at Lughnasa*.

11. For full reviews see *The Evening Press*, 25 April 1990: 5; *The Irish Independent*, 25 April 1990: 11; *The Guardian*, 1 May 1990: 22.

12. See 'The Abbey Stuns South Bank', *Sunday Independent*, 21 October 1990; 'Raves for Friel Play', *The Irish Times*, 20 October 1990; Julie Kavanagh, 'Friel at Last', *Vanity Fair*, 21 October 1991. *The Sunday Business Post* article appeared on 3 November 1991. The figure quoted was inaccurate: the actual amount predicted was $75,000. *The Irish Times* readers' competition was held in November 1991.
13. See, for example, *The Irish Times*, 24 November 1991: 3.
14. Brian Friel to Noel Pearson, 13 March 1991, Brian Friel Archive, National Library of Ireland, CB 119. Thanks to Joan Dean for sharing this reference.

3   Globalizing National Theatre: Sean O'Casey's *The Plough and the Stars*, 1926/1991/2002

1. This information is adapted from The Arts Council's *Annual Reports*, 1990–99. In 1990, the Abbey received €2,345,690 in funding – just over 54 per cent of all available funds for theatre in the Republic of Ireland. By 1999, funding to the Abbey had increased to €4,151,630. However, overall funding for theatre in Ireland had also increased, to almost €10.5 million, so that the Abbey by 1999 was only receiving 40 per cent of all available funding for theatre.
2. Blythe was director of the Abbey from 1941 to 1966, a period in which the theatre produced few works of lasting value, while infamously rejecting plays by the rising generation of Irish playwrights, such as John B. Keane, Tom Murphy, and Brian Friel.
3. This commentary is based on material consulted in the Abbey Theatre archive.
4. Comments about this production are based on attendance at a performance in April 1991 and viewing of a videotaped performance at the Abbey Theatre Archive in 2003. Comments on the 2002 production discussed below are based on attendance at performances in November 2002 and January 2003.
5. My thanks to Brian Jackson of the Abbey Theatre for confirming this information in 2003.
6. *The Plough* appeared at least once a year at the Abbey from 1926 to 1939; thereafter, productions became less frequent, appearing every four to seven years (ATA).
7. I have adapted this information from the CAIN website. See Malcolm Sutton, 'An Index of Deaths from the Conflict in Ireland', CAIN Web Service (http://cain.ulst.ac.uk/sutton/index.html) accessed 1 September 2004.
8. For an excellent consideration of what national theatres can achieve through theatre-in-education and outreach, see Deeney, 2007.
9. Lash and Lury (2007) offer an excellent analysis of the impact of branding on culture, drawing on Adorno and other theorists to analyse several different forms of mass-mediated event.

4   Globalizing the Brand: Dion Boucicault's *The Shaughraun*, 1874/2004

1. Plays by women at the Abbey in 2003 included Marina Carr's contribution to *Sons and Daughters*, Hilary Fannin's *Doldrum Bay*, and Stella Feehily's *Duck*, all of which were presented on the Peacock stage. Since 2000, the only other

plays by women who were either born or resident in Ireland were Elizabeth Kuti's *Treehouses* (2001) and Marina Carr's *Ariel* (2002). Plays in Irish included Tom McIntyre's *Caoineadh Airt Ui Laoghaire* (1998) and *Cúirt an Mheán Oíche* (1999), Antoine O'Flaharta's *An Suas Dearc* (1995), and Eilis Ni Dhuibhne's *Dun na mBan Tri Thine* (1994) (ATA).

2. Commentary on the 2004 production of *The Shaughraun* is based on my attendance at three performances of the production in June and July 2004.

3. The production did in fact open in the West End in 2005, though it was not as successful as the producers hoped. A scheduled US tour did not go ahead; instead McColgan and his wife Moya Doherty invested in the ill-fated *Pirate Queen*, which in 2007 became one of the most expensive flops of all time on Broadway. My point about *The Shaughraun* is not that its Irish qualities guaranteed success, but that Boucicault's 'branded' version of Irishness provided a blueprint that was later developed by Irish writers who wished to achieve international success. I am therefore inclined to see the failure of McColgan's *Shaughraun* in relation to the insights of Gilmore and Pine, who show that products that seem inauthentic will not be well received by consumers. The problem with McColgan's production of Boucicault is that it used a branded version of Irish identity that was over-familiar, and thus devalued.

4. The Gate curated a 'Pinter Festival' at the Lincoln Center, New York in 2000.

5. Conor McPherson's *The Weir* was produced by the Royal Court Theatre, as was *The Steward of Christendom* (with Out of Joint), while *The Cripple of Inishmaan* was produced by the Royal National Theatre.

5 Globalizing Authorship: Martin McDonagh, 1996/2003

1. I wish to thank Karen Fricker for pointing out Rushdie's use of this character to me.

2. The reading took place at Druid's Chapel Lane Theatre on 20 April 1997 as part of the Cúirt International Festival of Literature, Galway.

3. Hynes was artistic director at the Abbey from 1991–93, and worked with Druid from 1975–90 and from 1994 to the present.

4. Thanks to Garry Hynes and Fergal McGrath for providing information about the original number of characters in this play.

5. McDonagh's statement was made in private to Nicholas Hytner, who passed it on to Eyre. It is not made clear whether he made this comment sincerely or in jest.

6. I wish to thank Joan Dean for making a copy of the *Galway Advertiser* article available to me.

7. 'You never see the INLA shooting Australians', states Davey in *The Lieutenant* (2001: 55), while Mairead's mother sends the following message to her: 'Good luck and try not to go blowing up any kids' (57).

6 Globalization and Cultural Exchange: *Angels in America* in Dublin

1. The statement that the average attendance at the Abbey in 1995 was 65 per cent is taken from O'Reilly-Hyland, 1998. All other figures were made available to me in 2003 by Brian Jackson.

2. Both parts of *Angels in America* were presented at the Dublin Writers Museum in the 1999 Fringe Festival in Dublin, presented by a company called 'You'll Be Sorry When We're Famous' (which, incidentally, has yet to stage another production). Both parts were produced in 2008 by the Bull Alley Theatre Training Company at the Civic Theatre in Tallaght, Dublin. As that production was presented by the graduating class of a training company, it seems inaccurate to call them 'professional'.

3. For the record, Mason was responding to a question put to him from the audience by me during a public debate about national theatres that was held as part of the theatre's 'abbeyonehundred' celebrations. See Abbey Theatre, 2004.

4. Dublin 4 is a postal district on the city's south side. McGahon uses it in this context as a dismissive shorthand for the wealthy liberal class that dominates the Irish media and much of Irish public life. I have taken these quotations from Kathleen O'Callaghan, 1995. Incidentally, O'Callaghan wrote approvingly of McGahon's contempt for what she perceived as 'political correctness'.

5. *The Gay Byrne Show*, RTE Radio 1, 8 June 1995, 9.10 am. This quotation, and all subsequent statements, are taken from an unpublished transcript (ATA).

6. Unless otherwise specified, descriptions of the production are based on a viewing of production photographs and a recording of one performance, consulted at the ATA.

7. This tendency can be seen in the titles of many histories of Irish drama, which are usually arranged chronologically according to authors, as we see in Tony Roche's *Contemporary Irish Drama – From Beckett to McGuinness* and Nicholas Grene's *Politics of Irish Drama – Plays in Context from Boucicault to Friel*.

8. Information adapted from the appendix to Lady Gregory's *Our Irish Theatre*, 1965: 265–6.

9. This information is adapted from the Druid Theatre online archive (www. druidtheatre.com/productions). Between 1975 and 1980, Druid staged 45 different plays, of which 21 were not Irish. Between 1981 and 1990, Druid produced 51 different plays, of which 17 were not Irish. From 1990 to 2007, Druid produced 49 different productions (if we count *DruidSynge* as one production), and of them only four were non-Irish.

10. This information is adapted from the Rough Magic online archive (www. rough-magic.com). Between 1984 and 1990, Rough Magic produced 32 different plays, of which two-thirds (21) were non-Irish. From 1991 to 2002, the company produced 22 different plays, with just three being non-Irish. Since 2002, the company has, on average, produced one new Irish play and one non-Irish play each year.

11. Mark O'Rowe provided this information during a pre-show talk before the Gate Theatre's production of *Crestfall* on 30 May 2003, and Conor McPherson confirmed it during a pre-show talk before Eugene O'Brien's *Eden* at the Peacock Theatre on 25 January 2001. For Carr on Williams, see Ni Anluain, 2000: 56.

12. *Liveline* is a daily RTE Radio talk show which tends to discuss topical issues. Dr Anthony Clare (1942–2007) was a distinguished psychiatrist and broadcaster. Fintan O'Toole is a well-known cultural commentator and critic who published work on Irish theatre (including books on Tom Murphy and Sheridan), while also writing several books about Irish society around the time that *Angels* was produced: *The Ex-Isle of Erin* (1996), *Meanwhile Back at the Ranch* (1994), and *Black Hole, Green Card* (1994) – all of them lively attempts to come to terms with the rapidly evolving Ireland.

13. Stagg was never charged with solicitation. He remains married to his wife, Mary Morris. He retained his government post despite his arrest, and was re-elected in 1997, 2002, and 2007. In the 2007 Irish General Election to Dail Eireann, no openly gay politician was elected.

14. Strictly speaking, the Irish tourist season lasts from St Patrick's Day (17 March) until mid-September. For the purposes of clarity, however, I am referring only to those productions that took place in June, July, and August. In many cases, this includes plays that opened in May (closing in June or July), and some plays which opened in August, running right up to the end of September.

15. All information provided was taken from lists of productions at the ATA. Three additional points can be made. First, it might be argued that Shaw's plays are not recognizably 'Irish' classics – but, particularly for *St Joan*, the cast used Irish accents to bring out themes in the play that would have been seen as 'Irish'. Second, *Observe the Sons of Ulster* was premiered in 1985 and would certainly be regarded as an Irish classic now, but that reputation is largely based on its 1994 and 1995 revivals, so I have not included it in the list of 'Irish classics' that might have attracted a tourist audience at that time. Finally, an interesting point to note about *Tarry Flynn* is that it made use of techniques inspired by Théâtre de Complicité, which had visited the Dublin Theatre Festival in 1994 with *Street of Crocodiles* – a good example of how international practice influenced the development of Irish work.

16. My comments about the queue for tickets to *The Guys* are based on personal experience: I arrived an hour before the box office opened to find at least 50 people already standing in line.

17. Mitchell also produced a version of *Iphigenia* at the RNT, London in 2004. See Solga, 2008, for a useful account of that production.

7 Globalizing Gender and Dramatic Form

1. *The Mai* and *Portia Coughlan* were presented on the Peacock stage of the Abbey; *by the bog of cats . . .* and *Ariel* were presented on the theatre's main-stage. *On Raftery's Hill* was premiered in Galway by Druid, before transferring to the Gate Theatre and the Royal Court.

2. Bold and Italics in this quotation have been added for emphasis. In Standard English, the passage would probably mean something like the following: 'You know well when Sonia became Champion the wonder horse and gal-loped her way to success back in Gothenburg, yeah? And Sonia stands on the winner's podium with the world medal, all a dangling from the pretty little neck as the national anthem blasted the fuck out of the sky, and the green white and porridge [the Irish flag] was all a-flutter in the breeze. And all the Irish around the track and in the world, and anybody who ever fucked an Irish person [?], they all have a little tear in their eye when they said "This is a great day for Ireland". Well Runt, *this* is a better day'.

8 Branding Identity: Irish Theatre in 2005

1. I am referring to Lo and Gilbert (2002), Pavis (1996), and Bharucha (1993, 2000). For a detailed consideration of interculturalism and multiculturalism

in Irish theatre, see Jason King's two articles from 2005, listed in Texts Cited.

2. *The Irish Times* website, in a special section, provides a good overview of the main issues involved in the Citizenship Referendum, together with detailed analysis of the various claims made in relation to it. It was shown as the debate progressed that the number of women travelling to Ireland very late in their pregnancies was tiny; and the managers of the country's maternity hospitals issued a joint statement denying that such women were placing their services under strain. The referendum was passed by an overwhelming majority of 80%. Quotations from McDowell are taken from his contribution to the website (see www.ireland.com/focus/referendum2004/guide.html).

3. This issue was publicly debated on RTE's television show *The View*, broadcast on 8 February 2005 (see www.rte.ie/tv/theview/archive/20050208.html). The Ambassador Theatre Group staged the play in London; their website shows how reviews from British critics present in Dublin were used to market the play: Benedict Nightingale, for instance, wrote that 'Britain should see it. Soon' (see www.theambassadors.com/comedy/sp_p2009.html).

4. Joseph O'Connor's faux Victorian novel *The Star of the Sea* (New York: Harcourt, 2003) plays skilfully with this construction in its presentation of Irish characters crossing the Atlantic on a New York-bound steamer.

5. The description of Ireland as a 'Third World country' is particularly common in Irish political discourse. For instance, the Irish Department of Health was nicknamed 'Angola' by the TD Brian Cowen, so dysfunctional and chaotic did it seem to him. In 2004, Liz McManus TD stated that 'our health care system is reminiscent of a Third World country' (Dail Eireann, 2004). In a 2001 debate, a Junior Minister stated that 'anyone who read the contributions of Opposition Members during the debate on the motion last night could be forgiven for believing that Ireland is a Third World country when it comes to the provision of sporting facilities' (Dail Eireann, 2001).

Conclusion: Our Global Theatre

1. For an interesting treatment of how the reception of authors is influenced by celebrity culture, see Joe Moran, 2000.

2. I am not suggesting that all theatre from or about Northern Ireland can be seen as globalized. Rather, I use the example of McDonagh to show how globalization, not post-colonialism, has become the dominant paradigm in Irish theatre production.

3. During the late 1990s, numerous policy initiatives were launched by the Department of Education in Ireland to tackle illiteracy. Illiteracy rates among the workforce (ages 16–65) had been found to be relatively higher in Ireland than in many other countries, with one in four Irish adults rated completely illiterate in the findings of the International Adult Literacy Survey of literacy carried out in 22 industrialized countries between 1994 and 1998. For a full description of the survey and Ireland's position relative to other OECD countries, see OECD, 1997 and 2001.

Texts Cited

Abbey Theatre (2002) *The Plough and the Stars: Page and Stage* (Dublin: Abbey Theatre).
—— (2004) 'National Theatre and the Nation', Transcript of Abbey Debate, 31 January 2004. (www.abbeytheatre.ie/news)
Adams, Laura L. (2007) 'Globalization of Culture and the Arts', *Sociology Compass* 1, 1, pp. 127–42.
Allen, Theodore (1994) *The Invention of The White Race* (London: Verso).
Anderson, Benedict (1991) *Imagined Communities* (London: Verso).
Ang, Ien (1985) *Watching 'Dallas': Soap Opera and the Melodramatic Imagination* (New York: Routledge).
Appadurai, Arjun (1996) *Modernity at Large: Cultural Dimensions of Globalization* (London and Minneapolis: University of Minneapolis Press).
Arts Council, The (1990–2003) *Annual Reports, 1989–2002* (Dublin: The Arts Council).
Associated Press (1995) 'Gay Group Demands A Permit To March On St. Patrick's Day', *The Record,* 22 February 1995, p. A04.
AT Kearney/Foreign Policy (2002) *The 2002 AT Kearney/Foreign Policy Magazine Globalization Index* (Washington DC: Foreign Policy).
Bakhtin, M. (1986) *Speech Genres and Other Late Essays* (Austin: University of Texas Press).
Barber, Benjamin (1995) *Jihad vs. McWorld* (New York: Times Books).
Battersby, Eileen (1997) 'The Image Maker', *The Irish Times,* 12 June 1997, p. 13.
Bauman, Zygmunt (1998) *Globalization: The Human Consequences* (Cambridge: Polity Press).
—— (2001) *The Individualized Society* (Cambridge: Polity Press).
Beck, Ulrich (1997) *The Re-invention of Politics: Re-thinking Modernity in the Global Social Order* (Cambridge: Polity Press).
Beckett, Samuel (1986) *Complete Dramatic Works* (London: Faber & Faber).
Behan, Brendan (1978) *The Complete Plays* (New York: Grove Press).
Benjamin, Walter (1992) *Illuminations* (ed. and trans. Hannah Arendt) (London: Fontana).
Bennett, Susan (1997) *Theatre Audiences* (London and New York: Routledge).
—— (2005) 'Theatre/Tourism', *Theatre Journal* 57, 3 (October), pp. 407–28.
Bhabha, Homi K. (1994) *The Location of Culture* (London and New York: Routledge).
Bharucha, Rustom (1993) *Theatre and the World: Performance and the Politics of Culture* (London and New York: Routledge).
—— (2000) *The Politics of Cultural Practice – Thinking Through Culture in an Age of Globalization* (London: Athlone Press).
Billington, Michael (1992) *One Night Stands* (London: Nick Hern).
—— (2002) 'US Stars on the London Stage: Enough is Enough', *The Guardian,* 30 May 2002, p. 21.
—— (2007) *Harold Pinter,* revised edition (London: Faber and Faber).

Blumenthal, Dannielle (1997) *Women and Soap Opera: A Cultural Feminist Perspective* (New York: Greenwood Press).

Borreca, Art (1997) '"Dramaturging" the Dialectic: Brecht, Benjamin, and Declan Donnellan's Production of *Angels in America*', in Deborah R. Geis and Steven F. Kruger (eds), *Approaching the Millennium – Essays on Angels in America* (Ann Arbor: University of Michigan Press).

Boucicault, Dion (1987) *Selected Plays* (Gerrards Cross: Colin Smythe).

Bradley, Jack (1997) 'Making Playwrights'. *The Cripple of Inishmaan* programme (London: Royal National Theatre).

Brantley, Ben (2003) 'An Acting Lesson, With A Grovel and A Strut, in Two Plays', *New York Times*, 21 January 2003. (www.nytimes.com)

Bratu Hansen, Miriam (2001) 'The Mass Production of the Senses', in Christine Gledhill and Linda Williams (eds), *Reinventing Film Studies* (New York: Hodder Arnold), pp. 332–50.

Brook, Peter (1987) *The Shifting Point* (London: Methuen).

Brown, Stephen (2006) 'Fail Better! Samuel Beckett's Secrets of Business and Branding Success', *Business Horizons* 49, pp. 161–9.

Brundson, Charlotte (2000) *The Feminist, the Housewife and the Soap Opera* (Oxford: Oxford University Press).

Burke, Patrick (1997) '"As if Language no Longer Existed": Non-Verbal Theatricality in the Plays of Friel', in William Kerwin (ed.), *Brian Friel: A Casebook* (New York and London: Garland Publishing).

Carpenter, Edmund and Marshall McLuhan (1970) *Explorations in Communication* (London: Cape).

Carr, Marina (1998) *By the Bog of Cats* (Oldcastle: Gallery Press).

——— (2002) *Ariel* (Oldcastle: Gallery Press).

Casanova, Pascale (1999) *La République Mondiale des Lettres* (Paris: Seuil).

Castells, M. (1998) *The Information Age: Economy, Society and Culture, Volume 3. End of Millennium* (Cambridge: Blackwell).

Cave, Richard Allen (1996) 'The City Versus the Village', in Mary Massoud (ed.), *Literary Inter-Relations: Ireland, Egypt, and the Far East* (Gerrards Cross: Colin Smythe), pp. 281–96.

Caves, Richard E. (2000) *Creative Industries: Contracts Between Art and Commerce* (Cambridge and London: Harvard University Press).

Chambers, Lilian, Ger Fitzgibbon and Eamonn Jordan (eds) (2001) *Theatre Talk: View of Irish Theatre Practitioners* (Dublin: Carysfort Press).

Chisholm, Caroline (1997) 'Three of a Kind', *The* [Sydney] *Daily Telegraph*, 5 December 1997, p. 45.

Christalis, Angelique (2002) 'National's Desire for Hollywood Stars Upsets Local Talent', *The Guardian*, 23 August 2002, p. 11.

Clapp, Susannah (2003) 'Pack Up Your Troubles', *The Observer*, 30 November 2003, p. 14.

Clarke, Brenna Katz and Harold Ferrar (1979) *The Dublin Drama League* (Gerrards Cross: Colin Smythe).

Cleary, Joe (2000) *Literature, Partition and the National State: Culture and Conflict in Ireland, Israel and Palestine* (Cambridge: Cambridge University Press).

Clum, John M. (1994) *Acting Gay: Male Homosexuality in Modern Drama* (New York: Columbia University Press).

Coult, Tony (2003) *About Friel – the Playwright and His Work* (London: Faber and Faber).

Crawley, Peter (2003) 'Thicker than Water', *The Irish Times*, 25 September 2003, *The Ticket*, pp. 2–3.

——— (2005) 'His Name in Lights', *Irish Theatre Magazine* Volume 5, Number 23, Summer.

Cullingford, Elizabeth Butler (2001) *Ireland's Others: Gender and Ethnicity in Irish Literature and Popular Culture* (Cork: Cork University Press).

Curtis, Liz (1984) *Nothing But the Same Old Story: The Roots of Anti-Irish Racism* (London: Information on Ireland).

Curtis, L.P. (1996) *Apes and Angels*, revised edition (Washington DC: Smithsonian Institute).

Dail Eireann (2001) 'Parliamentary Debates, Tuesday 31 January 2001'. (www.gov.ie/debates-01/31jan/sect5.htm)

——— (2004) 'Select Committee on Health and Children', Thursday, 29 April 2004. (www.gov.ie)

Dawkins, Richard (2006) *The Selfish Gene* (Oxford: Oxford University Press).

Dean, Joan Fitzpatrick (2003) *Dancing at Lughnasa* (Cork: Cork University Press).

Deane, Seamus (1990) 'Introduction' to Terry Eagleton, Frederic Jameson, Edward Said, *Nationalism, Colonialism and Literature* (Minneapolis: University of Minnesota Press).

Deeney, John F. (2007) 'National Causes/Moral Clauses?: The National Theatre, Young People and Citizenship', *Research in Drama Education* 12, 3, pp. 331–44.

Delgado, Maria M and Paul Heritage (eds) (1996) *In Contact with the Gods? Directors Talk Theatre* (Manchester: Manchester University Press).

Dening, Penelope (1997) 'The Wordsmith of Camberwell', *The Irish Times*, 8 July 1997, p. 12.

——— (2001) 'The Scribe of Kilburn', *The Irish Times*, 23 April 2001, p. 12.

Dickens, Charles (1985) *Bleak House* (Harmondsworth: Penguin Classics).

Doyle, Roddy (1988) *The Commitments* (London: Minerva).

Dromgoole, Dominic (2001) *The Full Room* (London: Methuen).

Dublin Theatre Festival (2001) *Official Programme* (Dublin: Dublin Theatre Festival).

——— (2007) *James Son of James – Official Programme* (Dublin: Dublin Theatre Festival).

Dyer, Richard (1997) *White*. (London: Routledge).

——— (1998) *Stars*, revised edition (London: BFI Publishing).

Eccles, Jeremy (2000) 'Freak Redefines Beauty', *Canberra Times* (Australia), 12 August 2000, Section A, p. 12.

Eyre, Richard (2003) *National Service* (London: Bloomsbury).

Fisher, James (2001) 'Troubling the Waters: *Angels in America*', in James Fisher (ed.), *The Theater of Tony Kushner: Living Past Hope* (New York and London: Routledge).

Fisher, Mark (2001) 'Has Scotland Answered the National Question?', *The Irish Times*, 4 December 2001, p. 12.

Fitz-Simon, Christopher (1983) *The Irish Theatre* (London: Thames and Hudson).

——— (1994) *The Boys: A Biography of Micheál MacLíammóir and Hilton Edwards* (London: Nick Hern).

——— (2003) *The Abbey Theatre* (London: Thames and Hudson).

Flusty, Stephen (2004) *De-Coca-Colonization: Making the Globe from the Inside Out* (London: Routledge).

Foley, Imelda (2003) *The Girls in the Big Picture: Gender in Contemporary Ulster Theatre* (Belfast: The Blackstaff Press).

Foster, R.F. (1993) *Paddy and Mr Punch* (Harmondsworth: Penguin).

—— (2003) *WB Yeats – A Life, Volume 2* (Oxford: Oxford University Press).

Fricker, Karen (1995) 'At Ireland's Abbey Success Takes a Toll', *Variety*, July 24–30 1995, p. 55.

—— (1999) 'Dancing Like It's 1990 in Eire', *Variety*, 12–18 July 1999, p. 43.

—— (2002) 'Same Old Show: The Performance of Masculinity in Conor McPherson's *Port Authority* and Mark O'Rowe's *Made in China*', *Irish Review* 29 (Autumn), pp. 84–94.

Friel Festival (1999) 'Directors', *Friel Festival Programme* (Dublin: Abbey Theatre).

Friel, Brian (1970) *Crystal and Fox and The Mundy Scheme* (New York: Farrar, Straus and Giroux).

—— (1984) *Selected Plays* (ed. Seamus Deane) (London: Faber and Faber).

—— (1990) *Dancing at Lughnasa* (London: Faber and Faber).

—— (1994) *Molly Sweeney* (Oldcastle: Gallery Press).

—— (1997) *Give Me Your Answer, Do!* (Oldcastle: Gallery Press).

—— (1999a) *Essays, Diaries, Interviews: 1964–1999* (London: Faber and Faber).

—— (1999b) *Plays 2* (London: Faber and Faber).

—— (2005) *The Home Place* (Oldcastle: Gallery Press).

Gadamer, Hans-Georg (1989) *Truth and Method* (trans. Joel Weinsheimer and Donald G. Marshall), second, revised edition (London: Continuum Press).

Galway Advertiser (1996) 'New Druid Playwright is a "Natural"', *Galway Advertiser*, 11 January 1996, p. 23.

Gibbons, Luke (1996) *Transformations in Irish Culture* (Cork: Cork University Press).

—— (2003) 'Gaelic gothic: race, ethnicity and the other', unpublished paper.

—— (2004) 'Unapproved Road: Post-Colonialism and Irish Identity', *Zonezero Magazine* online. (www.zonezero.com/magazine/essays/distant/zrutas2.html)

Gillespie, Marie (1994) *Television, Ethnicity and Cultural Change* (London: Routledge).

Gilmore, James H. and B. Joseph Pine II (1999) *The Experience Economy* (Boston: Harvard Business School Press).

—— (2007) *Authenticity – What Consumers Really Want* (Boston: Harvard Business School Press).

Gilroy, Paul (1999) *Against Race* (Cambridge: Harvard University Press).

Gleik, James (2000) *Faster* (London: Abacus).

Goldberg, David Theo (2002) *The Racial State* (Oxford: Blackwell).

Graham, Colin (2001) *Deconstructing Ireland* (Edinburgh: University of Edinburgh Press).

Grant, David (1997) '*Tangles*: Addressing an Unusual Audience', in Eibhear Walshe (ed.), *Sex, Nation and Dissent in Irish Writing* (Cork: Cork University Press), pp. 235–51.

Gregory, Lady Augusta (1965) *Our Irish Theatre* (New York: Capricorn).

Grene, Nicholas (1999) *The Politics of Irish Drama* (Cambridge: Cambridge University Press).

—— (ed.) (2002) *Talking About Tom Murphy* (Dublin: Carysfort Press).

Guillen, Claudio (1993) *The Challenge of Comparative Literature* (Chicago: University of Chicago Press).

Hardt, Michael and Antonio Negri (2001) *Empire* (Cambridge: Harvard University Press).

Harrington, John (1997) *The Irish Play on the New York Stage, 1874–1966* (Lexington: University Press of Kentucky).

Harvey, David (1989) *The Condition of Postmodernity* (Oxford: Blackwell).

Hastings, Michael (2004) *Calico* (London: Oberon Books).

Heaney, Seamus (1990) *New Selected Poems: 1968–1987* (London: Faber and Faber).

Hobson, Dorothy (2003) *Soap Opera* (Cambridge: Polity Press).

Hodge, John (1995) *Shallow Grave* (London: Faber and Faber).

Hoffman, Alison (2003) 'American Nightmare', *The Guardian*, 25 February 2003.

Hogan, Robert and Richard Burnham (1992) *The Years of O'Casey* (Cranbury: Associated University Presses).

Hoggard, Liz (2002) 'Playboy of the West End World', *The Independent*, 15 June 2002, pp. 10–3.

Holden, Wendy (1994) *Unlawful Carnal Knowledge: The True Story of the 'X' Case* (London: Harper Collins).

Huber, Werner (2002) 'Contemporary Drama as Meta-Cinema: Martin McDonagh and Marie Jones', in Margarete Rubik and Elke Mettinger-Schartmann (eds), *(Dis) Continuities: Trends and Traditions in Contemporary Theatre and Drama in English* (Trier: WVT), pp. 13–24.

—— (2005) 'From Leenane to Kamenice: The De-Hibernicising of Martin McDonagh?', in Christopher Houswitsch (ed.), *Literary Views on Post-Wall Europe: Essays in Honour of Uwe Boker* (Trier: WVT), pp. 283–94.

Hughes, Declan (1997) *Plays 1* (London: Methuen).

—— (2000) 'Who the Hell Do We Still Think We Are?', in Eamonn Jordan (ed.), *Theatre Stuff* (Dublin: Carysfort Press).

Hunt, Hugh (1979) *The Abbey: Ireland's National Theatre 1904–1979* (Dublin: Gill and Macmillan).

IDA Ireland (2006) *Annual Report 2005* (Dublin: IDA).

Ignatiev, Noel (1996) *How the Irish Became White* (New York and London: Routledge).

Irish Times, The (1990) 'Raves for Friel Play', 20 October 1990.

—— (2001) 'Breaking News', 7 February 2001. (www.ireland.com/newspaper/breaking/2001/0207/breaking63.html)

Jackson, Joe (1999) 'Free Spirit', *Hot Press*, volume 23, number 19, p. 16.

Jeffries, Stuart (2003) 'Give My Regards to Hammersmith Broadway', *The Guardian*, 21 May 2003, p. 15.

Jones, Marie (2000) *Stones In His Pockets and A Night In November* (London: Nick Hern).

Kavanagh, Julie (1991) 'Friel at Last', *Vanity Fair*, 21 October 1991.

Keane, Madeleine (2006) 'When A Lack of Culture Rings Out', *Sunday Independent*, 2 April 2006.

Kearney, Richard (1997) *Postnationalist Ireland: Politics, Culture, Philosophy* (London: Routledge).

Keough, (1998) Review of *Jackie Brown. Boston Phoenix* 1 May 1998 (posted 13 May 2006) <http://www.filmvault.com/filmvault/boston/j/jackiebrown2.html>.

Khokhar, Ahmer (2007) 'Drink nearly killed me: McPherson', *Sunday Independent*, 3 June 2007. (www.independent.ie/national-news/drink-nearly-killed-me-mcpherson-690739.html)

Kiberd, Declan (1995) *Inventing Ireland* (London: Cape).

—— (2001) *Irish Classics* (London: Granta).

Kilroy, Thomas (1999) 'Friendship', *Irish University Review* 29, 1 (Spring/Summer), pp. 83–9.

Kilroy, Thomas (2000) 'A Generation of Playwrights', in Eamonn Jordan (ed.), *Theatre Stuff* (Dublin: Carysfort Press).

King, Jason (2005a) 'Black Saint Patrick: Irish Interculturalism in Theoretical Perspective and Theatre Practice', in Ondrej Pilny and Clare Wallace (eds), *Global Ireland* (Prague: Litteraria Pragensia), pp. 45–57.

—— (2005b) 'Interculturalism and Irish Theatre: The Portrayal of Immigrants on the Irish stage', *The Irish Review*, 33, pp. 23–39.

Kirby, Peadar, Luke Gibbons and Michael Cronin (eds) (2002) *Re-Inventing Ireland* (London: Pluto Press).

Klein, Naomi (2001) *No Logo* (London: Flamingo).

Korzeniewicz, Miguel (1993) 'Commodity Chains and Marketing Strategies: Nike and the Global Athletic Footwear Industry', in Gary Gereffi and Miguel Korzeniewicz (eds), *Commodity Chains and Global Capitalism* (Westport, CT: Greenwood Press), pp. 247–65.

Kramer, Mimi (1997) 'Three for the Show', *Time Magazine*, 4 August 1997, p. 71.

Kushner, Tony (1992) *Angels in America Part One: Millennium Approaches* (London: Nick Hern).

—— (1994) *Angels in America Part Two: Perestroika* (London: Nick Hern).

Kuti, Elizabeth (2005) *The Sugar Wife* (London: Nick Hern).

Lanters, José (2000) 'Playwrights of the Western World: Synge, Murphy, McDonagh', in Stephen Watt, Eileen Morgan and Shakir Mustafa (eds), *A Century of Irish Drama: Widening the Stage* (Bloomington: Indiana University Press), pp. 204–22.

Lash, Scott and Celia Lury (2007) *Global Culture Industry* (Cambridge: Polity Press).

Lawson, Hilary (1985) *Reflexivity – the Post-modern Predicament* (London: Hutchinson).

Leonard, Hugh (1991) 'The Plough and the Stars', *Sunday Independent*, April 1991.

Lipton, Martina (2007) 'Celebrity versus Tradition: "Branding" in Modern British Pantomime', *New Theatre Quarterly* 23: 2 (May), pp. 136–51.

Lloyd, David (1999) *Ireland After History* (Cork: Cork University Press).

Lo, Jacqueline and Helen Gilbert (2002) 'Towards a Topography of Cross-Cultural Theatre Praxis', *The Drama Review* 46, 3 (Fall), pp. 31–53.

Low, Lenny Ann (2003) 'Gulpilil on Side for Director's Fight Against "the Bullies"', *Sydney Morning Herald*, 30 September 2003. (www.smh.com.au)

Luckhurst, Mary (2004) 'Martin McDonagh's Lieutenant of Inishmore: Selling (-Out) to the English', *Contemporary Theatre Review* 14: 4, pp. 34–41.

Luckhurst, Mary and Jane Moody (2005) *Theatre and Celebrity in Britain 1660–2000* (London: Palgrave Macmillan).

Lyotard, Jean-Francois (1984) *The Postmodern Condition: A Report on Knowledge* (Minneapolis: University of Minnesota Press).

MacBride, Sean and Colleen Roach (1989) 'The New International Information Order', in Erik Barnouw (ed.), *International Encyclopaedia of Communications*, 4 volumes (Oxford: Oxford University Press).

Mac Dubhghaill, Uinsionn (1996) 'Drama sails to seven islands', *The Irish Times*, 27 November 1996, p. 12.

Manovich, Lev (2001) *The Languages of New Media* (Cambridge: MIT Press).

McCloskey, Gerry (1995) '*Angels in America*', *The Sunday Times*, 11 June 1995.

McConachie, Bruce and F. Elizabeth Hart (2006) *Performance and Cognition – Theatre Studies and the Cognitive Turn* (London and New York: Routledge).

McDonagh, Martin (1997) *The Cripple of Inishmaan* (London: Methuen).
——— (1999) *Plays 1* (*The Beauty Queen of Leenane, A Skull in Connenara, The Lonesome West*). (London: Methuen).
——— (2001) *The Lieutenant of Inishmore* (London: Methuen).
——— (2003) *The Pillowman* (London: Faber and Faber).
McGuinness, Frank (ed.) (1996) *The Dazzling Dark: New Irish Plays* (London: Faber and Faber).
——— (1999) *Dolly West's Kitchen* (London: Faber and Faber).
McKeon, Belinda (2004a) 'Call for Abbey's Artistic Director to be Dismissed', *The Irish Times* 6 September 2004, p. 6.
——— (2004b) 'Difficult Questions at the Abbey', *The Irish Times* Weekend Supplement, 11 September 2004.
McLuhan, Marshall (1970) *From Cliché to Archetype* (New York: Viking Press).
McNair, Brian (2002) *Striptease Culture: Sex, Media and the Democratisation of Desire* (London and New York: Routledge).
McPherson, Conor (2000) *Four Plays* (London: Nick Hern).
——— (2004) *Plays 2* (London: Nick Hern).
Meany, Helen (2004) 'Review of *The Shaughraun*', *The Irish Times*, 4 June 2004, p. 12.
Merriman, Victor (1999) 'Decolonisation Postponed – The Theatre of Tiger Trash', *Irish University Review* 29, 2, pp. 305–17.
——— (2001) 'Settling for More: Excess and Success in Contemporary Irish Drama', in Dermot Bolger (ed.), *Druids, Dudes and Beauty Queens: The Changing Face of Irish Theatre* (Dublin: New Island Books).
——— (2004) 'Staging Contemporary Ireland: Heartsickness and Hopes Deferred', in Shaun Richards (ed.), *The Cambridge Companion to Twentieth-Century Irish Drama* (Cambridge: Cambridge University Press), pp. 244–57.
Mirzoeff, Nicholas (2002) 'The Subject of Visual Culture', in Nicholas Mirzoeff (ed.), *The Visual Culture Reader*, second edition (London and New York: Routledge).
Moran, Joe (2000) *Star Authors* (London: Pluto Press).
Morash, Christopher (2002) *A History of Irish Theatre, 1601–2000* (Cambridge: Cambridge University Press).
Moretti, Franco (2000) 'Conjectures on World Literature', *New Left Review* 2, 1, (January/February), pp. 54–68.
——— (2001) 'Planet Hollywood', *New Left Review* 2, 9 (May/June), pp. 90–101.
Morgan, Joyce (1998) 'Aussie Soaps: McDonagh Comes Clean', *Sydney Morning Herald*, 8 January 1998, p. 27.
Mumford, L.S. (1995) *Love and Ideology in the Afternoon: Soap Opera, Women, and Television Genre* (Bloomington: Indiana University Press).
Murray, Christopher (1997a) '"Recording Tremors": Friel's *Dancing at Lughnasa* and the Uses of Tradition', in Kerwin, *Brian Friel: A Casebook* (New York and London: Garland Publishing).
——— (1997b) *Twentieth-Century Irish Drama: Mirror up to a Nation* (Manchester: Manchester University Press).
NBC News (1998) 'Playwright Martin McDonagh Takes Broadway By Storm', *Today Show*, 16 April 1998.
Ness, Fiona (2004) 'Artistic Director to Quit Abbey Next Year', *The Sunday Business Post*, 4 July 2004. (http://archives.tcm.ie/businesspost/2004/07/04/story89912768.aspc)

Ni Anluain, Cliodhna (2000) *Reading the Future: Irish Writers in Conversation with Mike Murphy* (Dublin: Lilliput Press).

O'Callaghan, Kathleen (1995) 'So There's One For the Boys', *Irish Independent*, Weekend Supplement, 10 June 1995.

O'Casey, Sean (1998) *Plays 2* (London: Faber and Faber).

OECD (1997) *Literacy Skills for the Knowledge Society* (Paris: OECD).

—— (2001) *Education at a Glance* (Paris: OECD).

O'Hagan, Sean (2001) 'The Wild West', *The Guardian*, Weekend, 24 March 2001, p. 24.

O'Kelly, Donal (1997) *Catalpa* (Dublin: New Island Books).

O'Kelly, Emer (1995) 'Review of *Angels in America*', *Sunday Independent*, 11 June 1995, p. 18.

Omi, Michael and Howard Winant (1994) *Racial Formation in the United States From the 1960s to the 1990s* (New York and London: Routledge).

O'Reilly-Hyland, Emer (1998) 'Filling up cracks in the Masonry', *The Sunday Times*, 20 September 1998.

O'Rowe, Mark (1999) *Howie The Rookie* (London: Nick Hern).

O'Toole, Fintan (1996) 'Failures Raise Issue of Public Subsidy', *The Irish Times*, 4 June 1996, p. 10.

—— (1997a) 'Nowhere Man', *The Irish Times*, Weekend Supplement, 26 April 1997, p. 1.

—— (1997b) 'Murderous Laughter', *The Irish Times*, 24 June 1997, p. 12.

—— (1997c) 'Marking Time: From *Making History to Dancing at Lughnasa*', in Alan J. Peacock (ed.), *The Achievement of Brian Friel* (Gerrards Cross: Colin Smythe).

—— (2000) 'The State of the Art', in Eamonn Jordan (ed.), *Theatre Stuff: Critical Essays on Contemporary Irish Drama* (Dublin: Carysfort Press).

—— (2001) 'Review of *My Brilliant Divorce*', *The Irish Times*, 30 November 2001, p. 9.

—— (2003a) 'Silence, cunning, exile – so what next?', *The Irish Times*, 3 March 2003, p. 12.

—— (2003b) *Critical Moments* (Dublin: Carysfort Press).

—— (2006) 'A Mind in Connemara: The Savage World of Martin McDonagh', *The New Yorker*, 6 March 2006, pp. 40–7.

Pavis, Patrice (1996) *The Intercultural Performance Reader* (London and New York: Routledge).

Pettitt, Lance (1989) 'Gray Fiction – 2', Graph, 7, p. 13.

PGIL-Eirdata (2008) 'Brian Friel'. (www.pgil-eirdata.org/html/pgil_datasets/authors/f/Friel,Brian/life.htm)

Phelan, Mark (2008) 'Performing "Authentic" Ireland: (Dis)connecting the Cultural Politics of the Irish Revival and the Celtic Tiger on the Irish Stage', in Paul Murphy and Melissa Sihra (eds), *Contemporary Irish Theatre* (Gerrards Cross: Colin Smythe).

Phoenix Magazine (1995) 'Review of *Angels in America*', July 1995, p. 18.

Pilkington, Lionel (2001) *Theatre and the State in Twentieth-Century Ireland: Cultivating the People* (London: Routledge).

Pinter, Harold (2005) *Various Voices – Prose, Poetry, Politics, 1978–2005* (London: Faber and Faber).

Pogrebin, Robin (2003) 'Proposing a National Theater Downtown', *New York Times*, 9 September 2003. (www.nytimes.com)

Rebellato, Dan (2006) 'Playwriting and Globalisation: Towards a Site-Unspecific Theatre', *Contemporary Theatre Review* 16, 1, pp. 97–113.

Redmond, Sean (2006) 'Intimate Fame Everywhere', in Su Holmes and Sean Redmond (eds), *Framing Celebrity: New Directions in Celebrity Culture* (London: Routledge), pp. 27–53.

Richards, Shaun (2003) '"The Outpouring of a Morbid, Unhealthy Mind": The Critical Condition of Synge and McDonagh', *Irish University Review* 33, 1–2, pp. 201–14.

Richtarik, Marilyn (2004) 'The Field Day Theatre Company', in Shaun Richards (ed.), *The Cambridge Companion to Twentieth-Century Irish Drama* (Cambridge: Cambridge University Press), pp. 191–203.

Roberts, Robin (2003) 'Gendered Media Rivalry: Irish Drama and American film', (eds Brian Singleton and Anna McMullan) *Australasian Drama Studies Special Issue: Performing Ireland* 43 (October), pp. 108–27.

Robertson, Roland (1992) *Globalization: Social Theory and Global Culture* (London: Sage).

Robinson, Jo (2007) 'Becoming More Provincial? The Global and the Local in Theatre History', *New Theatre Quarterly* 23, 3, pp. 229–40.

Roche, Anthony (1995) *Contemporary Irish Drama: From Beckett to McGuinness* (Dublin: Gill & Macmillan).

—— (2006) 'Contemporary Drama in English, 1940–2000', in Margaret Kelleher and Philip O'Leary (eds), *The Cambridge History of Irish Literature*, Volume II (Cambridge: Cambridge University Press), pp. 478–530.

Rockett, Kevin and Emer Rockett (2003) *Neil Jordan* (Dublin: Liffey Press).

Roediger, David R. (1999) *The Wages of Whiteness*, revised edition (London: Verso).

Rosenthal, Daniel (2001) 'How to Slay 'Em in the Isles', *The Independent* (London), 11 April 2001, p. 10.

Ross, Michael (2003) 'Hynes Means Business', *The Sunday Times*, Culture Section, 18 May 2003, p. 10.

Rushdie, Salman (1999) *The Ground Beneath Her Feet* (London: Vintage).

Sassen, Saskia (2000) 'Territory and Territoriality in the Global Economy', *International Sociology* 15, pp. 372–93.

Segal, Victoria (2004) 'They Could Have Danced All Night', *The Sunday Times*, Culture Section, 8 August 2004, p. 9.

Seiter, Ellen *et al.* (eds) (1991) *Remote Control: Television Audiences and Cultural Power* (London: Routledge).

Shore, Robert (2001) 'Animal Harm', *The Times Literary Supplement* 5121, May 2001, p. 25.

Sierz, Aleks (2001) *In-Yer-Face Theatre: British Drama Today* (London: Faber).

Sihra, Melissa (2004) 'Marina Carr in the US: Perception, Conflict and Culture', in Nicholas Grene and Christopher Morash (eds), *Irish Theatre on Tour* (Dublin: Carysfort Press).

Simpson, Alan (1962) *Beckett and Behan and a Theatre in Dublin* (London: Routledge and Keegan Paul).

Singleton, Brian (2004) 'The Revival Revised', in Shaun Richards (ed.), *The Cambridge Companion to Twentieth-Century Irish Drama* (Cambridge: Cambridge University Press).

Smyth, Gerry (2001) *Space and the Irish Cultural Imagination* (Basingstoke and New York: Palgrave).

Solga, Kim (2008) 'Body Doubles, Babel's Voices: Katie Mitchell's *Iphigenia at Aulis* and the Theatre of Sacrifice', *Contemporary Theatre Review* 18, 2 (May), pp. 146–60.

Standage, Tom (1999) *The Victorian Internet* (New York: Berkeley Publishing Group).

States, Bert O. (1985) *Great Reckonings in Little Rooms – On the Phenomenology of Theater* (Berkeley and Los Angeles: University of California Press).

Stearns, David Patrick (1996) '*Riverdance* Re-invents Irish Folk Dance', *USA Today*, Life Section, 4D, 7 October 1996.

Stembridge, Gerard (1996) *The Gay Detective* (Dublin: New Island Books).

Stiglitz, Joseph (2002) *Globalization and Its Discontents* (New York: Norton).

Stowe, David W. (1996) 'Uncolored people: The Rise of Whiteness Studies', *Lingua Franca 6, 6 (September/October)*, pp. 68–77.

Sunday Independent (1990) 'The Abbey Stuns South Bank', *Sunday Independent*, 21 October 1990.

—— (1995) 'Angels rush in where Performers Fear to Tread', *Sunday Independent*, 18 June 1995, p. 3.

Synge, J.M. (1982) *Complete Works*, Vol. IV. Plays: Book II (ed. Ann Saddlemyer) (Gerrards Cross: Colin Smythe).

Tarantino, Quentin (1999) *Pulp Fiction* (London: Faber and Faber).

—— (2000) *Reservoir Dogs* (London: Faber and Faber).

Taylor, Lib (2003) 'Shape-shifting and Role-spilling: Theatre, Body and Identity', in Naomi Segal *et al.* (eds), *Indeterminate Bodies* (London: Palgrave), pp. 164–91.

Taylor, Paul (2005) Review of *The Plough and the Stars*. *The Independent*, 29 January, p. 40.

Thackaberry, Frank (1991) *Theatre Ireland* 27, pp. 12–13.

Therborn, Goran (2000) 'Globalizations. Dimensions, Historical Waves, Regional Effects, Normative Governance', *International Sociology* 15, 2, pp. 151–79.

Thornton, Niamh and Padraic White (2002) 'Interview with Enda Walsh', *Film and Film Culture* 1, 1, pp. 11–20.

United Nations Development Programme (2004) *Human Development Report* (New York: UN).

Vandevelde, Karen (2000) 'The Gothic Soap of Martin McDonagh', in Eamonn Jordan (ed.), *Theatre Stuff* (Dublin: Carysfort Press).

Vanek, Joe (1993) 'In Search of *Lughnasa*', *Theatre Ireland* 31, pp. 8–10.

Wallerstein, Immanuel (1974) *The Modern World System* (New York and London: Academic Press).

—— (1991) 'The Construction of Peoplehood: Racism, Nationalism, Ethnicity', in Etienne Balibar and Immanuel Wallerstein (eds), *Race, Nation, Class – Ambiguous Identities* (London and New York: Verso).

Walsh, Enda (1999) *Disco Pigs*, in John Fairleigh (ed.), *Far From the Land* (London: Random House).

Ward, David (2001) 'RSC Fires Off Warning Shot to Patrons', *The Guardian*, 7 April 2001, p. 8.

Waters, Malcolm (2001) *Globalization,* second edition (London and New York: Routledge).

Watt, Stephen (1991) *Joyce, O'Casey and the Irish Popular Theatre* (New York: Syracuse University Press).

—— (2004) 'Late Nineteenth-Century Irish Theatre – Before the Abbey and Beyond', in Shaun Richards (ed.), *The Cambridge Companion to Twentieth-Century Irish Drama* (Cambridge: Cambridge University Press), pp. 18–32.

Welch, Robert (1999) *The Abbey Theatre 1899–1999: Form and Pressure* (Oxford: Oxford University Press).

West, Michael (2001) *Foley* (London: Methuen).

Whelan, Gerard and Carolyn Swift (2002) *Spiked* (Dublin: New Island Books).

White, Victoria (2000) 'A New Stage for the Abbey', *The Irish Times*, 17 February 2000, p. 12.

——— (2002) 'Abbey Could Move', *The Irish Times*, 15 February 2002, p. 5.

Wilde, Oscar (2000) *The Major Works* (Oxford: World's Classics).

Williams, Tennessee (1970) *The Glass Menagerie* (New York: New Directions).

Witchell, Alex (1993) 'Life May be a Madness, but it's Also a Poem', *New York Times*, Section 2, 17 October 1993, p. 5.

Wolf, Martin (2004) *Why Globalization Works* (New Haven: Yale University Press).

Wu, Chin-Tao (2002) *Privatising Culture: Corporate Art Intervention Since the 1980s* (London: Verso).

Yeats, W.B. (1990) *The Poems* (ed. Daniel Albright) (London: Everyman).

——— (1998) *Autobiographies* (London: Macmillan).

Zemer, Lior (2006) 'Contribution and Collaboration in Joint Authorship: Too Many Misconceptions', *Journal of Intellectual Property Law and Practice* 1, 4, pp. 283–92.

Zimmermann, Georges Denis (2001) *The Irish storyteller* (Dublin: Four Courts Press).

Index